Gary Finley

THE CHURCH AND
ORGANIZED MOVEMENTS

SUBJECTS OF THE COMMISSIONS

The full membership of the Commissions is given at the end of this volume.

The CHURCH and ORGANIZED MOVEMENTS

RANDOLPH CRUMP MILLER

Editor

The
INTERSEMINARY
Series

VOLUME TWO

HARPER & BROTHERS · PUBLISHERS
New York and London

THE CHURCH AND
ORGANIZED MOVEMENTS

Copyright, 1946, by Harper & Brothers
Printed in the United States of America

F-W

CONTENTS

CONTENTS

PREFACE

THE INTERSEMINARY SERIES

The five volumes which comprise "The Interseminary Series" have three main purposes: to outline the character of the contemporary world which challenges the Church; to proclaim afresh the nature of the gospel and the Church which must meet that challenge; and to set forth the claims which ecumenical Christianity makes upon the various churches as they face their world task. Although the perspective of the volumes is American, it is nevertheless comprehensive in that it views the Church as the Body of Christ in the world, performing a mission to the whole world.

The immediate occasion for the publication of the series is a national conference of theological students scheduled for June, 1947, under the auspices and initiative of the Interseminary Movement in the United States. The volumes will serve as study material for the delegates to the conference.

From the outset, however, it has been the desire and aim of those sponsoring the project that the volumes might have a wide appeal. They have been designed for the Christian public in general, in the hope that there may be in them help toward our common Christian task in the fateful postwar days.

To produce the volumes, the Interseminary Committee outlined the five major questions and organized the Commissions listed elsewhere in this volume. Each Commission met once, and in the course of a two-day meeting outlined, first, the chapters for its respective volume, and, second, the main elements to be contained in each chapter. Authors were assigned from within the Commission. A first draft of each paper was submitted to Commission members and the chairman of the Commission for criticism, returned and subsequently rewritten in final form. The fifth volume, which is a summary interpretation of the preceding statements, is written by a single author. It should be specially noted that the work of Commission I-B was graciously undertaken by the already organized Pacific Coast Theological Group to which were added a few guests for the purpose at hand.

The volumes thus represent a combination of group thinking and individual effort. They are not designed to be completely representative statements to which the Commissions, or the Interseminary Movement, would subscribe. They are intended, rather, to convey information and to stimulate thought, in the earnest hope that this may in turn contribute to a more faithful performance of our Christian mission in the world.

For the National Interseminary Committee:
ROBERT S. BILHEIMER
Executive Secretary

THE AUTHORS

BUELL G. GALLAGHER holds the B.A. degree from Carleton College, the B.D. degree from Union Theological Seminary, the Ph.D. degree from Columbia University and the D.D. degree from Oberlin College. He is professor of Christian ethics in the Pacific School of Religion. His publications include *American Caste and the Negro College, Color and Conscience: The Irrepressible Conflict* and *Portrait of a Pilgrim: A Search for the Christian Way in Race Relations.* Dr. Gallagher is a member of the Congregational-Christian Church.

GEORGE HEDLEY, who was born in China, received his early education at Tientsin School and at Ashville College in England. His B.A. degree is from the University of Southern California; his M.A. and B.D. degrees from Maclay School of Religion; and his D.Theol. from Pacific School of Religion. Dr. Hedley is associate professor of economics and sociology at Mills College. His publications include *A Christian Year, The San Francisco Strike As I Have Seen It* and *In Brief* (verse). Dr. Hedley is a member of the Methodist Church.

RANDOLPH CRUMP MILLER has his A.B. degree from Pomona College and his Ph.D. from Yale University. He has studied also at Episcopal Theological School. His publications include *What We Can Believe, A Guide for Church School Teachers, The Challenge of the Church* and *Christianity and the Contemporary Scene* of which he was the co-editor. Dr. Miller is assistant professor of philosophy of religion and lecturer in Christian ethics and Christian education in the Church Divinity School of the Pacific, and is a member of the Protestant Episcopal Church.

PIERSON PARKER holds the A.B. degree from the University of California and the M.A. degree as well as the Th.D. degree *magna cum laude* from the Pacific School of Religion. He is associate professor of Biblical literature and lecturer in homiletics and comparative religion in the Church Divinity School of the Pacific. In addition to articles in the *Journal of Biblical Literature* and the *Anglican Theological Review*, his publications include a contribution to *Christianity and the Contemporary Scene*. Dr. Parker is a member of the Protestant Episcopal Church.

EDWARD L. PARSONS, whose A.B. degree is from Yale University and whose B.D. is from Union Theological Seminary, has also studied at the University of Berlin and Episcopal Theological Seminary. He holds the D.D. degree from the Pacific School of Religion, Yale University and Episcopal Theological Seminary, and the LL.D. degree from the University of California. His publications include *What Is the Christian Religion*, *Victory with Christ* and *The American Prayer Book* (with B. H. Jones). Dr. Parsons is Retired Bishop of California of the Protestant Episcopal Church.

DWIGHT C. SMITH, whose B.A. and B.D. degrees are from Yale University, holds the Ph.D. degree from the University of Edinburgh. He is the minister of the United Churches in Olympia, Washington. His publications include "Transcription of Gifford Lectures by Albert Schweitzer" (article in *Christendom*, 1936), "Robert Browne" (article in *Church History*, 1937), *The First Hundred Years of Washington Congregationalism* and *What I Believe*. Dr. Smith is a member of the Congregational-Christian Church.

HOWARD THURMAN, until 1946 professor of systematic theology at Howard University, is now co-pastor of the Fellowship

Church of All Peoples in San Francisco. His B.A. and D.D. degrees are from Morehouse College, and he holds the B.D. degree from Colgate-Rochester Divinity School. Among his publications are *Greatest of These* and *Deep River*.

ELTON TRUEBLOOD, whose S.T.B. degree is from Harvard University and Ph.D. degree is from Johns Hopkins University, was until 1945 Chaplain of Stanford University. In the autumn of 1946 he assumed new duties as professor of philosophy at Earlham College. His latest publications include *The Logic of Belief*, *The Predicament of Modern Man*, *Doctor Johnson's Prayers* and *Foundations for Reconstruction*. Dr. Trueblood is a member of the Society of Friends.

ROBERT FREDERICK WEST holds the B.A. degree from Lynchburg College and the B.D. and Ph.D. degrees from Yale University. Until the spring of 1946 he was chairman of the Department of Religion at Texas Christian University, and professor of Christian doctrine at Brite College of the Bible. In the autumn of 1946 he assumed new duties as professor of religion at Wabash College. He is the author of *Alexander Campbell and Natural Religion*. Dr. West is a member of the Disciples of Christ.

HUGH VERNON WHITE holds the A.B. degree from the University of California, the B.D. degree from the Pacific School of Religion, the S.T.M. degree from Harvard and the Ph.D. degree from Stanford University. His publications include *A Theology for Christian Missions* and *A Working Faith for the World*. Dr. White is professor of Christian theology and world Christianity in the Pacific School of Religion. He is a member of the Congregational-Christian Church.

INTRODUCTION

Randolph Crump Miller

The purpose of this volume is to evaluate various organized movements in the United States today in the light of their usefulness in achieving the Christian hope for man. We have defined that hope in terms of standards of behavior, of loyalty within the society, and of commitment to the will of God.

The problem is clear in its outline and purposes, but the complexities of adequate evaluation provide difficulties in stating cogently and persuasively what one's specific decisions should be. In some cases, including the organized churches, there are elements of resistance to the achievement of Christian goals. In other cases, including communism with its anti-Christian bias, there are elements of resource for making society more Christian.

In the attempt to provide guidance for the Christian in specific situations, the implied standards of judgment have been clarified. Christians derive the basis of their moral decisions from their theology, and their theology is alive in so far as it stems from the experience of belonging to the Christian community, and their church membership is dynamic in so far as it is a means for furthering their personal and social relationships with the living God of history. For this reason, a brief statement of theological background has been included as the basis for the standards of judgment and loyalty in determining resistance and resource.

We recognize that God is at work in the world, and that the Church exists as a society within a society by an act of God to further His purposes. The attitude of Christianity toward the world situation involves also the attitude of the Church toward other organized movements which may prove to be opponents or allies, or in which there are elements of both resistance and resource. Paul Tillich has described the situation as follows:

> Protestant orthodoxy can hold aloof from the present world situation, at least to a considerable extent. Roman Catholicism can look forward to the moment when anti-Christian totalitarianism will be replaced by a revived Catholic totalitarianism. Liberal Protestantism can go neither way. It must, however, solve the problem of its relation to the present stage of civilization. It must not return to a position of servant to a social and cultural system whose contradictions have now become manifest. On the other hand it must not follow the totalitarian way in either its pagan or its Catholic form. Only if liberal Protestantism becomes truly "Catholic" can it meet the needs of the hour.[1]

In this sense, this volume represents "liberal" Protestantism seeking the Christian answer in a specified field or fields. Its theology is grounded in the liberal and ecumenical approach, and there is a degree of transcendence in the emphasis on God's judgment standing over against the world—including the Church. The writers of the various chapters represent quite different theological backgrounds, and the area of their agreement on some matters is limited, but all of them fit roughly into what might be called "the central trend" of American theology. They would agree with this statement by Edward Lambe Parsons:

> Barth and Brunner, Maritain, Temple, and Niebuhr must all have their place in the contemporary theological field as Athanasius and Augustine, Aquinas and Calvin and Luther have in the past. It is true that the picture this gives us is that of an uncomfortably big Church, too

[1] Henry P. Van Dusen, ed., *The Christian Answer* (New York: Charles Scribner's Sons, 1945), p. 39.

Catholic for our limited vision; but it is nevertheless the only picture which paints reality. We have tried to paint the picture otherwise and failed. The Church has never been Catholic enough.[2]

The Church, conceived in this wide scope within the framework of ecumenical Christianity—and even this framework limits its true "catholicity" for it omits the Roman Church—is at work in the world. It is looking for allies in various organized movements; and it is also seeking to find its enemies. But just as there are friends and foes of Christ within the churches, so there are both allies and enemies within many organized groups. Where there is active opposition, antagonism, unfair criticism, highly developed self-interest, refusal to seek Christian goals, and limited or conflicting loyalties, we find resistance to the Christian hope. There is active opposition among some atheistic groups, there is unfair criticism from many intellectualist and some labor groups, there are limited loyalties among some social welfare agencies and service clubs, but in these cases we must also look for positive features. In facing this problem, the writers of this volume part company with Protestant orthodoxy (as described by Tillich).

It is important to know how we can co-operate with various organized movements so that their power for good will be realized and their evil potentialities will be restricted. These groups have partial goals; they are serving a class, or a vested interest, or an economic or laboring stratum of society. The churches also fall into this trap, but at least the churches should be aware of their universal responsibility to serve all men equally and thus they should stand consciously under the judgment of a just, righteous and loving God. Most of the groups mentioned in this volume do not operate as religious institutions (except for the cults and non-Christian religions), but

[2] Randolph C. Miller and Henry H. Shires, eds., *Christianity and the Contemporary Scene* (New York: Morehouse-Gorham Company, Inc., 1943), p. 114.

from the Church's point of view they stand equally under the judgment of God.

The questions thus become clearer. How can we co-operate with those social radical movements which seem to be achieving political and social goals which an unaided Church cannot attain? How can we discover fascist tendencies in organizations with other announced purposes? To what extent does social work actually fulfill the ideal of Christian charity? Why do Christians and non-Christians find release for their religious urges in service clubs and lodges? What ideals are to be found in nontheistic humanism, scientism and vocationalism which aid in making society more Christian? How can Christians within the ecumenical movement find ways of dealing with various cults, and which cults should be declared outside the Christian tradition? What is the Christian approach to other religions in the new world situation? What are the resources, opportunities and powers within the Christian Church by which it may accomplish its task?

The particular assumptions, standards and methods of assessment which may be useful guides to the reader are outlined in the opening chapter. The second chapter points to the live options available in terms of what is called "The New Comparative Religions." Part II consists of six chapters listing the facts, giving an interpretation of those facts and evaluating the degrees of resistance and resource for the Christian today in certain specified fields. (Some obvious areas, especially in economics and politics, have been deliberately omitted because they are covered in Volume I of this series.) These chapters are partly for the sake of information especially in fields where it is difficult to obtain knowledge of the facts, partly for the sake of guidance particularly where the neophyte might find himself involved beyond his understanding, and partly by way of illustrating the methods which can be used in assessing and evaluating any contemporary movement from a Christian perspective. It is not a course in propaganda analysis; it is rather an exercise in Christian judgment in the light of a deep and ecumenical

Christian faith as applied to elements of the American scene. Part III brings the particular problems into a wider view, as the resources of the Christian faith are examined in terms of the missionary task, and as the Church is seen in terms of its opportunity, its fundamental moral integrity and stability, its faith which interprets total experience, and its invincible spiritual power.

This volume was undertaken by the Pacific Coast Theological Group, implemented by several guests, at the request of the Interseminary Movement, and the group has met regularly during the year of preparation. Almost ten years old, this fellowship had a mutual understanding and love which made frank and creative criticism possible. The first draft, prepared by a committee between meetings, was discarded along with the papers which had been written. As a result of group thinking, in which Elton Trueblood served as the catalytic agent, the outline was thoroughly revised and new writers were assigned. The chapters were thoroughly discussed at subsequent meetings and further revisions followed. In May of 1946, the chapters of this volume were finally accepted by the group.

The writing of this volume would have been impossible without the aid of the Hazen Foundation, to which the Pacific Coast Theological Group is indebted for financial support. The presence of Robert Bilheimer of the Interseminary Movement provided guidance in terms of policy and frequent specific criticisms. The members of the group and guests who did not write chapters were the able critics who insisted on the caliber of scholarship and sound judgment which these chapters may have, although each writer is responsible for the final result.

PART I

The General Perspective

CHAPTER 1

The Discovery of Resistance and Resource

RANDOLPH CRUMP MILLER

CHAPTER 2

The New Comparative Religion

ELTON TRUEBLOOD

1

THE DISCOVERY OF
RESISTANCE AND RESOURCE

Randolph Crump Miller

Introduction. 1. The theological framework: the Church, history, man. 2. Christian standards of judgment. Sources: the Bible, the Church, conscience, the Gospel. The religious foundations of ethical judgments and life. 3. Methods of assessment: deduction, induction, the combined method. 4. Basic attitudes of Christians in the Church. 5. The necessity of a comparative study of today's live options.

~~~~~~

The Church is at work in the world. It is a society within a society seeking to achieve specific ideals and purposes which it equates with the will of God—or considers as an approximation of His will. Because the Church is an institution within society, it is faced with other organized movements which are seeking also to realize particular goals. Some of these groups are considered as allies, some as competitors, some as active opponents. In every organized movement, the Church is bound to seek out the elements of resistance to the gospel and elements of resource for accomplishing Christian ideals.

In order to provide guidance for the individual Christian, for the leaders within the Church and for the Church acting as a corporate organism ("the Body of Christ"), a careful and penetrating discipline is necessary. The Church itself must be placed within a theological framework, the Christian standards of judgment in ethics and theology must be made evident, the problems of loyalty must be clarified, the methods of assessment for the collecting and manipulating of data must be provided, and the basic attitudes of the Church toward all organized movements must be described before particular evaluations of specific groups can be established. The purpose of this chapter is to make clear some presuppositions which may prove helpful in reading the remaining chapters of this volume.

1. THE THEOLOGICAL FRAMEWORK

The Church

The relation of the Church to God is of primary importance. The Christian Church finds its historic roots in Judaism. The relationship between Yahweh and his people, as recorded in the Bible, establishes God as Lord of history, who is righteous and loving and who entered into a covenant relationship with His people. Through the life, work, death and resurrection of Jesus Christ, God entered into a new covenant relationship with the Christian community. The coming of Jesus Christ in history through the Church is a continuation of the old covenant, ratified by the life and death ("the blood") of Jesus Christ.

The Church, then, is the people who have entered this covenant relationship, this agreement, with the Father of Jesus Christ. Whether the Church be conceived as "given" or "gathered," the sovereignty of God and His priority are recognized in making the covenant relationship central. It is God's purposes which are being worked out through the Church, and this is the only theological reason which justifies the existence of the Church.

The Church exists to fulfill God's purposes in history and to point to God's will beyond history. The visible Church is in the world, with all of the historical, political, economic and social limitations which finite existence places upon it. At the same time, the Church stands over against all other social organisms, claiming to pronounce judgment upon the world from a non-worldly point of view. It is this paradox of the absolute and the relative, of the ideal and the prudential, of the elect society and the mixed society, which faces the Church as we find it in human experience.

As a society within a society, the Church is not cut off from the world; it is the chief means by which the divine initiative enters the life of the world. The Church we experience as a mixed body never fully represents God's will, and sometimes fails even to approximate it, and the visible Church is evident only in the many churches which constitute the universal Church. It is this complexity of relationships which further befogs the issue for this volume.

The societies of the world have relationships on many levels, including the national, political, economic, cultural, racial, religious and others. They interact and overlap. The Church cuts across all of them with greater or less intensity. The Church not only faces these various organized movements at different levels, but the Church as a mixed society is not always constant in its own willingness to accept criticism from within or from without. The Church and the churches, therefore, also stand under the judgment of God. There is always the possibility and need of reformation within the churches, and in order for the Church to evaluate either its own way of life or that of other organized movements it must see the general principles of its philosophy of history and of its ethical standards.

History

The Christian philosophy of history underlies the doctrine of the Church. The meaning of life is found in a living God and not in an idea. God is known as He reveals Himself in the historical process as Lord of history—history itself being an act of God. Only as the Church is seen as a product of God's work does the covenant relationship become intelligible. A free and personal God, controller of history and of the destinies of men, entered into this relationship with his people—at first with the Israelites and then with the new Israel. Out of the Jewish-Christian tradition came the Church by the act of God. Jesus

Christ lived and died and rose from death that men might come to believe in a living God who would redeem His people. The Incarnation and the Atonement are events of history and the center of Christian theology. "Christ Jesus came into the world to save sinners."

As theology becomes metaphysical, it translates the revelations found in history into a philosophical perspective. History is not the end of religion, but it provides the matrix in which our religious knowledge is to be discovered. Neither Christianity nor the Church is exhausted by the meanings found in historical revelation, and the wider view of a metaphysical theology is necessary to complete the picture.

Man

The Christian doctrine of man underlying most of these chapters should also be made clear. That men are made in the image of God is never forgotten in the insistence that men are also disobedient and even treasonable children of God. They are sinners; they are also dupes, and the element of self-deception becomes increasingly clear as we analyze the conflicting loyalties of men. If Christianity at its best is the commitment of the total self to the living God as revealed in Jesus Christ, with the expectation of receiving God's power to do good, then many of us are foolish and ignorant dupes of our own deceptions and of the false claims of organizations seeking our loyalty.

This balanced view of man as a child of God and still a sinner, as able to achieve positive goodness in freedom and only by the grace of God, as seeking the kingdom and receiving it only from God, as in a tragic human situation and living the abundant life, as saved through the atonement of Jesus Christ and needing to be saved through repentance and commitment, as an individual and finding sanctuary in the Church, as loved of God and suffering God's judgment, is an anthropology which has developed from a profound and Biblical approach to man's present predicament.

Against this theological background, it will be easier for the reader to discover the theological implications underlying the chapters which follow. It is an attempt to stand in "the central tradition" of American theology, liberal in intent and sane in reference to tradition, which gives hope of intelligent analysis and decision in discovering standards and implementing action in the areas of competing organized groups.

We ask, what happens to the Church, to the God of Jesus Christ, and to man as a child of God among the secular radicals, among those fascists who masquerade under various banners, in social welfare, in the service clubs and lodges, in organized education, among the cults, and in other religions? What kind of Christianity will be influential enough and persuasive enough to continue to exist among the "new comparative religions?" Can we make our ethical judgments in these fields an inseparable part of our theology?

2. CHRISTIAN STANDARDS OF JUDGMENT

In evaluating the organized movements of our time, we need to clarify our standards of judgment. We make judgments and say, "This is Christian," and, "This is unchristian," and "This is partly Christian." Sometimes we make such a statement synonymous with "the good" and thus reduce Christianity to ethics — although Christianity is profoundly ethical. As we examine the resistance to the Christian purpose and the resource for the Christian goal, we need to be sure of our sources of judgment and of the standards by which we act.

Sources

(1) The Bible as an authority has always presented many problems. It has always been the Bible as interpreted by groups or individuals, and the use of scripture to provide authority for almost any enterprise illustrates what happens when the fundamental Christian motives are disregarded. A literalistic interpretation leads to unending confusion and the opposite extreme of free rendering places the authority outside the Bible.

Paul's use of "the mind of Christ" as a means of judgment lacks the clarity of legal and literal renderings of authority, but it provides a perspective in terms of basic attitudes by which the remainder of the Bible can be understood. The doctrine of "the mind of Christ" has the objectivity of the teachings of Jesus in the Synoptic Gospels (except for the most radical critics), but it also includes the insights of history and the subjective elements of the individual's own choice. This solution does not provide an absolute authority, for God's will becomes relative the moment he expresses it in the historical process.

(2) The Church also hands down standards of judgment, but the pluralism of the churches often suggests that "the mind of Christ" is divided. Roman Catholics sponsor "bingo" while some Protestant groups frown on dancing or contract bridge; Roman Catholics follow the Vatican line in politics and support Franco while the richer Protestant groups vote a straight Republican ticket. All agree that it is wrong to break the Ten Commandments, but this primitive code dates back at least to 750 B.C. The judgments of various Protestant groups vary with geographic, economic and cultural conditions even on such profound issues as race prejudice, social work, economic goals and political action—as well as on the minor "sins" of smoking, dancing and card playing.

There is, however, a new recognition of authority in the non-Roman Christianity of today. Just as the ecumenical councils of old carried an authority which holds even to the present day, so the modern ecumenical conferences are developing a persuasive authority for many non-Roman churches concerning the most profound issues of the modern world. The increasing influence of such organizations as the Federal Council of the Churches of Christ in America is also seriously to be considered.

(3) In the last analysis, the individual must make his own choice on these matters. He is faced with various alternatives, where he can choose between the statements of different churches, conflicting Biblical interpretations, and modern non-Christian moral standards. He must live with his own conscience.

But the conscience is also far from infallible, and its content depends upon previous conditions. The conscience draws upon the insights of others, especially of the Bible and the churches which are not infallible either, and thus the modern man is caught in a perplexing circle of relativity. In the proper blend of these resources, the devoted Christian can find many helps, for the environment provided by the Church with all its wisdom of the ages contains some of the content upon which his conscience can act, but he still has no infallible guide.

(4) The deeper source of Christian judgment lies in the religious dimension, for the chief power of the Christian Church is that it has a *Gospel*. The good news of Jesus Christ, who was sent by God to save sinners, to redeem men, to reconcile the world to God, provides at once the corrective for the relativities of human judgment, for the weaknesses of the Church and for the reforming of the Church to save the world in this atomic age.

As long as the Church keeps true to the Gospel, the Church will find a basis for judging its competitors in the world. As the Church becomes more nearly the community of its Master, it will go out into the highways and byways seeking men who have been made or marred in the rough-and-tumble world of industry, business, agriculture, politics and war, showing the relevance of the Gospel to them.

Church, Bible and conscience, when properly blended in relation to the Gospel, can provide a guide for our prudential task of living in the world. Whenever God's will is translated into human terms, it ceases to be absolute and becomes permeated with the relativities of human experience. The Church as a worshiping community finds resources in God's grace to do unexpected things, for in the personal relationship between a loving God and men of faith the power of the Gospel is set forth to remake the world and to fulfill the prayer, "Thy kingdom come, thy will be done."

The ethical problem is not purely ethical

We do not ask, "Is this good?" but, "Is this good for something?" And the Christian makes this more specific, "Is this good for furthering the will of God?" The Christian has a religious solution for moral problems, and the absolute is not an ethical ideal or standard but the will of the living God. Yet the will of God is known only through the insights of men, and thus God's will as men relate it to the world is relative. The formation of standards by which we can judge the actions of ourselves and others is fraught with difficulties and relativities. There is no absolute bar of justice short of God himself, and no exact way of establishing that any organized movement is absolutely good or absolutely evil. The standards must be provided by the sources of Christian judgment. In so far as these standards are prudential, they are limited to the highest and best that men can conceive.

(1) The Christian is enjoined to "love his neighbor as himself." An organization is not to be tested chiefly in terms of developing the qualities of its particular members, but in terms of whether it concerns itself with the good for everyone. The ideal can never be achieved on the utilitarian basis of the greatest good of the greatest number; the Christian ideal has no such limitations and insists that every person is an end in himself, although he may use himself as a means. If communism sponsors one class against another, and if the classless society means the liquidation of opposing classes, that is the good—or a good—of the greatest number; but it falls short of the Christian goal precisely in its lack of recognition of every person as valuable in the sight of God. If Roman Catholicism argues for freedom of propaganda for true believers only, and by implication says that therefore only Catholics are free to spread their religion, there is a limitation on freedom—even the freedom to choose error and thus learn the truth. Legislation concerning racial equality or economic rights or educational opportunities must be evaluated on the basis of the Christian doctrine of man. If a service club enhances the fellowship of its members at the cost of being oblivious to the real needs of others in the vicinity, it has thereby limited its field of usefulness.

Except for the ideal Church, all social groupings are partial. They are, in some cases, pressure groups seeking their own aggrandizement at the expense of others. As one of the later chapters makes clear, the real advantage of Christianity over these other organized movements is that it contains all of their objectives and many more. *The Church deals with the whole man and all men in their total environment, and when the churches fail to reach the high ideal of the Church they also fall under the judgment of God.*

(2) Christian standards are frequently summarized in terms of the golden rule: "Do unto others as you would have them do unto you." This is a generalized standard which needs paring down to specific situations without being distorted into self-interest or evaporated into pious mouthings. It is a question of respect for personality in terms of the total life situation of every human being. It means a society organized so that every *child* will receive his due.

It is, however, too subjective a standard to stand on its own basis. The danger is that the giver's needs or wants will be projected onto the recipient, or, on the other hand, that the wants of the one who receives are not his true needs. There is a demand here for *empathy*, whereby the giver can see in his imagination what the recipient actually sees in terms of real needs.

Thus, as we examine the relevant data concerning the organized movements in competition with, or parallel to, the Christian Church, our question is: Does it minister fully to the real needs of the person involved? Does it give him a chance to fulfill his potentialities for good in the service of God? Does it make him a better person in all his relations with others? In so far as the organization in question fulfills these requirements, it may be a resource for the achieving of the Christian hope; in so far as it is in conflict with this ideal, it is in resistance to the Christian goal, even though it might be an organization of the churches.

(3) The third standard applies to the social order in which Christians find themselves. We are concerned that the social order shall be sufficiently Christian to provide freedom, social fellowship and opportunity for service for every man. This becomes specific in the statement issued by the leaders of the

three major religious traditions of England: "The resources of the earth should be used as God's gifts to the whole human race, and used with due consideration for the needs of present and future generations."[1]

This puts squarely before men the need for a social conscience that will go to any length to achieve fairness of distribution and conservation of natural resources. It presents the command of God to the "have" nations to deal generously with the "have-not" nations. It underscores the advances made in social legislation in many countries of the world. It looks toward the equalizing of opportunity and puts the emphasis on the collective good.

As we examine the claims and achievements of various organized movements, the questions become clearer: Have the secular radicals achieved goals beyond the announced purposes of the churches in caring for the whole human race? Can the fascists contribute anything that is good to the social order? Does organized social work achieve a just distribution of goods in the light of respect for personality? Do service clubs concern themselves with the needs of the human race or even of the surrounding community? Does humanism provide a basis for claiming that all men should share the fruits of the earth? Have the cults sought to alleviate suffering on a world-wide scale? Do the other religions have a universal concern for all races of men?

(4) A different kind of standard is required in the relations of the Church to contemporary culture. A certain amount of political and social liberty is essential if the Church is to be free to seek its own announced goals. The Church was forced underground in Germany and Norway, it was banned in Russia, it is narrowly circumscribed in Mexico, and it is not free to be Protestant in countries where the Roman Church is in the majority. A satisfactory relationship between Church and State

---

[1] No. 10 of "Ten Peace Points" published by the London *Times*, December 21, 1940, over the names of Archbishop Lang, Archbishop Temple, A. Cardinal Hinsley and Dr. Walter H. Armstrong. It was also used as a basis for the "Malvern Manifesto" of January, 1941. Cf. *A Christian Basis for the Post-War World*, edited by A. E. Baker (New York: Morehouse-Gorham Company, Inc., 1942), pp. 106-109.

can do much to provide the type of religious freedom which permeates the whole culture.

Within any culture, there are different attitudes expressed by various groups. As we look at the live options facing the world today, there are some which hinder the freedom of the Church by cynical indifference. It is as if they were saying, "You are free to be a Christian, if you are fool enough to swallow their superstitions." When this influence hits youth, as, for example, on college campuses, it actually limits the freedom of the churches to do effective work. There are subtle opposing forces which must be recognized. The opposition of the Church to much of modern educational philosophy centers at this point.

Then there are the groups which oppose Christianity by ignoring it. Their partial goals, which are often good in themselves, can be reached without benefit of the Church. Although the various economic and labor interests frequently seek the support of the clergy, the basis of their operations is usually free from any religious presuppositions and the Church is considered a luxury. These groups use the Church for their own ends, but will not stand for criticism by the Church.

Some groups, however, are actively opposed to the Church, and would either eliminate its influence in social affairs or seek to operate under its banner. Such new groups as Youth for Christ stay within the Christian fold. Coughlin and Gerald L. K. Smith make use of their Catholic and Protestant connections to further their schemes. The Communists have officially considered religion an opiate, and are now using the Church as an instrument.

Our primary concern is not with the continued existence of particular churches; but the living witness of the Church as the bearer of the Gospel is the deep responsibility of every Christian, and thus he must ask of every group: "Do you mean to allow the Church to continue its witness for Christ in every area of human living, or do you mean to sabotage, capture or oppose the Church to foster your own ambitions?" Within a free society, the Church can ask such questions and act in terms of the answers given.

(5) The judgments of Christian ethics are not fundamentally

in terms of external standards. Christian ethics examines one's loyalty, motives and inner attitudes, in order to discover what the direction of character is. The heart of religion is found in loyalty rather than belief, in faithfulness rather than concepts, in allegiance rather than creed, in devotion rather than ceremonial, in fealty or homage rather than lip service. Loyalty is difficult to measure, for while behavior can be adequately observed, the question of loyalty can be answered only introspectively by the individual Christian.

In relation to the discovery of resistance and resource, the question of loyalty to God, of devotion to the highest conceivable values, must be faced squarely. It is more difficult to obtain objective measurements of loyalty as an attitude than it is of patterns of behavior, but in each problem that faces us these six questions can be asked:[2]

(a) *What kind of God demands man's loyalty?* The Christian believes in the God of Jesus Christ, a living and personal God who deserves man's absolute trust and loyalty. He is the God of all men, who created the world and who seeks to bring men into the way of love. He is dependable, answers prayer, but is not a conjuror who pulls miracles out of heavenly silk hats. He demands that we seek social justice and He pronounces judgment upon unrepentant sinners. He forgives sinners who turn from their evil ways. He is the source of all that is good, true and beautiful. He is revealed in and through men, and especially in Jesus Christ who died to show that God cares enough for men to give His Son at the hands of wicked men. Such a God deserves man's absolute loyalty.

(b) *To what degree is a man's loyalty to God complete?* This completeness of loyalty is not predicated upon demonstrated knowledge except to a limited degree. It is simply a willingness to follow the commands of God, no matter where they may lead. It is the full integration of a personality-going-in-the-right-direction.

[2] Cf. Henry Nelson Wieman & Regina Westcott Wieman, *The Normative Psychology of Religion* (New York: Crowell), pp. 38-41, 363-390.

> I know not where the road will lead
> I follow day by day,
> Or where it ends; I only know
> I walk the King's Highway.[3]

It is difficult to be sure that a man is on the right track, and it is easy for him to deceive himself. It is likely that a man will assume that respectability is a synonym for loyalty. In regard to every competitor of the Church, this question of completeness of loyalty is pertinent. There are conflicts of loyalty, there are subordinate loyalties, there are complete loyalties to organizations which do not reveal the fullness of God's purposes for men. Where these institutions (which deserve a place in the realm of subordinate loyalties) demand absolute loyalty, there is idolatry —whether in terms of family, business, political party, labor group, social club or any other competing or parallel organized movement.

(c) *How efficient is a man's loyalty?* Christian ethics derives its profoundest insights from a man's inner attitudes, but the question of efficiency points to the connection between motives and results. Character education is of no value if it stops with talk. The history of Christianity has been written by men whose loyalty was effective, illustrating the saying of James: "Show me your faith apart from your works, and I by my works will show you my faith. So faith by itself, if it has no works, is dead."[4]

The appeal of many groups, especially the social radicals, lies in their efficiency. The power of many labor leaders lies in their specific achievements, and any slackening of effort to achieve higher wages or better working conditions or a share in management jeopardizes their positions. The high ideals professed by the Christian Church are not genuine competition for its rivals unless it demonstrates its efficiency by getting things done. Other-

[3] Evelyn A. Cummins, *The Hymnal 1940* (New York: Church Pension Fund), p. 432.

[4] James 2:18b, 17. From the Revised Standard Version of the New Testament. (Copyright, 1946, by the International Council of Religious Education.)

wise it rightly may be accused of being an opiate of the people.

(d) *How sensitive is a man's loyalty to God?* One of man's greatest weaknesses is his lack of sensitivity to the sufferings of those beyond his immediate experience or knowledge. Furthermore, he is frequently blind to the potentialities of value residing in a specific experience. Just as it takes a trained ear to appreciate the finest music, so it takes a discriminating sense of value to see where God can best be served. It is in this realm that the Hebrew prophets were so effective, for they pointed out the evils of the time, being sensitive to suffering and injustice and various other forms of moral evil. They would not let men escape from responsibility into the release provided by deliberate ignorance or by the routine of daily work. The Church and its competitors are often lacking in this practical kind of sensitivity, where new values can be intuited and brought into existence by applying consecrated imagination to the situation at hand.

(e) *Are a man's loyalties progressing?* Religious living is a process of growth. St. Paul talks frequently of "growing in grace," which means simply that God can work more easily and effectively through men who consciously seek to serve Him, whose loyalty is becoming more complete, more effective and more sensitive. As the Church comes into contact with its competitors, there is need for growth on all sides. No organism can remain static, and new features are always coming into the picture, so that there must be constant reintegration around new and higher factors.

In judging between the various options, there is need to investigate the possibilities of growth in the groups and among their members. If there is a fixed idea around which the group is integrated, the Church will find resistance to the degree that spiritual growth is rendered impossible.

(f) *Are a man's loyalties socially effective?* This throws us back on the standards derived from Christian theology: justice for all regardless of nationality or race or class, fellowship across all existing barriers, achievement of real freedom within and between nations, a free Church in a free state. The Church officially believes in these goals for society, but often the means for achieving them lie outside the Church.

The social effectiveness of the Christian's loyalty to God is expressed in and through the Church and also through organizations in some degree different from and perhaps opposed to the Church. Some of the vital options suggested in the succeeding chapters provide for the partial fulfillment of these goals. The Church member needs to be an active and patriotic citizen, working through various organizations to achieve what values are actually possible. This may involve working through unions, service clubs, social agencies, pressure groups, special agencies of the churches, or through political and educational channels. It makes mandatory the discovery of resistance and resource in every organization which the Christian can be expected to join.

(6) There has been a shift in Christian thinking on social ethics. No longer do we believe that a social gospel can exist in a theological vacuum. No longer is man "building" God's kingdom as a perfect society. At the same time, there is no cessation of man's attempt to construct a good society. It is simply the recognition that the religious dimension is primary, and that ethics is in the religious dimension. Furthermore, moral idealism and God's will cannot be simply equated, for it is conceivable and even likely that God's purposes are often contrary to man's conception of God's intentions. The coming of the kingdom is God's act and man prepares for it.

The tragedy is that most Church members do not make their judgments from theological perspectives. They are either caught in a legalism of moralistic codes, or they assume that the surrounding culture is Christian and behave according to the standards of respectability, or they see the Christian standards and deem them irrelevant. The same danger faces those using the standards of judgment and norms of loyalty suggested in the preceding paragraphs, unless it is clearly affirmed that the Christian religion is deeply rooted in the historical process of which God is the sovereign ruler. What is called for, therefore, is a revolution in the habits of moral judgment, and there is no sign that this will be forthcoming. We are always forced back from moral judgments as such to religions judgments which include moral judgments, and thus the theological answer of repentance is placed in a social context and provides hope that a revolutionary change might take place under God's leadership. The theological basis of sociological analysis must be kept in mind as we turn to the problem of getting at the facts.

3. METHODS OF ASSESSMENT

Getting the facts is not easy for the average churchman. He needs skill in analyzing propaganda, for he cannot rely on the secular press for unbiased accounts, his own prejudices intervene, and self-interest cannot be kept out of the picture. The average layman does not have access to the information he needs to make intelligent judgments, and thus he is open to various persuasions unless the leaders of the Church make it available. Our problem, then, is to suggest methods of assessment for the lay and clerical leaders of the churches rather than for the rank-and-file membership.

The deductive approach

The deductive approach operates from self-evident principles as a basis of judgment, without too great regard for the facts. If a group denies the principles held to be sacred, it is therefore providing resistance to the Christian cause. It looks as if deduction is irrelevant, for it deals with the logical implications of a self-evident proposition rather than with facts. Moral judgments are frequently made in the realm of ideas without consideration of the facts of moral achievement. A good example of this is the attitude of the Roman Church toward communism and fascism. The communist ideology is officially atheistic, there is a long-time development of antagonism in the realm of power between Moscow and the Vatican, and therefore communism is evil per se no matter what good it may achieve. Fascism, on the other hand, makes a place for the Roman Church in its structure, by signing a concordat or by giving it political power, and thus fascism and Catholicism go hand in hand in Franco Spain and Argentina. That this deductive approach is shared by many Protestants is indicated by the record of the United States in the Spanish Civil War. It is also the basis of much Protestant bickering about "blue laws," reform government, and various minor moral matters.

The inductive approach

The inductive approach is more realistic and difficult, and cannot operate successfully without the aid of deduction. Induction derives its principles from the observation of facts, and thus its generalized conclusions are only relative guides to action. Therefore, no organization is likely to be judged either fully Christian or non-Christian, and degrees of resistance and resource will be discovered in the partial objectives of each group. From the standpoint of values achieved, the inductive approach finds more good in atheistic communism than in Catholic-dominated fascism; it sees more good in John Dewey's instrumentalism than in Coughlin's Catholic politics; it sees values in the humanism and scientism of the college campuses which, with all the dangers, may prove superior to the fundamentalism and low standards of some denominational colleges. But the inductive approach also sees the resistance to the Christian hope in these same movements and in movements which the deductive approach might find wholly good.

To let the facts speak for themselves means accurate knowledge of the facts. Statistics can be distorted as easily as can deductive judgment, and Christian moral judgments need more cross-checking than has previously been available. There are several sources of data available to Church members and others: (1) The special information services of the ecumenical movement and of the various churches contain statements of facts untouched by commercial interests and relatively free from bias. Departments of social relations in various churches have access to information which does not appear before the general public and frequently this information is invaluable in forming judgments. (2) The Church press, while not always accurate, is relatively free from economic pressures and makes available facts which should be known by intelligent Christians. (3) While the secular press is often slanted in the reporting of news, it is possible to discount the bias; often, however, the bias is very subtle among both magazines and books. (4) Where technical judgments depend upon experts, as is frequently the case, the churches have access to the findings. Of course, experts differ in their opinions and predictions, but it is sometimes possible for trained leaders in the churches to make their own evaluation of the moral implications derived from the facts. (5) The sciences and social studies provide much help in giving technical data to the churches. (6) Even if our factual judgments are reasonably accurate, they do not provide an adequate basis for predicting the future, for the element of personal freedom to change the use of facts within any group may alter the whole situation; the policy of a particular group does not necessarily guarantee its future actions.

The combined approach

The inductive-deductive approach attempts to avoid the dogmatism of the latter and the relativity of the former. Whitehead has said that induction and deduction are two ends of the same worm. Logical certainty (as deduction) is operative in obtaining practical and highly probable truth. In the premises of the syllogism, the major premise would be a generalization based upon widespread experience, the minor premise would be a specific observation of relevant and immediate data, and the conclusion would follow with as high a degree of probability as the underlying facts could afford. The conclusion, however, awaits empirical verification. Deduction makes articulate the experience of the past; induction draws new information from specific and observable data and enriches future deductions, thus increasing the degree of probability in knowledge.[5]

[5] Harold Bosley, *The Quest for Religious Certainty* (Chicago: Willett, Clark & Company, 1939), pp. 61-77.

In any thoroughgoing functional analysis, the inductive-deductive approach is used. For example, the anthropologist sees each institution or organized movement integrated on a certain principle which satisfies the needs of that group. The family is seen not merely in its basic functions of reproduction and sex, but in terms of education, citizenship and its relations to the surrounding culture. The historical point of view not only provides perspective for evaluating a group, it also provides pointer readings which can predict elements of future behavior even if factors of change are introduced. This principle of "selective conservatism," as Malinowski calls it, does not eliminate the possibility of revolutionary changes, but the basic assumption is that only great effort will bring it about.[6]

Drawing upon the methods of the inductive-deductive approach and upon all the aids which the social studies can provide, the Church seeks to determine the degrees of resistance and resource among the various live options. It begins with an accurate description of the facts, and then it passes relative judgments upon the competing systems of thought and organized movements in terms of possible resistance and resource, seeking for allies to achieve in practice what the Church asserts in ideal. Using the ideal standards derived from Christian theology and strengthened by the grace that comes from the living God in Christ, the Church stands as a witness to the religious dimension of all living; for the Church is a people-Church in a covenant relationship with the God of Jesus Christ, bound to do God's will as far as it can be ascertained in each situation.

4. BASIC ATTITUDES OF CHRISTIANS IN THE CHURCH

The Christian in the Church has various live options before him. He lives in a world where there are many organized movements seeking to achieve their own ends. In the Church he can find strength and comfort and guidance, provided through wor-

[6] Bronislaw Malinowski, *The Dynamics of Culture Change* (New Haven: Yale University Press), pp. 62-63.

ship, fellowship, education, pastoral aids, missionary ideals and the overcoming of national and racial barriers. In his loyalty to the Church, he works in and through the Church to bring about the realization of Christian ideals within the "Body of Christ."

The Christian is aware, more than others, that the Christian community to which he belongs falls short of being an ideal Church. It is divided from Christians of other names. It is open to all the shortcomings, mistakes and sins of a society in which individual members do not always see eye to eye or share the same degree of devotion. Within the churches, there are always critics who delight in pointing out the obvious or hidden weaknesses, whether they be moral, theological or broadly cultural. The fully loyal Christian will welcome such criticism, for it points to where the Church is in itself providing resistance to the will of God. The Church, when it is fully Christian, welcomes reformation and self-criticism; but too often the weakness of the churches comes from the stiff-necked refusal to open their eyes to the errors of their ways when they are described

Criticism of the Church needs careful examination, for too often the criticism is from a partial point of view or from a limited or inadequate grasp of the facts. If the Marxist criticism of religion seemed to be justified when applied by Communists to the Czarist Russian Orthodox Church, that does not provide sufficient evidence for the generalization that religion is an opiate of the people. If John Dewey's criticisms of religion fit a certain type of fundamentalism, that does not mean that they apply with equal force to dynamic Protestantism. If it is true that a particular denomination appeals to a class of people with greater education or wealth, that does not mean that Christians are therefore a bourgeois group. If it is true that the churches have fostered racial distinctions in many areas, that does not mean that Christianity is necessarily a white man's religion. The Christian can learn from all of these criticisms, but he must always take into account the non-Christian perspective from which many such criticisms are made.

The Christian, living in the world, expresses his basic loyalty to the God of Jesus Christ through membership in many other groups, including his family, his work, his play, his political allegiance and his community fellowship. Some of these organizations do not come into competition with the Church. They are legitimate parallel organizations, seeking goals which neither strengthen nor weaken the work of the Church. Yet they impinge upon the time and money given to the Church and may serve far lower ends.

The competitors of the Church are sometimes unconscious ones, which are really competing instrumentalities such as commercialized recreation, motion pictures, radio and the like. No one conceives of these instrumentalities as competing for the loyalty of the people in the same sense that one lives for an ideal. The problem becomes serious when these instrumentalities fall into the hands of people who misuse them, and then we are faced with the opposition of an organized or unorganized movement, such as the new fascism, low moral standards or some other genuinely live option.

Social groups may be actual competitors of the Church even though they are not consciously opposed to the Church. This may be true of some service clubs, social welfare agencies, educational organizations and labor unions. They seek their goals and consider them good without reference to God or to the aims of the Church. The whole problem of a rising secularism comes into the picture here, and it is not always easy to see where a highly ethical humanism provides either resource for, or resistance to, the Christian hope. At the point where the theological basis of Christianity is denied, however, the Christian must protest.

Other organizations are actively opposed to the Church or at least to Christian ideals. A Communist will follow the party line at this point by opposing or using the churches. There are hidden opponents who give lip service to the Church while plotting the destruction of its power; the various American fascist groups masquerading under the guise of Christianity are examples, and to these the Christian must be unalterably opposed.

The Christian in the Church, faced with opportunities to work in and through other organizations, has to make important moral and religious judgments. The options are live ones and he must make a choice, coming to terms with the world without losing his "citizenship in heaven."

5. THE NECESSITY OF COMPARATIVE STUDY OF TODAY'S LIVE OPTIONS

There is a "new comparative religion." While Shinto is not a live option in the United States, communism, fascism, Christian Science, Dewey's humanism, scientism and various other organized movements are live choices for many people. The spirit of secularism is vital not only on college campuses but at every educational level in this country; it pervades the economic and political scene and expresses itself in recreation and leisure.

The leaders of the Church need adequate bases for judgment and sufficient channels of information in order to know what action is necessary. Those who choose to co-operate with labor unions and employers, with the National Association of Manufacturers and the C.I.O.-Political Action Committee, with Youth for Christ and the Humanist Society, with the Rotary Club and the Christian American, with social agencies and pressure groups, with Christian Science and British Israel, need to know enough not to get burned. There is need for a morally religious realism, where the facts are allowed to speak for themselves. There is need for astute leadership in the churches, so that the churches can make use of these organizations in so far as these groups provide resources for achieving Christian goals and so the churches can oppose these organizations in so far as they provide resistance to the realization of the Christian hope. "To be as wise as serpents and as harmless as doves" is essential if one is to be an intelligent Christian in the atomic age. The important thing is to discover God's will and to do it. To this challenge the Church must find an answer for today.

FURTHER READING

BENNETT, JOHN. *Christian Realism*. New York: Charles Scribner's Sons, 1941.

BOSLEY, HAROLD A. *The Quest for Religious Certainty*. Chicago: Willett, Clark & Company, 1939.

BRUNNER, EMIL. *Justice and the Social Order*. New York: Harper & Brothers, 1946.

HOLT, ARTHUR E. *This Nation Under God*. Chicago: Willett, Clark & Company, 1939.

KEAN, CHARLES D. *Christianity and the Cultural Crisis*. New York: Association Press, 1944.

McMAHON, FRANCIS E. *A Catholic Looks at His World*. New York: Vanguard Press, 1945.

MILLER, RANDOLPH CRUMP, and SHIRES, HENRY H., eds. *Christianity and the Contemporary Scene*. New York: Morehouse-Gorham Co., Inc., 1943.

NIEBUHR, REINHOLD. *Christianity and Power Politics*. New York: Charles Scribner's Sons, 1940.

TEMPLE, WILLIAM. *Christianity and Social Order*. New York: Penguin Books, Inc., 1942.

The Nature of the Church: A Report of the American Theological Committee. Chicago: Willett, Clark & Company, 1945.

2

THE NEW COMPARATIVE
RELIGION[1]

Elton Trueblood

Introduction. 1. The influence of Christianity. 2. The real divisions of Christianity. 3. The rivals of Christianity: the faith of labor, Marxism, scientism, anthropocentric humanism, nationalistic mysticism. 4. Levels of co-operation.

The average thoughtful person in the life of the West, if he is asked to consider possible alternatives to Christianity, is likely to mention some of the historic world religions, such as Buddhism, Mohammedanism and Hinduism. He may do this because he once pursued a course in college called "Comparative Religions" or because he has done some general reading concerning what are called "The World's Living Religions." The general supposition is that there are nine or ten such living faiths and that Christianity is one of them. Most of us, when the subject is brought up, wish we might have time to study more carefully these other religions of which we know so little even though we are aware that they number their adherents by the millions.

The person who reacts in this familiar way is making a sharp

[1] Because of the unavoidable absence of Dr. Trueblood from two out of three meetings of the Group, the present treatment was not subjected to the same process of criticism employed for the other chapters. Therefore the Group must note that it cannot be responsible for certain matters of emphasis here in the same degree as in regard to other chapters, although the chapter as a whole is representative of the mind of the Group.

distinction, and a wholly proper one, between faiths which are living and faiths which are dead. We may have some interest in the religions of Egypt or Babylonia, we frequently study Greek and Roman religion, and we even delve somewhat into the ancient Druidical or Teutonic faiths, but we do not ordinarily look upon these as live options. We rightly look upon recent efforts, directed to the resurrection of Teutonic religion, as wholly bizarre and as no longer a serious threat. By the same token no one is tempted to become a Druid.

Though the current distinction between living and dead religions is important, it does not go far enough. If we follow the logic of this situation further we soon realize that many contemporary religions are really no more living options for twentieth-century Western man than are the ancient religions of Mesopotamia. The truth is that most of the nine or ten world religions about which we frequently read are not for us genuine alternatives to Christianity. They are, of course, real possibilities in Asia, but they are not real possibilities in *Western* civilization. They are valid objects of study, but they are little more.

Most of the world faiths do not entice the average Westerner to acceptance. He is no more tempted to embrace Shinto than he is tempted to make graven images. Even Judaism is not a live option for most of our people, though it does not seem bizarre. Theoretically Judaism is a universal religion, welcoming converts, but most of the Gentile millions of the Western world have no more thought of seeking entrance into the Jewish community than they have of seeking entrance into the fold of Islam.

Our tendency to present the various world religions *as though* they were the live alternatives to Christianity in the Western world may do incalculable harm. The student or the general reader is likely to come away from a recital of world religions with considerable knowledge, but no important convictions. He has found out how quaint religion can be and it is hard for him to avoid the conclusion that all faiths are equally quaint. He has had a conducted tour through a contemporary museum and he feels toward all the exhibits the detachment which usually characterizes any museum mood. He has not looked upon the faiths he has studied as live alternatives for him in his time. He is tempted to suppose that religion is a subject to study rather than a faith to endorse or to reject. He does not realize the degree to which religion, rightly understood, always produces a forced option.

The sense of commitment is the differentiating mark of true religion, and many of the genuine religious alternatives of Western culture, therefore, lie wholly outside Christianity or at least outside the Church. Though very few of us are ever tempted to join the historic religions of the East, millions may be tempted to join an atheistic idealism, like that of Marxism or even the incipient paganism of a naturalized fascism. On less ambitious levels the real faith of men and women may become centered in the parent-teacher association, the labor movement or a study circle.

To an increasing degree in our time the honest Comparative Religion, so far as Western man is concerned, will include only the various forms of Christianity and the growing secular religions indigenous to our culture. There are, perhaps, nine or ten live possibilities in the new Comparative Religion, as there were in the old list, but they appear in a variety of combinations. Several of the living faiths of our day can be held simultaneously without mutual conflict, or in any case it seems so to the people who hold them.

Even our Comparative Christianity must be seen in new alignments and with new alternatives if we are concerned with live options. The most important reason why a merely denominational description of Christianity is insufficient is that denominational divisions do not, for the most part, represent the genuine divisions in Christendom. The real divisions cut across all denominational lines. Though this is less true in regard to Protestant-Catholic relationships, there are striking evidences of the working of this principle even here. In any case it is true that Protestant Christianity, which is still the dominant form in the major life of the West, presents horizontal divisions running across all sectarian lines. It is almost an axiom in some denominations, that great numbers find a deeper fellowship with the like-minded of other denominations than they find with many who are supposedly in their same fold.

We are living at a time when the lines between religions are being rapidly reformed. The new alignments are coming so rapidly that we can hardly keep pace. The lines between Protestant denominations are so greatly broken that it is now the rule rather than the exception for our people to change their affiliations when they move from one city to another. Ours is an uprooted time. Many still want to belong, but the live alternatives are vastly different from what they were a quarter of a century ago. Some of the new fellowships that are forming are still so embryonic that we cannot even guess what their developed form will be.

1. THE INFLUENCE ON CHRISTIANITY

Any realistic study of religion must recognize the decline of Christianity in our Western civilization. Our civilization in the past has, of course, been most imperfectly Christian, but some conscious loyalty to the Christian faith has been, for centuries, the accepted standard. In the time of our fathers a man who joined a labor union did not normally suppose that he joined the labor union *instead* of the Church. He might easily have some kind of affiliation with some church and be interested in the labor movement at the same time. Though the majority of labor leaders are today professed Christians, relatively few of them take an active part in church life.

Christianity, in the Western world, has ceased to have the favored or dominant position and is now *one* of the religions which Western man may choose. The wide recognition that both Nazism and communism have been real, though inadequate, religions has brought this home to the consciousness of millions. What Berdyaev understood so well more than twenty years ago is now common knowledge. "Christianity," he said, "is going back to the state she enjoyed before Constantine; she has to undertake the conquest of the world afresh."[2]

It has been the curious and tragic fate of Christianity to raise up enemies to itself. The Church has reared children who have opposed her. The most conspicuous examples of this are found in the development of nontheistic humanism, on the one hand, and in the development of technology, on the other. By the insistence of Christianity on the truth that man is infinitely precious and that institutions were made for man, rather than man for them, we have been led to the man-centered thought which so stresses the humanities that it despises and neglects theology. By means of the beneficent Christian nationalism, which has founded universities, with their sciences, there has been produced a highly efficient technology which has made man arrogant in his self-reliance. "The forces that have done most violence to man's natural life," says V. A. Demant, "have sprung from a perversion of energies released in Europe by the Christian religion." The result of this development is that the only influence of Christianity in many circles is that of unconscious remnants.

To be sure, there are some areas for which this is not true. We refer frequently to the secularism of our age, but the secularism is seldom complete. All of our people still date their letters from the beginning of the Christian era and look upon Mussolini's effort to make his march on Rome a dateline as both humorous and fantastic. This, some may say, is a trivial remnant, but more serious examples may be found. One regards marriage. While serial polygamy is clearly on the increase, there is still a widespread respect for the sanctity of marriage which Christianity has encouraged so assiduously, and there is much more chastity before marriage than would exist apart from the centuries of Christian teaching. Another important example of such a Christian remainder is our widespread and unargued philanthropy.

[2] Nicolas Berdyaev, *The End of Our Time* (New York: Sheed & Ward, 1933), p. 170.

One of the most significant of Christian remnants, and one revealed by the war, is the fact that most of our people, who have allowed their own working standards to be detached from the Christian root, are nevertheless genuinely shocked by the frank acceptance of unchristian standards elsewhere.[3] Though most of our people would consider it wholly quaint for an intelligent man to champion the Gospel with evangelical vigor, it remains true that they are still close enough to that Gospel to be equally shocked when they hear Christianity openly denounced or rejected. To reject it openly is as truly bad form as to champion it openly.

We may say, then, that whatever the census reports may reveal, the majority of the people in the West make no active avowal of Christianity, but likewise they do not deny it or have any intention of forbidding it. Most of them are extremely tolerant toward those of their neighbors who continue to consider Christianity important. They believe in freedom of religion, partly because they suppose it is essentially harmless. The open and vocal enemies of the Christian religion are few. But the residual Christianity is so slight and so thinly spread that millions who represent this position are easily induced to champion rival faiths in the West and many have already championed them.

2. THE REAL DIVISIONS OF CHRISTIANITY

Having said all this, however, we must recognize—indeed, insist upon—the fact that an unapologetic Christianity is one of the live alternatives before Western man at this juncture. Any frank statement of this position is exciting, partly because it is rare. One of the most refreshing of such statements is that made by Howard Foster Lowry whose inaugural address as the president of the College of Wooster has recently been printed:

[3] On this point see John Baillie, *What Is Christian Civilization?* (New York: Oxford University Press, 1945), p. 39.

The College holds that behind all life is a great and loving Father who works through man, who gave man the free choice of good and, therefore, the possibility of evil; who exacts justice but loves mercy; and who, through the sheer miracle of love, gave his only begotten Son that man might have everlasting life. The logical result of any such belief is *evangelical* Christianity. It has to be because evangelical Christianity is the only kind of Christianity there is.[4]

The difference between such a "Fellowship of the Unashamed" and the watery Christianity of so many of our people who tend to apologize for the little faith that they have, is a fundamental difference and represents one of the real divisions in our new Comparative Religion.

The consciously organized Christianity of our day appears, in the main, in the following forms:

(1) *Ecumenical Christianity.* This is the faith which now cuts across many denominational lines and is represented by the men who are writing the present series of essays. The people who support the major Protestant seminaries, who read the major Protestant journals and attend the ecumenical councils belong to this faith. The men who preach at the universities which have chapels are so much of one mind on major issues that no outsider can guess the denominational affiliations of the different men. They are usually loyal to their own denominations, because they know that there can be no Church unless there are churches. They have many differences among themselves, but they all belong to a universe of discourse which makes intelligent discussion and conference possible. These people, who constitute the major leadership and much of the laity of the great Protestant bodies, are the true *Catholics* in the modern world because they are serious in their fellowship with one another and because they extend their fellowship even to those groups who do not extend fellowship to them.

(2) *Dogmatic Christianity.* This is the faith of those Christian

[4] See "Sketch for a Family Portrait," *The College of Wooster Bulletin*, September, 1945, p. 43.

groups who are wholly inflexible in their relations with other Christians, because they consider all others as heretics. Their strength lies in their definiteness of belief, in the higher degree of certainty they encourage and in the conviction that they occupy a favored position. This makes them aggressive and frequently successful in adding numbers. They are found in all churches, perhaps most powerfully concentrated in the Roman Catholic Church, but in large numbers throughout Protestant churches as well. The chief defect of this form of Christianity is that it is not *catholic*, and it is by this inelastic temper of mind and spirit that they are to be identified.

(3) *Neo-Revivalism.* The revivalistic Christianity, which has often been supposed dead or ready to die, continues to show an astonishing vitality. This is particularly true in America, but the phenomenon may be observed in all Anglo-Saxon countries. In many large cities, including those supposedly most sophisticated, the churches which strive for the public avowal of conversion, and use essentially vaudeville tactics to accomplish this result, continue to be both prominent and successful. The numerical showing which the Youth for Christ movement has been able to make is one evidence of the importance of this variant of the Christian religion, and the steady appearance on the radio of men who foster this kind of experience, is another.

(4) *Fringe Movements.* Fundamentally different from the three types of Christianity just described are the scores of small movements which appear to be out of the main Christian stream. These range all the way from "respectable" movements for the upper classes to cults which draw chiefly from the underprivileged. Most of them show whatever vitality they possess by virtue of the fact that they are largely lay religions, that they adopt unconventional procedures, and that they demand complete devotion as a qualification for membership.

3. THE RIVALS OF CHRISTIANITY

Important as it is to understand the main variants of contemporary Christianity in the West, it is far more important to

understand the genuinely rival faiths which have already arisen
and are continuing to rise. We may be certain that the number
of live alternatives will be more numerous a few years from
now than they are today.

It is a common practice in consciously Christian circles to
deplore the rise of these rival faiths, and their rise is often
truly deplorable, but most of them involve some aspects of
potential or actual nobility. All of these faiths now offer some
resistance to the Christian gospel, but all of them are potential
resources as well. All have much to contribute to a total
faith adequate for this time. Our task is therefore that of careful
evaluation, looking to eventual employment of what is truly
valuable. Many of the people dissociated from Christianity, or
at least from Christian institutions, are sensitive people, who
are finding new outlets for their spiritual energies. A memorable
illustration of this is seen in Rebecca West's account of a meeting at a schoolhouse in an English village, a meeting called to
hear a report, by two officers, on the actual facts of Buchenwald.
All of Rebecca West's account of the meeting is interesting, but
it is her conclusion that bears so strongly on our present
problem:

> We were conscious, as we listened to the tales of Buchen-
> wald, in our village school, that such danger might be over-
> hanging us; and I think we were all halfway to suspecting
> that it might be as Christopher Burney tells us and that
> there is no way of averting that danger, save for each one
> of us to resolve that all our lives long we should prefer
> the agreeable to the disagreeable, love to hatred, and good
> to evil. Such resolutions, in the past, were usually re-
> inforced in the village church. But though a fair proportion
> of us attended the meeting at the village school that Satur-
> day night, not many of us would meet at church on Sunday
> morning; and I do not know the answer to the problem
> implied in that disharmony.[5]

[5] See "From England," *Harper's Magazine,* January, 1946, p. 25.

This statement is as revealing as it is disarming. The Christian religion apparently seemed irrelevant to most of Rebecca West's neighbors, yet they were highly serious, full of moral earnestness, and intent on finding new ways of providing themselves and others with a living faith. The illustration is important because it is truly characteristic of our time.

We must never forget that a great part of the secularism which represents such a serious challenge to Christian civilization has arisen from a lofty motive and as a noble gesture. Many of the men who reject the Christian gospel, and especially the older ones, have thought of themselves as helping to free mankind from ecclesiastical tyranny and from the shackles of false piety. Their opposition to Christianity has often been ignorant and uninformed, but it has been a revolt which involves a basically valid element, the opposition to inadequate religion. Reinhold Niebuhr has performed an important service in reminding us that "the primary conscious motive of this secularism (whatever may have been its unconscious and more sinful motives) was to break the chains which a profane Christianity had placed upon man."[6]

The fundamental secular rivals of contemporary Christianity in Western civilization are potentially numerous. The following are suggested as examples of what we may expect:

The faith of labor

Though the Christian faith has been largely responsible for keeping alive in the world most of the social passion which brought the labor movement into existence in the beginning, there are few groups of men in the modern world who feel farther from Christianity than do those who give their nights and days to organized labor. That these men have found an alternative faith cannot reasonably be denied. They have not only lost the Christian gospel; they have found another gospel.

The labor movement now has its own heroes of the faith who

[6] See Reinhold Niebuhr, *Christianity and Power Politics* (New York: Charles Scribner's Sons, 1940), p. 218.

are, in many cases, followed with unquestioning loyalty. These saints of labor must be rough and tough, and they may be corrupt, but they know how to make men follow them.

Though most of the men who make up the rank and file of the labor movement are wholly innocent of conscious doctrine or theory, they are really held together by a kind of truncated idealism. No matter how debased a union may become in the corruption of its leaders and in its strategy of terror, there is enough of this truncated idealism to hold the movement together. They start with a recognition of the injustices of our social order, they are continually conscious of the widely different standards of living of labor and management, and they tend to have some sense of identification with the oppressed everywhere. This has led, in some labor circles, to a better record in regard to anti-discrimination on ground of race than is shown in some Christian communities. Conspicuous evidences of this are to be noted in the official stand of Soviet Russia and in the official position of the Congress of Industrial Organizations. The surrogate for religious experience, in conventional labor circles, is a genuine sense of solidarity.

Marxism

Though most of the leaders, as well as the followers, of the labor movement are relatively untouched by theory and certainly are not Marxists, there is a vigorous minority, represented by some persons in the labor movement and by some in intellectual circles, for whom Marxism is the very breath of life. That their position is that of a religion there can be no doubt, since they hold their ideas with that sense of commitment which is everywhere the differentiating mark of genuine religion. The group inspired by the Marxist faith is not yet relatively large in most parts of the West, but it is highly vocal, and of great potency in the creation of the future.

The potential strength of the Marxist faith is vastly increased by the fact that one great country, Russia, appears to be a political embodiment of this faith. Actually the divergence of

Russia from orthodox Marxism is great, but the connection is sufficiently close to seem significant to the faithful. The Marxist faith, in its conventional form, is an atheistic idealism, looking, with prophetic enthusiasm, toward a society organized, not for the benefit of one class, but for the achievement of complete classlessness. That there is a marked contrast between this lofty dream and the actual practical policies of the Soviet Union, many of which are extremely devious, is what the critic who is familiar with the history of religions ought to expect.

Any serious combination between the Marxist faith and the Christian faith is extremely difficult at the present stage of events because both, when true to their own genius, demand the whole of life of all followers. A period of mutual accommodation may come eventually, but for the immediate present, the option is sharper at this point than at any other. For several years to come the question on which millions will divide most sharply in Western civilization is the question of Russia.

Scientism

The faith of science, though, does not represent so many persons as does the faith of labor, nor is it as intense as Marxism, but it has a great influence in our society and is an important alternative to Christianity. It is important because of the present prestige which science has and because of the excellent character of the majority of the men who have adopted this alternative.

There are many natural scientists who are devout and unapologetic Christians. In fact, it is often noticed in our universities that there are more devout Christians among the physical scientists than are to be found among the social scientists. Perhaps this is because the scientific reputations of chemistry and physics are so firmly established that they are not endangered by a public attachment to the supposedly outmoded Christian faith.

When this has been said we must go on to say that a very large proportion of active natural scientists, probably the majority, are wholly unconscious of any affiliation with Christianity or any debt to the Gospel. The average working scientist, on Sunday morning, passes by the place of worship and goes on to his laboratory.

The essential faith of many of these men is almost pathetically simple. They have found a technique that works and they therefore believe in it. They are frequently so absorbed in their experimentation that they neglect to ask the troublesome but highly relevant questions which plague the minds of more philosophical men. Many, who understand very well the little technique they follow, would be hard pressed if asked to explain the genuine logical difficulties involved in verification. Many are simple-minded technicians. Many have no notion of the fact that there is no necessary connection between science as a method and the naturalistic metaphysic so often associated with it.

The great merit of the scientific faith is the degree of personal and intellectual honesty which inspires it and is, in turn, encouraged by it. Most active scientists would accede to the dictum of one of their number that the purpose of science is to set limiting values to a man's preconceptions. The golden rule is Huxley's admonition, "Sit down as a little child before the fact," and the procedure is to follow the evidence and let the prejudices take care of themselves.

These values of science are qualitatively religious just as the Marxist demand for social justice is religious. Both are elements of any genuinely good society. The pity is that, in both cases, the single leaf has been torn from the larger book and so much of the meaning thereby lost.

Anthropocentric humanism

The first and third examples of alternatives to Christianity in contemporary life are based largely on occupational interests. The fourth example is less so. The most vocal representatives of this alternative are found among writers and scholars in the humanistic disciplines, but not among them alone. It has become the supposedly adequate faith of a truly alarming number of public school teachers and has been strongly entrenched in the teachers' colleges. It has had a wide vogue also among the general reading public.

It is necessary to call this faith anthropocentric humanism to distinguish it from the older or theocentric humanism. The great majority of those who call themselves humanists today would consider theocentric humanism quaint. Most of them do not make a specific rejection of belief in God and are not usually forced into a position in which this is necessary. They do not bother to denounce the Christian religion as false; they are merely convinced that it is wholly irrelevant. It is in this group that religious toleration is most warmly espoused and for the reason given above, viz., that religion is harmless. What they call tolerance, therefore, is really indifference.

The most common position is not that of express denial of the existence of the God and Father of our Lord Jesus Christ, but rather the contention that the good life is possible, *wholly without reference to the existence or nonexistence of God*. Philip Wheelwright has put his finger on the crucial point in his re- mark that "the ethics of humanism, being derived from the nature of man, is logically independent of a belief in God or in any other metaphysical entity."[7]

It must be noted that there is a certain nobility in this de- tached humanistic ethic. Man stands alone in his moral life; his ethical position does not even derive from theology. Such a position has been clearly championed by Walter Lippmann in *A Preface to Morals*, by W. T. Stace in *The Destiny of Western Man*, by Alexander Meiklejohn in *Education between Two Worlds*, and by many more.

Though theism is not specifically rejected in the cultivated circles which are satisfied with this alternative, a little analysis usually reveals that the metaphysics assumed is in any case naturalistic. John Bennett has pointed out that, in a volume

[7] Philip Wheelwright, *A Critical Introduction to Ethics* (New York: Doubleday Doran and Company, 1935), pp. 188-9.

I Believe, consisting of the personal credos of thirty-seven con-temporary intellectuals, not more than two represent an avowed Christian position.

The strength of the anthropocentric humanism in our day consists largely in the fact that it seems to many people to keep what religion formerly attempted to cherish. It is assumed, often with no effort to deal at all with contemporary theology, that the Christian religion cannot be defended intellectually; but, they say, we must somehow keep faith in "spiritual values." Much is said about "the aspiring spirit of man," and the notion of the essential brotherhood of man is widely accepted, with few to ask the embarrassing question, how men can be brothers when they have no common Father. The encouragement of the "Humanities" has been one of the practical results of this humanistic faith and conferences have been held which make those who cherish this gospel have a sense of participation in a common enterprise.

If the strength of this movement lies in its emphasis on "spiritual" and human values, the danger lies in the subjectivity and groundlessness of these values and in the pride which such uprooted humanism engenders. Those who are concerned with spiritual things, but are not subject to the humbling discipline of prayer, are in danger of a smugness more terrible than any ever known in Christian circles. Anthropocentric humanism is very popular and is often productive of some human good, but it can never be a really adequate faith because it leads inevitably to a sinful, though delusive, sense of self-sufficiency.

Nationalistic mysticism

We often speak of the paganism of our civilization, but, for the most part, this is a loose use of language. Certainly we ought not to speak of those wholly devoid of religious faith as pagans, if we propose to keep anything of the historical meaning of the term. In the ancient culture the pagans were the country people who went on believing in the old divinities after the advent of Christianity. Their error lay not in failure to have religious belief, but rather in believing *too much*. Paganism stands, not for irreligion, but for false religion.

The nearest approach we have had to paganism in the modern world is the Nazi experiment. This was a conscious secession from Christendom on a large scale, and an effort to recover something of the old Nordic faith. The latter was wonderfully adapted to the needs of racism, encouraging the requisite self-confidence of the Germans, and especially of the German youth. It was nationalistic mysticism, carried to the extreme.

This particular form of paganism is now discredited both by world judgment and by military defeat. It may live on, among fanatical German groups, as a lost cause, but, in this form it is not a live option for modern man. If it is to become a live option in the West it must appear in various clever disguises and it must seem wherever it appears to be a home-grown variety.

That there is much of this kind of faith existing in our society we cannot doubt. A common form of it is the glorification of the white man as against those who may eventually challenge his place and power. There are many who champion openly the doctrine of white supremacy. Only a slight shift in public opinion would be required to make this generally acceptable to the public. It might easily become the chief faith for which men would work or fight. Whatever mythology were added to such a faith it would be directly opposed to Christianity and therefore an alternative to it.

Most of the nationalism of the modern world does not reach the fanatical and deeply malevolent form which it reached in Germany, but the love of country is the nearest thing to a religion which millions in our democratic populations know. It is not uncommon to observe religiously detached or even religiously attached groups singing "God Bless America" with all the fervor which once was to be observed in the singing of gospel songs.

Much of this patriotic faith reaches a fairly noble level, a level close to poetry if not to true religion. An example of such loftiness of sentiment is provided by the following words of a young R.A.F. officer, killed in action, who wrote his mother a letter which she was to read in case he did not return:

> My death would not mean that your struggle had been in vain. Far from it. It means that your sacrifice is as great as mine. Those who serve England must expect nothing from her; we debase ourselves if we regard our country as merely a place in which to eat and sleep. . . .
>
> However long time may be, one thing can never be altered—I shall have lived and died an Englishman. Nothing else matters one jot nor can anything ever change it.[8]

No one who cares about the Christian gospel or about the fate of our civilization can fail to be moved by such a testimony. The faith it expresses is inadequate; it may be dangerous; but it is not ignoble. It is alarmingly close to the faith of some young Nazis, among whom were undeniably idealistic men. It can be matched in many nations and will continue. In short, it is something with which we must be prepared to reckon all our days.

4. LEVELS OF CO-OPERATION

In our new Comparative Religion we have now mentioned four levels of Christianity and five examples of alternative faiths. There is, of course, a considerable degree of overlapping, since the lines are not sharp, though they are getting sharper. In some senses each of these alternatives is opposed to Christianity, and, in other senses, all of them are potential allies. Each one of the living faiths can be shown to contain elements that are genuinely valuable and that would be immeasurably strengthening to the Christian institutions, if they could be kept inside, instead of becoming secular sects outside. Christianity needs the sense of solidarity which unites labor, she needs the

[8] *Modern English and American Literature*, W. Somerset Maugham, ed. (Philadelphia: The Blakiston Company [New Home Library], 1943), p. 26.

fierce loyalty exhibited by Marxists, she needs the intellectual honesty which is the faith of science, she needs the aesthetic sensitivity of the humanities, and she needs the will-to-sacrifice of mystic nationalism.

It is a sad fact that these human interests have been allowed to separate themselves from the universal Gospel, with the result that millions are limited to small loyalties, when they might have cherished larger ones. But it is a still sadder fact that other millions seem to have no essential loyalties at all! They are spiritually empty. They have given up Christianity, at least in any vigorous sense, and they have not as yet adopted anything else.

It is said, sometimes, that these millions have something to live for, in that they are materialists. They live for new cars and for country houses. While there is manifestly some truth in this, it is not a very important truth, because mere material possessions are never sufficient to inflame men's souls. Though men may appreciate good plumbing, they will not live and die for it. Materialism may be a hindrance to the Gospel, but it is not really an alternative, and it it not a serious menace because it is not a gospel. All the really dangerous men of the world preach a gospel, and they are frequently relatively independent of material comfort. It is always religions that are dangerous. Materialism, inadequate as it is, is not yet a religion and shows no signs of becoming one. Many with the most material goods are the most empty.

We cannot contemplate these empty and uprooted millions without thinking of the gospel parable of the empty house. The demon of half belief is gone, the house is swept and garnished, but will seven other devils worse than the first one enter in? The condition of emptiness is always a great danger, because men will not remain empty. Bizarre new faiths, such as we have hardly imagined as yet, or which may now exist in undeveloped forms, may fill this spiritual vacuum. One thing is clear: the men of this age will adopt inadequate and dangerous faiths unless they are provided with an adequate and beneficent faith, for the adoption of a faith is a forced option.

As the historical movements of our time advance with cumulative speed, we begin to see some of the ways in which a high level of co-operation can supersede a condition of resistance. The striking example of this, just now, is provided by many scientists, especially those who have been responsible for the spectacular developments in nuclear physics. Much of the mood of science has altered since August 6, 1945. The present mood is more chastened, more humble, more concerned. It is no exaggeration to say that the members of our society who are most deeply concerned now about the enlistment of our moral resources, to forestall danger while there is yet time, are the physicists and particularly the atomic physicists. These men are more aroused than any other group in our society, and that for two reasons. First, they know far better than laymen know the extent of the damage which their invention makes possible, and, second, they feel a keen sense of personal responsibility.

This new burst of moral seriousness on the part of so many of our scientists is exciting in every way. Many of these are sensitive men and the perplexities of their situation have made them seeking men. They have experienced many of the preconditions of spiritual insight. One result is that they are not proud. The production of the most astounding scientific invention of all time has not led to rejoicing or to self-glorification.

This experience gives us an important clue to our vocation. In the first place, our task is to make the most of the new openness among men of science while it lasts, welcoming them, with true humility, into spiritual fellowship. There is an important level of co-operation which is possible in this area even without full agreement in belief. "Full Christian virtue," says T. S. Eliot, "cannot exist without full Christian belief, but there is natural virtue about which Christian and non-Christian can agree."[9]

[9] *Christian News Letter*, No. 97.

Even more important than this particular co-operation is the constant effort to watch for similar possibilities at other points. We must be continually alert. Many movements which truly inflame men's souls may conceivably be shorn of their abuses and turned into an active ally of the Christian faith, providing thereby new richness in the total Christian fellowship of our day. The new Comparative Religion, therefore, with its discovery of resistance and resource, is a necessary discipline for all who commit themselves to the way of Christ.

FURTHER READING

BAILLIE, JOHN. *What Is Christian Civilization?* London: Oxford University Press, 1945.

BENNETT, JOHN. "Christianity and Its Alternatives." *Christendom*, 1941, Vol. VI.

BERDYAEV, NICOLAS. *The End of Our Time.* New York: Sheed & Ward, Inc., 1933.

HAYMAN, ERIC. *Worship and the Common Life.* New York: The Macmillan Company, 1944.

VAN DUSEN, H. P., ed. *The Christian Answer.* New York: Charles Scribner's Sons, 1945. (Especially Theodore M. Greene, "Christianity and Its Secular Alternatives.")

PART II

Contemporary Live Options

CHAPTER 3

The Anti-Opium League (Secular Radicalism)

GEORGE HEDLEY

CHAPTER 4

The Fascist Masquerade

HOWARD THURMAN

CHAPTER 5

Welfare Work: Ally or Alternative?

BUELL G. GALLAGHER

CHAPTER 6

The Church and Organized Fraternalism

DWIGHT C. SMITH

CHAPTER 7

Christianity and Organized Education

FREDERICK WEST

CHAPTER 8

The Cults

PIERSON PARKER

3

THE ANTI-OPIUM LEAGUE
(SECULAR RADICALISM)

George Hedley

1. Organizations. Antireligious radical groups: left-wing parties, nonpolitical leftism, intellectual leftism. Nonreligious radical groups: political, labor, liberal and special economic groups. 2. Attitudes. Radical, church and Christian attitudes. The fuller Gospel.

~~~~~~

1. ORGANIZATIONS

While controversy of many kinds has raged furiously within religious circles, and between religious groups, there has been in America only one persistent, organized attack upon religion as such. Stemming from the socioeconomic doctrines of Karl Marx, it has been conducted by the several parties and economic organizations which profess Marxist theory. The present chapter will discuss first those radical groups which are consciously antireligious, and then those (more characteristic of the general American pattern) which express no decisive attitude toward religion, but which by ignoring it become negative in total effect.

Antireligious radical groups

(1) THE MARXIST VIEW:

Man makes religion; religion does not make man. Religion, indeed, is the self-consciousness and the self-feeling of the man who either has not yet found himself, or else (having found himself) has lost himself again. . . . Religion is the sigh of the oppressed creature, the feelings of a heartless world, just as it is the spirit of unspiritual conditions. It is the opium of the people. The people cannot be really happy until it has been deprived of illusory happiness by the abolition of religion.[1]

Thus in 1843, four years before the writing of *The Communist Manifesto*, Karl Marx declared war on religion as he knew it. The qualifying phrase is important. The religious patterns which Marx knew at first hand were those of the Orthodox Judaism in which he had been born and which his family had abandoned,[2] the officially otherworldly Lutheranism into which they had been baptized, and the Catholicism of the Rhineland and of Paris. Marx's judgments of these religious traditions and groupings proved applicable also to the Orthodox Church of Czarist Russia, and were enthusiastically applied by the revolutionaries of 1917.

Orthodox Marxism remains in essence antireligious. Rejecting the method of revolution, the Social Democratic party of Germany preserved the remainder of Marxist doctrine, so that to be a Social Democrat was automatically to be an atheist. Needing in the recent war both internal unity and external good will, the Soviet government relaxed its antireligious laws and professed to discourage "Godless" propaganda. It may thereby have erased from Russian Christianity the marks which once made it anathema, for it seems that the Russian church has become a bulwark not of the old order but of the new.

[1] Karl Marx, *Zur Kritik der Hegelschen Rechtsphilosophie*, Deutsch-Französische Jahrbücher, Sec. 1. Quoted in Otto Rühle, *Karl Marx: His Life and Work*, tr. Eden and Cedar Paul (Philadelphia: The Blakiston Company [New Home Library], 1943), p. 57.

[2] When Marx was six years old. His bitterness against German Jewish culture is well seen in his essay on "The Jewish Question," also published in the Deutsch-Französische Jahrbücher, 1844.

(2) LEFT-WING PARTIES:

By no means the first American party professedly Marxist, but the most important in our time, is the Communist party. A "Communist Propaganda League" was formed in 1918 with the avowed intent of capturing the American Socialist party for a revolutionary program in harmony with, and in support of, that of Soviet Russia. That attempt did not succeed, though expulsions and secessions greatly weakened the older Socialist body. The pro-Russian group organized an independent Workers' party in 1921. After numerous factional fights, in which the Third (Communist) International intervened, William Z. Foster gained ascendancy over his rivals. In 1929 the name "Communist party" was adopted.

Until the mid-1930's the Communist "line" was strictly of the revolutionary Marxist type. Thus Communist propaganda included vigorous opposition to practically all the existing institutions of American life, including religion and the Church. More than one loyal Communist, on trial under criminal syndicalism laws or (as was common practice) for "vagrancy," made his conviction certain by advertising his atheism before a middle-class American jury.

Then came, in 1935, the Seventh Congress of the Third International. Faced by the acute threat of Nazism, Soviet and Comintern policy shifted to "collaboration with bourgeois democracy" in collective security through the League of Nations. The "new line" immediately became apparent in the United States. Politically the Communists swung to definite if not explicit support of the New Deal. Propaganda against religion was dropped, and young Communists in particular joined Christian groups, seeking to swing them toward Communist economic, racial and international policies.

A sudden turn in the opposite political direction appeared in August, 1939, with the announcement of the Russo-German nonaggression pact. Soon Britain and France were portrayed as fighting an "imperialist war," which friends of the working classes must oppose. The method of infiltration into the American churches had proved so successful, however, that instead of being abandoned it was intensified—though of course redirected. Formerly seeking alliance with interventionists, the Communists now attempted (and largely achieved) active collaboration with devout Christian pacifists. The "American Peace Mobilization," Communist-inspired and Communist-controlled, gained the adherence of many Christian individuals and of some organized Christian groups.

When Hitler attacked Russia, in June of 1941, the position again was reversed. Overnight the "American Peace Mobilization" became the "American People's Mobilization," and the tocsin was rung for war on behalf of democracy. Already the Communist party, pressed by federal legislation restricting agencies of foreign governments, had formally severed its connection with the Comintern. Early in 1944 it took the further step of dissolving itself as a party, assuming the new name (and marginally the new form) of the "Communist Political Association."[3]

With the end of the European war, and the increasing visibility of tensions between Russia and the Anglo-American allies, the pendulum swung yet once more. Earl Browder, who as general secretary had been the foremost spokesman for collaboration, was deposed in August, 1945, and the "old, old line" was resumed with Foster in command. As yet there are few signs of general antireligious propaganda, though controversies between Moscow and the Vatican have been reflected in sharp anti-Catholic editorials in *New Masses* and the *Daily Worker*. The policy of association with church groups appears to be continued, with labor and race issues as major points of contact.

The Communist "line" at any given moment may be identified by reading *New Masses*, the *Daily Worker* (New York) and the

---

[3] An acute observer has remarked that this change came very shortly after the "Big Three" conference at Teheran, and the revival of the Communist party soon after the death of President Roosevelt.

Daily People's World (San Francisco).[4] In brief, despite the severance from the Comintern and the later dissolution of that body, the determining factors in American Communist argument and activity are to be found in the policy and interests of the Soviet Union.

The present Socialist party in the United States was organized in 1901, as an outgrowth of the Social Democratic party of Eugene V. Debs and Victor Berger. At the outset it included among its leaders a number of influential trade unionists, and its policies were so gradualist as substantially to exclude Marxist theory. As Presidential candidate Debs polled almost a million votes in 1912, and again in 1920 (the latter while he still was a Federal prisoner for opposition to the first German war).

In 1924, after the left-wingers had joined the Communist ranks, the Socialist party supported the "Progressive" candidature of the elder La Follette. When Debs died, two years later, the party leadership passed into the hands of intellectuals and liberal religionists. Norman Thomas, a former Presbyterian minister, has been the Presidential nominee in the past five elections, with a maximum vote of 884,781 in 1932, dropping to 80,518 in 1944.

In the early 1930's a "Revolutionary Policy Committee" became active within the party, and eliminated almost all the remaining conservatives and trade unionists. Some of these subsequently organized the Social Democratic Federation, a gradualist body which became actively interventionist. A temporary infiltration of Trotskyists into the Socialist party was followed by mass expulsion, though the Trotskyists retained control of the Young People's Socialist League. Many former Socialists, including numerous members of the "I-voted-once-for-Norman-Thomas Club," decided that practical progress was most likely to be achieved through the New Deal.

Under the leadership of Thomas and such intellectuals as

[4] This last does not admit Communist affiliation; but its editorial policy has not been known to vary from the party's "line" as of any given date.

Maynard Krueger of the University of Chicago, the program of the Socialist party has become increasingly difficult to identify. During the period of Communist isolationism, 1939-1941, the only difference between the two groups which an outsider was likely to note was that the Socialists criticized Soviet Russia as fiercely as they did capitalist America. During the war Socialist propaganda was mildly pacifist, but not so vocally as in the time of Debs.

The Socialist party never has stressed anti-religionism. Indeed it has drawn much of its membership, and still more of its vote, from the ranks of religious liberals. (That vote in general scarcely represents conscious approval of the party's program; it has been rather a protest against things as they are, voiced through an agency less unpopular than the Communist party.) The Socialist party's chequered organizational history to date, and its lack of a consistent and coherent program, suggest that in itself it is not likely ever to become a major force in American life. Nevertheless many of the specific measures it has advocated now are part of the law of the land, and to its credit must be recorded the capable Socialist municipal administrations in Bridgeport, Connecticut, and in Milwaukee.

The Socialist Labor party is the oldest continuing American group professing a Marxist orientation. Organized in 1876 as the Workingmen's party of the United States, immediately after the dissolution of Marx's First International, it adopted its present name in 1877. Its major emphasis throughout has been upon the importance of political action by trade union groups. For the first quarter century of its history it made a considerable stir in organized labor circles. Supplanted in public attention by the Socialist party and later by the Communist, the Socialist Labor party has retained a small but faithful following. With its candidates on the Presidential ballot only in a few states, it polled 45,336 votes in 1944.

The typical Socialist Laborite is highly logical in statement of Marxist theory as he interprets it, patronizing about the errors both of capitalism and of rival left-wing groups, precisely informed on the details of internecine war among the leftists. This is perhaps the most stable of the "true churches" of the left; and as such it inevitably makes slight appeal to shifting popular opinion. While anti-religionism is part of the accepted dogma, its presentation by the Socialist Labor party has little effect upon the public mind.

The followers of Leon Trotsky in America have changed their party name with amazing frequency. As the October Revolution was reflected in the formation of the American Communist party, so the expulsion of Leon Trotsky from the Soviet Union led to a major split in American communism. Trotsky's adherents, at present calling themselves the Workers' party, are strict believers in world revolution. They count the Communist party guilty of mortal heresy, and oppose the Soviet regime so thoroughly that some of their spokesmen have been welcomed as special writers for the Hearst press.

While the Communist party has been driven to relative realism by the practical problems faced by the Soviet state, the Trotskyists, having no objective situation to defend, can afford to be consistent. Accordingly they proclaim Marxism practically in its original form, including the antireligious aspect. Nevertheless in the American scene they have laid little stress upon this point, perhaps because in various attempts at a "united front" they have found themselves supported by "innocent" church groups when the Communists followed their standard procedure of trying to have all Trotskyists expelled. The official current statements of the Trotskyist view are to be found in the magazine *Fourth International*.

The story of controversies within the left wing is inconceivably complex, and there is sure to be a new outcropping of separatist groups before the present text can reach the public. It will suffice here to note the existence of such "splinters" as the Gitlowites and Lovestoneites, such political units as the Proletarian party (which seems to have no proletarian constituency), and the Workers' Socialist party (perhaps the most doctrinaire of all).

In general the points of conflict are matters of detailed
exegesis of the Marxist scriptures. The antireligious position,
however, is an item of formal unanimity. The argument tends to
remain in the nineteenth-century area, with the attack centered
upon traditional religious patterns such as those which Marx
himself opposed. As has been noted, official anti-religionism
often is subordinated in practice to the effort to secure the co-
operation of religious groups in a variety of specific causes.

(3) NONPOLITICAL LEFTISM:

Anarchism, as the negation of all authority, inevitably rejects religious institutions, standards and practices along with
the other mores of our society. Holding to the absolute right of
the individual to do as he pleases, and therefore defending the
most extreme aberrations from accepted behavior patterns, the
anarchists have been easy and obvious victims of public hysteria.
Lacking organization, and unable to create it because in their
way of thinking any attempt at organization would be "un-
anarchist," they have no group stability and consequently little
strength.

The major public outcries against the anarchists have been
at the time of the Haymarket bombing in Chicago, in 1886,[5]
and at that of the Sacco-Vanzetti case of 1920-1927.[6] In both
cases murder charges were brought on dubious evidence, and
convictions were secured in an atmosphere of social passion
rather than of judicial calm. Contrary to popular notions, many
professed anarchists are mild in the extreme, some carrying
personal nonviolence to the point of conscientious vegetarianism.
The number of anarchists never has been large, and is not

[5] See Henry David, *The History of the Haymarket Affair: A Study in the
American Social-Revolutionary and Labor Movements* (New York: Farrar
& Rinehart, Inc., 1936).

[6] See Michael A. Musmanno, *After Twelve Years* (New York: Alfred A.
Knopf, 1939). Two letters of Sacco, and one of Vanzetti, may be found in
Bernard Smith, ed., *The Democratic Spirit: A Collection of American
Writings from the Earliest Times to the Present Day* (New York: Alfred
A. Knopf, 1941).

likely to be. As individuals they are almost as various as are Republicans or Democrats, and much more varied than Communists. Their one point of identity is their absolutist contention for absolute freedom.

The Industrial Workers of the World constitute the most authentically American of all the leftist movements that this country has seen, and the most completely free from the influence of nonworking-class intellectuals. Temperamentally and ideologically the I.W.W. is anarcho-syndicalist, accepting just enough organization to work toward destruction of the existing order. Its propaganda is in American language: "strike on the job," "the government is the executive committee of the boss class," "labor leaders are labor fakers," "fellow workers." Wholly opposed to political action, it seeks its goals by immediate economic pressures only. It rejects collective bargaining contracts as unjustified "class collaboration," and seeks (though it seems scarcely to define) "abolition of the wage system."

Organized by Socialists in 1905, in opposition to the American Federation of Labor, the "Wobblies" adopted their present emphasis in 1912. They conducted vigorous strikes in the textile mills of the East and in the mines and lumber camps of the West. Furious prosecutions in Washington and California in the early 1920's eliminated their best leadership and broke their strength. Today the I.W.W. survives largely as a debating society of old-timers, faithful to the tradition and devoted to the memory of its martyrs. Occasionally it attempts labor organization among the unskilled, but it has had scant success in competition with the C.I.O. Its weekly organ, *The Industrial Worker*, assails with equal enthusiasm both major labor federations, the federal government, the "bosses," and the Soviet Union.

Whether anti-religionism among the "Wobblies" has any Marxist roots is uncertain. It certainly is not expressed in the terms of Marx's critique of Hegel. The "Wobblies" love to sing

(chiefly gospel song tunes). One of their classics is set to the
tune of "The Sweet By-and-By." It runs, in part:

> Long-haired preachers come out every night,
> Try to tell you what's wrong and what's right;
> If you ask them for something to eat,
> They will answer, in accents so sweet:
>   "You will eat, by-and-by,
>   In that beautiful land up in the sky;
>   (*Basses:* 'Way up high!)
>   Work and pray, live on hay,
>   You'll get pie in the sky when you die.
>   (*Basses:* That's a lie!)"

There is something honest, healthy and humorous about the
whole I.W.W. approach. Almost alone among the leftist groups,
the "Wobblies" habitually invite as speakers at their forums
those who do not agree with them. It behooves the visiting
speaker to prepare well, for nowhere will he meet a more
acutely critical and gaily contentious audience. The history of
the I.W.W. probably is a matter of the past; but it is a history
of native American response to actual American conditions,
and it commands the respectful attention of all students of the
shifting American scene.

(4) INTELLECTUAL LEFTISM:

As has been said, much of the present leadership of the left-
wing political parties comes not from the working class but
from "intellectual" circles. The characteristic patterns of urban
intellectual leftism are to be found in Greenwich Village in New
York, on Telegraph Hill and Russian Hill in San Francisco.
Here anti-religionism, both theoretical and applied, is most
frankly accepted and most decisively proclaimed. These intellectuals have read enough religious history to know some of the
absurdities of historic religion, and are so free from social con-
trols as to fear no criticism from their associates.

A fair sample of Saturday night discussion in such a milieu
is provided by Edna St. Vincent Millay in her *Conversation at*

Midnight. Some who have sat through the endless arguments, and the still longer monologues, will pronounce the participants half-baked, and will enlist among the scorners of the "parlor pinks." In truth the Village- and Hill-dwellers have not proved to be socially very effective, and when they have gained control of political movements they commonly have wrecked them. There may be ground, too, for believing that many of them ultimately become wearied of the atmosphere and graduate into fairly stuffy respectability.

Cognate to the metropolitan leftist coteries are groups on most large university campuses and at some small colleges. There used to be a recognizable and regular student cycle from family Republicanism to Christian socialism to orthodox Communism to violent Trotskyism to weary indifference. Student radicalism of the acute sort frequently is found to be a reflex of family maladjustment. Nevertheless it often is deeply sincere, and occasionally it proves lasting. In some colleges there are faculty members who become almost professional leaders of student dissent, and who seem to encourage secularism with special delight. Their spiritual homes, of course, are with the urban intelligentsia, and their general cultural level is in the same mid-zone between innocence and wisdom.

The problem of intellectual anti-religionism is precisely the problem of pseudo sophistication. Despite individual defections, the type is likely to multiply as higher education makes increasing contacts with the world outside the colleges. It cannot be met by repeating the old phrases, though sometimes it can be laughed out of countenance. Both in the cities and on the campuses, this constitutes one of the nice problems with which the Church of tomorrow will have to deal.

Nonreligious radical groups

Perhaps as disconcerting to the religious person as is Marxist anti-religionism, and certainly not less dangerous to the future of religion, is the indifferentism which in our secular age is far more widespread than is any conscious opposition. The majority of radical movements in the United States—certainly the majority in membership if not in number of organizational units—express no opinion about religion. They merely ignore it.

(1) POLITICAL GROUPS:

In addition to the consciously Marxist parties, American political history has seen the birth and death of many small and often regional movements to the leftward of the Republicans and Democrats. Among the principal examples of early days may be noted the Greenbackers of the 1870's and the Populists of the 1890's, both representing debtor interests and therefore supporting inflationary policies. The most vigorous third-party movement of recent times was that of the "Bull Moose" campaign of 1912, which carried six states for Theodore Roosevelt and threw the election to Woodrow Wilson. The name of the Progressive party was used again in 1924 for the La Follette-Wheeler ticket, which secured the electoral vote of the single state of Wisconsin. The Union party of 1936, with Lemke of North Dakota as its standard-bearer, drawing its support from various dissident elements, polled almost 900,000 votes.

More strictly regional groups of this type, which locally have gained some electoral success, are the Nonpartisan League (North Dakota), the Farmer-Labor party (Minnesota), the Commonwealth Federation (Washington), and the Progressive party of Wisconsin. The Nonpartisan League carried North Dakota in 1922, and by 1923 had both United States Senators. The Farmer-Labor party elected Floyd Olson Governor of Minnesota in 1930 and again in 1932. The Commonwealth Federation has sent a number of its nominees to the State Legislature. The Wisconsin Progressive party was almost a personal possession of the La Follette family, twice sending Robert Jr. to the Senate and in 1936 electing his brother, Philip, governor. In March of 1946 it dissolved itself, with a majority of its convention voting to affiliate with the Republicans. All of these groups have represented uneasy coalitions of agrarian and labor interests, and all have suffered from repeated Communist attempts to take over control.

A regional party of a different type is the American Labor party of New York. Because of the structure of the New York election system, it has commonly chosen to back one or another major party (or fusion) candidate rather than to present candidates of its own. It was a major force in support of Mayor La Guardia, and it is credited with a large share in the New York victories of Franklin Roosevelt. Recently it has suffered a split between factions approximately representing Communists and Socialists, the latter seceding to form the Liberal party. Dominant opportunism is indicated by the support which the majority (allegedly Communist) group gave in the mayoralty campaign of 1945 to the Democrat (Tammany) O'Dwyer.

Not calling themselves "parties," but constituting political movements of some consequence, were the Epic ("End Poverty in California") enthusiasts who in 1934 captured the Democratic gubernatorial nomination for Upton Sinclair, and who lost the election only after a campaign of terrific sound and fury; and the Utopian Society which appeared in Los Angeles in the same year and for a few months afforded the chief local subject of discussion. The membership in these two movements was largely overlapping. It was drawn from the economic fringes of depression society, from bankrupted small enterprisers and unemployed skilled workmen, and their wives and widows. Its culture was principally Midwestern, with a decided emotional quality and a fondness for revivalist methods. While these movements are dead, their like will appear when next the economic cycle drives the "little man" to the wall. Whether then they will embrace genuinely progressive causes, or will be drawn into quasi-fascism, depends upon the development of political thinking and political education in the interim.

(2) LABOR GROUPS:

Largely the personal creation of Samuel Gompers, the American Federation of Labor has had only three national presidents in the sixty-five years of its history.[7] That perhaps is an accurate index of its conservative mood and cautious procedure. Under Gompers' influence the A. F. of L. concentrated on tightly knit organizations of skilled workers, preferred economic pressures to political action, cared little about public opinion. While nominally a federation of autonomous craft unions, the A. F. of L. has become increasingly a centralized body controlled by its national Executive Council. In its early days it went through many violent conflicts. More recently, with its status relatively assured, it has deprecated violence and has sought to keep on good terms with employers.

Anti-religionism never has been officially promoted by the A. F. of L., but indifference toward religion has been common. The man who works hard at union activities finds in them many of the personal satisfactions that others discover in the Church, and almost inevitably he feels that he does not have time for both. Women's auxiliaries to the unions often are socially equivalent to ladies' aid societies, giving dinners, holding parties and raising special funds, in almost exactly the same ways.

Late in 1935, dissatisfied with official A. F. of L. indifference to organization of unskilled workers in mass production industries, ten A. F. of L. unions of the industrial type set up within the Federation a voluntary Committee for Industrial Organization. These ten unions, promptly suspended by the Executive Council, later were expelled by the National Convention. In 1937, retaining the initials which by then had gained publicity value, nine[8] of the dissident unions set themselves up as the Congress of Industrial Organizations.

Today the C.I.O. claims as many members as the A. F. of L.: about seven million. Dominantly, though not absolutely, its

---

[7] Only two of major importance, Gompers and William Green. The third, McBride of the Mine Workers, served only 1894-1895, as the result of a short-lived Socialist triumph in the Federation.

[8] The International Ladies' Garment Workers' Union declined to enter the new Congress, and after about a year of independent activity re-entered the A.F. of L.

structure is industrial ("vertical"), with union affiliation determined by employment relationship rather than by craft assignment. The C.I.O. always has engaged in political action, and in general has favored government determination of labor issues. Accordingly it has needed, and consciously has attempted to create, a favorable public opinion. Its Political Action Committee lent weighty support to Roosevelt in 1944, and seems to have been determinative in some Congressional contests. Recognizing that the Church does much toward establishing public attitudes, the C.I.O. has sought actively the friendship and support of church groups.

There is reason to suppose some connection between this policy and the similar procedure of the Communist party. While relatively few C.I.O. members are consciously Communist, a considerable proportion of C.I.O. leaders invariably follow the Communist "line." Among the major national C.I.O. unions, the Amalgamated Clothing Workers and the United Steel Workers appear to be actively anti-Communist. In the United Automobile Workers non-Communists have controlled the top positions, though some Communists are active as local officers. The National Maritime Union,[9] the Transport Workers' Union and the International Longshoremen's and Warehousemen's Union, have followed a uniformly Communist pattern of action. So also have the small but vocal white-collar groups: the State, County and Municipal Workers, the United Office and Professional Workers, and the Federation of Architects, Engineers, Chemists and Technicians.[10] Control of Newspaper Guild units varies as among local branches.

While the C.I.O. talks much of democracy, its structure is in fact highly centralized, and policies are determined chiefly from the top down. The general membership is not much better

[9] Early in 1946 Joseph Curran, Catholic president of the Union, broke openly with the Communist group with which hitherto he had co-operated; and which had been his active and consistent supporters.

[10] These two last were amalgamated, under the former's name, in March of 1946.

informed than in the older federation, commonly has had much slighter union experience, and shows little more personal interest in union affairs. In so far as Communists are in places of power, a basic anti-religionism exists. In practice, however, as in the case of the Communist party itself, antireligious attitudes recently have been subordinated to active efforts to win church support.

The great unions outside the two major federations are the four Railway Brotherhoods, the "aristocracy of American labor." Recently John L. Lewis' United Mine Workers, successively A. F. of L. and C.I.O., and then "independent," has returned to the A. F. of L. Dubiously to be classified as "independent" is the "company union," outlawed by the National Labor Relations Act but not yet quite extinct.

For the railwayman his "lodge" (as commonly he calls his union local) performs practically all the functions of fraternal order and of church. Here he meets those who share his interests, and at hours set conveniently for his irregular and complicated working schedule. In railway division towns the social life of the community (apart from the local business and professional men) centers quite naturally in the railway "lodges." Much the same is true of the miners' unions in mining towns. "Company unions" by their very nature claim little loyalty and make small drains upon the energy of their members.

(3) LIBERAL GROUPS:

The American Civil Liberties Union always has taken a single, clearly defined position, and seldom has been tempted into inconsistency. Its one concern is freedom under the law: freedom for the expression of every point of view, freedom of legitimate action for every group. Accordingly it has defended with equal vigor the civil rights of Communists and of Bundists, has opposed social, political and economic prejudice of every kind. Damned by reactionaries for supporting radicals, the A.C.L.U. often is damned by radicals when it insists upon freedom of utterance for reactionaries.

The Civil Liberties Union engages in some propaganda activities, always on issues of positive freedom and equal justice for minority groups, but devotes most of its energy to actual court procedures. Sometimes it actually conducts the defense of those whom it considers victims of injustice, sometimes it intervenes as a "friend of the court," occasionally it has raised funds for defense conducted by attorneys other than its own. Such units as the International Labor Defense (Communist), the Workers' Defense League (Socialist), the General Labor Defense (I.W.W.), and the Nonpartisan Labor Defense (Trotskyist, now defunct), usually have preferred to conduct their own courtroom activities, because the single insistence of the A.C.L.U. on civil freedom often runs counter to the promotion of their own special points of view.

Founded by Jane Addams, the Women's International League for Peace and Freedom has been characterized in general by a pacifist approach. Increasingly it has tended to stress economic justice as a prerequisite to lasting peace. On both counts, therefore, it has been assailed by patrioteers as being a radical and subversive organization.

While many of its local chapters have betrayed a startling innocence of political realities (as did Miss Addams herself in her share in Henry Ford's "Peace Ship" venture), the W.I.L. has been extraordinarily successful in escaping ex parte control. In the average community its members are crusaders for the highest idealism. Its influence in practical affairs to date has been relatively slight.

Better informed than the W.I.L., and correspondingly more realistic, the League of Women Voters has concentrated its energies upon legislative action. It promotes vigorous educational programs both for its own members and for the public, endorses specific legislative proposals (though seldom specific candidates), and conducts lobbying campaigns both by organized letter-writing and by personal representation in state capitals and at Washington. Usually it comes out just a little to the left of center. For the past decade its position may be described as roughly equivalent to that of the New Deal.

The apparently "liberal" organizations which actually are Communist-controlled are so numerous, their names and emphases change so frequently, that no inclusive list can be made. Perhaps the most notable was the American League against War and Fascism, which later changed its name to the more positive American League for Peace and Democracy. After a long campaign for collective security, in harmony with the Litvinov policy, the League disappeared altogether after August, 1939. It was replaced by the isolationist American Peace Mobilization, which suddenly in June, 1941, became the interventionist American People's Mobilization.

"Youth movements" have been a special concern of Communist infiltration. The National Student League was the Communist-sponsored rival to the (Socialist) Student League for Industrial Democracy. In 1936, with the support of student idealists indifferent to party quarrels, the two were combined in the American Student Union. On most campuses, because of the greater energy and superior discipline of the Communist fractions, the A.S.U. units remained Communist-controlled. With the political shifts of 1939 the Communists in the major universities came out into the open as the Young Communist League. The general youth organization, including the college groups and many Christian societies, was the American Youth Congress. The A.Y.C. survived the 1939 change from interventionism to isolationism, but could not weather the reverse transition of 1941. Its place today is held by the American Youth for Democracy.

The National Negro Congress was the Communist "opposite number" to the National Association for the Advancement of the Colored People. The Interprofessional Association sought to rally the upper-level white-collar element for Communist causes. The League of Women Shoppers was a Communist-directed supporter of trade union activities (chiefly Trade Union Unity League, and more recently C.I.O.). The National Committee for the Defense of Political Prisoners was a rival to the A.C.L.U., but selective as to the prisoners' points of view. All of these organizations seem now to be extinct. The most active group of the kind recently has been the Joint Anti-Fascist Refugee Committee.

The general technique is to seize upon what persons of good will regard as a worthy cause, and to set up a society to promote it. Sincere liberals are persuaded to allow the use of their names on letterheads, and occasionally are encouraged to accept office. Paid employees, however, usually are selected by the party authorities, and local executives of the American League against War and Fascism were directly assigned by party headquarters.

Control is exercised principally through parliamentary procedure, in which a disciplined Communist fraction can rush or postpone action without the innocent members knowing what has happened. It is not necessary for the Communists to constitute a majority of the membership; all they need is a majority "present and voting," which after hours of wrangling is almost certain to be theirs by midnight. The willingness of Communist members to do routine "dirty work" also tends to put effective power into their hands. The Communist fraction usually may be identified not only by its faithful promotion of the current Communist "line," and by its custom of calling all opponents "Fascist," but also by its unwillingness to hear dissident speakers, and by its apparently unconquerable habit of trying to expel all Trotskyists.

(4) SPECIAL ECONOMIC GROUPS:

The consumers' co-operative movement, which in Britain and Scandinavia has become a powerful economic force and has rendered notable public service, has had hard going in the United States. American individualism works against it, and relative American prosperity has weakened its appeal. Occasionally successful for small groups in restricted local areas, it has proved effective neither over long periods nor on a nation-wide scale.

Part of the weakness is chargeable to inept leadership, scarcely to be escaped because in the American pattern the smart businessman usually has preferred to operate on his own. As a consequence local managers of co-operatives too often have been small businessmen who have failed in private enterprise, and who do no better as agents of a society which exercises only casual supervision. The alternate choice ordinarily available for managership, that of an eager idealist without business experience, seldom is more productive of efficiency. Another major difficulty is the familiar one of attempts by political groups to gain control and to use the co-operatives for their own purposes. Much energy has been expended in these conflicts, and the bitterness engendered has caused numerous withdrawals from activity and membership.

While much genuine ethical zeal has been apparent in the formation of co-operatives, it has often lost its force with the passage of time, and in general has failed to be self-regenerative. The co-operative movement can make a sound case for itself in economic terms, but the difficulties of establishing it firmly in the face of private business competition and opposition demand a more intense and more persistent loyalty than the American consumers' co-operatives yet have exhibited. (It must of course be recognized that many so-called "co-operatives," both of the marketing type and of group buying by associated retailers, do not belong to the consumers' co-operative pattern at all, and have no place in a discussion of radical movements They are strictly business concerns, with no interest in socioeconomic change.)

The Townsend Old-Age Pension Plan appeared in California in the gubernatorial campaign of 1934. Endorsed by the Republican candidate (who was a Long Beach neighbor of Dr. Townsend), it captured popular support in Los Angeles and contributed to the defeat of Upton Sinclair and his "Epic" supporters. Rival pension enterprises, such as "Thirty Every Thursday" and "Ham and Eggs," have sprung up in almost every election year, and have spread to all states where there is a high proportion of elderly citizens.

The proposals urged by these pension groups would work havoc with the economy of the country. The source of funds would be a recurring transactions tax which would stifle business, and would turn a startling percentage of the national income into the hands of the few beneficiaries. But the adherents are not economists, and the propaganda is not conducted as economic discussion.

Still more strikingly than the labor unions, the pension groups have taken on the social coloration of the Protestant churches. They have dinners, parties, whist drives. Their personnel is much the same as that which became "Epic" or "Utopian": elderly, unsuccessful, unreflective, emotional. Their propaganda has been weakened during the war boom, but may be expected to revive (perhaps with new names and new details of procedure) as soon as depression supervenes.

Agrarian radicalism in the United States has been amorphous. Personally the farmer has tended to be rabidly individualist, and therefore reluctant to work in cohesive groups. Often, because of this individualism, he has been content with the program of the Republican party; only in times of acute depression does he turn elsewhere.

The inflationary drives of the "Greenbackers" and Populists were largely agrarian in their support, as was the "Free Silver" campaign of William Jennings Bryan. The Nonpartisan League of North Dakota, the Farmer-Labor party of Minnesota, and the left-wing Republicanism which elected Smith W. Brookhart Senator from Iowa, came from this same background. Occasionally the National Grange has espoused what city bankers would regard as radical proposals, but scarcely what a city worker would recognize as such.

The Southern Tenant Farmers' Union is the only decisively left-wing farmers' group of our time which has exercised any large influence. Much of its organizing was done by Socialist agents, and some later by Communist functionaries. Naturally the independent farmers of the northern states have no interest in a tenant enterprise. It is to be noted that some so-called farm groups, such as the Associated Farmers of California, actually are agencies of metropolitan financial interests.

2. ATTITUDES

Radical attitudes

It may seem that the foregoing account of secular radical groups is one of frustration if not of destruction. Yet a great deal not only of active human energy, but also of vital human loyalty, has been poured into the myriad movements that this country has seen. From the institutional point of view these movements have been largely ineffective. In broader terms they have succeeded not only in Communist achievements in infiltration, but also in the adoption by the body politic of many ideas once regarded as revolutionary. It is clear that often the leftists have been unwise, that sometimes they have worked both against their own interests and against those of the public. Shall we then join the Dies Committee in stamping them "subversive," or try with the Hearst press to wipe them out?

Before we make that decision, it will profit us to inquire into the personal and social attitudes that these movements have revealed. Doing so, we shall find that strength and weakness, positive and negative values, often are opposite sides of a single shield. Anti-religionism, for example, immediately strikes the religious person as being certainly unwarranted, and probably vicious. Yet seen in historical perspective, the Marxist "opium" dogma has much to support it: so much that it was expressed also by such Christian Socialists as Charles Kingsley and F. D. Maurice. Whether as an open supporter of a reactionary state (Orthodoxy in Czarist Russia), or as a nonparticipant in public affairs (Lutheranism in pre-Nazi Germany), or as a half-conscious proponent of middle-class shibboleths (traditional

Protestantism in America), Christianity often has become an influential deterrent of social progress.

He who for this reason thinks himself an "atheist" is ill-informed, confused and ultimately illogical, but he may be utterly sincere. Not only professional sophisticates, but also eager social reformers, have assailed organized religion because it seemed to them to have no relevance to human life. The paradox of devoutly religious opposition to religion is an obvious one in our time. The thinking of such opponents of what they understand to be "religion" no doubt needs to be redirected, but the intensity of their moral passion on no account may be denied, nor on any account be destroyed.

There is indeed here what Paul Tillich has called the "latent Church": a reservoir of moral passion which if rightly channeled can revitalize the dusty fields of human weariness. It must be recognized, however, that this Church is latent rather than actual, that as it exists it cannot fill all the needs of man. Christianity and socialism, even Christianity and communism, may have much in common. They are not identical; and to think them so is to run the danger of vitiating the Christian message. Christianity is incomplete without the social gospel, but certainly it is not complete as social gospel only.

Often it seems to the onlooker that radical movements notice only the sordid and the mean, that they choose to ignore the constructive and the beautiful in our exising world. The anarchists and the I.W.W., as opponents of all institutions of our present order, perhaps are the extremists on the negative side; but of necessity they are joined by all the others in a condemnatory approach to many aspects of our dominant culture. Things seldom are so bad as the radical propagandist alleges. Neither, however, are they so good as the self-satisfied middle-class citizen supposes. If the typical leftist overdoes denial of good in things as they are, the typical Christian is at least as guilty in his failure to admit the presence of evil. Radical realism about what is wrong becomes frequently a necessary contributor toward the establishment of right; and it has lessons to teach to those who assume that whatever has been is bound to be forever satisfactory.

All the radical groups claim that they seek economic justice. Unhappily most of them think it necessary to add "for labor," or "for farmers," or "for the retired," or perhaps, nowadays, "for the small businessman," as if justice were divisible. The line between economic justice and economic partisanship is not easy to draw, and it is one which no single economic class can draw so as to satisfy all others. It is possible, and sometimes essential, to condemn economic selfishness; but the passion for justice is not to be ignored, even when its plea is voiced by those who themselves are the sufferers from injustice.

All groups eagerly claim freedom for themselves, but few are willing to accord it to others. The anarchists do, and the I.W.W. in discussion but scarcely in action. The clearest record here is that of the American Civil Liberties Union, which contends for the full freedom even of those who themselves would deny freedom. Per contra, the Communist record is the worst, not only in Russia but also here: as witness Communist attempts to secure denial of public platforms to Gerald L. K. Smith, so shortly after Communist appeals to the Bill of Rights in seeking public meeting places for themselves.

He who asserts his own freedom merits full support at that point. He who would deny another's freedom must be challenged with equal vigor. The distinction must be carefully maintained, and ever and again re-examined, lest they who cry for freedom become themselves the creators of new tyranny. To establish now the precedent of suppression in order to silence Fascists, as the Communists frankly desire, would be to intensify the danger of Fascist suppression not only of Communists, but also of all liberals, in a later period of crisis.

In many cases the innocent liberal, enlisting in what he counts a worthy cause, finds that some ulterior motive actually dominates the effort. Locally, Communist-inspired efforts in behalf of racial equality demand careful examination to discover whether a given case has been brought up because of genuine human concern or merely as a means for creating social disturbance. On the world scale, current Communist support of "freedom" for the people of India and of Indonesia, and most recently for the Negroes of South Africa, must be assayed in terms of the extent to which such propaganda serves the political interests of the Soviet Union in its power struggle with Britain. In all such cases the shrewdest discrimination is necessary, and the strongest insistence upon principle for its own sake.

The American tradition makes much of the "embattled farmer" of 1776, and in general has tended ever since to encourage violent personal defense when personal rights are challenged. Very easily this slips over into organized violence as a considered group policy, whether on the part of conservatives (the American Legion in its earlier and more excitable years) or of radicals (the I.W.W. in its former practice and continuing theory). While it is true that much of the alleged labor violence of the United States has been initiated by employers, or by police or militia acting in their behalf, it cannot be pretended that organized labor's hands are wholly clean. Personal courage must be admired. Considered techniques of violence may not be condoned. Yet again the problem is one of precise discrimination applied to each specific case.

It is possible to portray the radical movements as wholly admirable or as wholly objectionable, depending upon whether we concentrate attention on courage, freedom, justice, realism, honesty, or on violence, intolerance, partisanship, negativity, anti-religionism. The positive values are the precise cognates of the negative forces. Can the Church, can Christianity, find ways to restrain the negative while conserving and advancing the positive?

Church attitudes

Facing the "opium" charges of the orthodox Marxist, the churchman commonly has replied by saying, "It's not so." If he is a well-informed churchman, he may exhibit legitimately the social and economic propaganda of the Hebrew prophets, the social implications of the Gospels, the revolutionary effect of Christianity in the Roman world, the ameliorative influence of the Church in the rugged Middle Ages, the social pronouncements of the Popes Leo XIII and Pius XI and of the Federal Council of Churches. All these are matters of record, and they have to their credit more than the words in which Hebrew-Christian idealism has been stated.

If the churchman be honest as well as well-informed, however, he will not claim too much. The prophets gave way to the priests, and social urgency to social control. The teachings of Jesus were understood chiefly in individual rather than in social application. Christianity conquered Rome by yielding to it, most strikingly so in the person of Constantine. Similarly the medieval church made terms with feudal society, and helped to maintain feudal social stratification. Not all Catholic laymen heed the labor encyclicals, and few Protestant vestrymen would vote for the Federal Council's resolutions. Religion has not been wholly an opiate, but neither has it proved itself uniformly to be a social stimulant.

Not content with efforts to defend their institutional positions against leftist attack, both Catholic and Protestant groups now and then have become active campaigners for social reaction. While the Vatican's labor pronouncements are far to the left of those of the National Association of Manufacturers, Rome's defensive opposition to communism turned into positive support of fascism in Italy and of the Franco regime in Spain. Today Catholic propaganda, in the United States as well as in Europe, lends itself readily to the purposes of those who insist that war with Russia is inevitable and who therefore want to bring it on immediately.

Similarly Protestant sentiment in the American South, accurately identifying radicalism with racial equalitarianism, has been swung to the support of quasi-Fascist movements; and Indiana, Oregon and California bear witness that this phenomenon is not a Southern monopoly. Revivalist sects, stressing an otherworldly view of the future, have been encouraged and not seldom financed by those who want no changes in the present world system. Surely it is not accidental that publicity for the individualist Youth for Christ campaign comes chiefly through the Hearst papers, opposed to liberalism not less virulently than to the most acute radicalism. Influential laymen in metropolitan churches, and an occasional cleric, have thought to identify Christian principles with "free enterprise," and on that ground have wielded considerable influence against any trend of economic heresy.

Such efforts have been only marginally successful. The special pleading of the economically advantaged is easy to recognize, and it has been met with indifference if not with active repudiation. At the same time the average Christian layman knows almost nothing about what is happening in radical circles, and lacks both means of finding out and interest in inquiring. Mildly approving of "free speech," he often adopts a "Hyde Park" attitude of toleration, declaring that it is wisest to "let the rabble-rousers get it out of their systems."

Seldom does he seem to realize that the rabble-rousers might say anything worth his own hearing. It is a legitimate charge against most radicals that they damn religion without finding out what religious persons of today are saying and doing. It is a grave weakness of many Christians that they have no information about radical positions, and that in their satisfaction with the *status quo* they have no notion of inquiring as to the nature of criticism, let alone as to its possible validity.

Beyond this point have gone many Christian young people of our time, and perhaps a majority of the younger clergy in the "standard" denominations. It is relatively easy for them to become aware of social maladjustments, and it is natural that they should ally themselves with such reform movements as come to their attention. Too often, unhappily, they know less about the movement itself than about the situation it has addressed itself to change. Thus one sincere liberal after another has had his fingers burned in the fire of partisan objectives. Sometimes he reacts by turning wholly to reaction, more often by becoming so cautious as to be ineffective. The cure is not to withdraw, but to learn the ways of effective and constructive action.

The contrasting danger, of course, is that disgust with Christian conservatives, coupled with the influence of non-Christian radicals, will draw these young enthusiasts altogether away from the Church and from the Christian position. Communists used explicitly to assert, and evidently still implement, the view that "fellow-travelers" should be so far identified with Communist activity as to make them useless in any other role in society. When this happens in the case of young Christians, as not infrequently it does, the blame lies quite as fully upon the Church as it does upon the Communist party

Christian attitudes

It is not to be inferred from the division between "church attitudes" and "Christian attitudes" that the present writer thinks there have been no Christian attitudes within the churches. He does hold, however, that a considered Christian approach to the problems of secular radicalism will be a wiser and better one than has characterized the majority of church groups up to the present time. How shall a mature, modern Christian look upon the social and economic stirrings in our society? How much shall he challenge? How much shall he sympathize? How much shall he participate?

What the Hebrew-Christian tradition contributes at this point is its basic concern for human values. Resting upon the fatherhood of God and therefore asserting the brotherhood of man, it seeks to make that brotherhood effective in human relations. Thus it is inevitably committed to personal freedom and to economic justice. These values of freedom and justice always are asserted, and often are sincerely sought, by the radical movements. Effective Christian participation will insist always upon the primacy of the human factor, will seek the greatest good not merely of a special group, nor even of the greatest number, but of everyone.

Maintenance of this criterion will help greatly toward accurate distinction between the constructive and the destructive elements in current radicalism A movement which ignores personal worth in the interests of a predetermined system is anti-Christian at that point if at no other, and as such may not claim rightfully the support of the sincere Christian. The loyal exponent of a cause may rightfully sacrifice himself in its interests. If the cause be Christian, he is not permitted to sacrifice to it any other human personality. Insistence upon this distinction often will clear the atmosphere of discussion of policy, and will serve to direct activity into truly constructive channels.

The continuing handicap of Christians involved in radical activities is that they have been too "innocent." It is essential that they should hold to their own ideals. It is just as requisite that they shall be aware of external realities. Scientific method must be applied both in the diagnosis of social ills and in the inquiry into proposed schemes of betterment. Communist "front" organizations would lose their power for ill if only all their members were fully aware of what goes on in parliamentary maneuvers and in the formulation of propaganda; and the members can become aware if they will pay the price of careful scrutiny. This is frankly a plea that we shall be as wise as the serpents with whom we have to deal; if we are not, we as doves may be wholly swallowed up. Nor is it to deny that serpents are among God's creatures; but we should be clear as to their anatomy and habits.

The knowledge of the facts in the case, once possessed, should be openly shared with all who are concerned. In particular, the institutional interests of many left-wing agencies, both political parties and labor unions, must be clearly differentiated from their professed (and often actual) objectives. It is true that the labor official, charged with perpetuating his organization at the expense of promoting his cause, rightly may say to the Church,

"You too." That excuses neither the Church nor the union. Rather it challenges both Church and union, and in particular it challenges the rank and file of their memberships, to recognize the temptation and to reject it.

Some sincere idealists hesitate publicly to admit any fault in leftist movements because they do not wish to join the ignoble company of "red-baiters." Again the question is that of the relative importance of the movement as such, and of the goal which the movement professes to seek. The unwarranted bitterness of some politicians and some military men toward Russia does not justify a white-washing of Russian policy by those who want to be fair. The indiscriminate blackguarding of some Congressional and legislative committees does not require that all the victims of their ire shall be defended at all points. The Soviet Union and the Communist party have contributed much negatively in their condemnation of capitalist injustice, and not a little positively in their maintenance of a very real equality among "racial" groups. When they assail wrong and maintain right they are to be commended and supported. When they assail competitors for power in the sole interest of their own power, they have no claim upon the loyalty of those whose concern is with right and wrong in their essence.

The cause of genuine economic justice and freedom will not be far advanced if it should turn out, late in the course of the campaign, that the major promoter has been controlled by ulterior interests. Both by his ideals of honesty and by considerations of ultimate strategy, the Christian is obligated to state the facts as he sees them, and to give credit and challenge where each is due. Only thus can he keep his own hands clean, only thus can he maintain his freedom fully to serve the causes to which he is committed.

Opinions differ, and will continue to differ, as to how far it is advisable for the religious person to align himself with specific radical causes. It is impossible to lay down any general rule applicable to all cases. Much depends upon the particular social and economic views which the individual holds (and there are many among which Christians rightfully may choose), and which of necessity will determine his preferences among agencies of action.

Individual participation commonly endangers the Christian enterprise less than does institutional affiliation. The involvement of Christian young people's groups, for example, in the American Youth Congress, led to sad disillusionment for many. The association of the World Peace Commission of the Methodist Church with the American Peace Mobilization, during the period of Communist isolationism, was scarcely less embarrassing than was the publicity that ecclesiastical body gave to the activities of Colonel Lindbergh and Senator Wheeler. Now the Communists may agree with the Christian, and now the Trotskyists; but Christian societies should avoid the risk of being expected always to agree with either.

Very occasionally sincere liberals have succeeded in wresting control of a movement from partisan and special-interest groups. Commonly this is difficult, because of the superior discipline maintained by the left-wing political units; and it should not be tried unless a similar parliamentary discipline can be established among those whose concern is wholly sincere. The history of "united fronts" in this country is discouraging, and therefore should be studied carefully by all who propose to engage in united action with groups whose structure and purposes are not fully known.

The case for the individual Christian's joining the labor union appropriate to his own employment is a fairly clear one. Not to join is to take sides with the employer, who commonly is in no great need of support. The power of the individual to promote his own ideals within the union depends partly upon his personal abilities, much more upon his willingness to invest time and energy. There is in unions at least as much general indifference as there is in churches, and the strength of a single energetic participant, therefore, is much greater than a count of heads would suggest.

The fuller Gospel

The final advantage which Christianity holds over the secular radical groups, and an absolute one, is that it includes all their objectives and much more besides. They are concerned with man's making of a living. The Christian can join heartily in that effort, while seeing it as the means toward the making of a life. He will not pretend that man can live without bread; but he will insist that beyond bread there are ultimate values which the well-fed, well-clothed, well-housed man and woman have within their reach.

Essential Christianity is much more profoundly radical than are any of the secular political and economic movements, for it reaches much more deeply into all the roots of life. Applied in full sincerity and without reserve, achieved in absolute personal dedication, Christianity would be more devastating to the ills of the existing order than any leftist party ever has dreamed of being. If, however, the truly radical character of Christianity is effectively to emerge, it must draw from the deepest roots of faith and experience far more richly than commonly it has. Christianity has resources of continuing strength, of self-restoration, which secular radicalism conspicuously has lacked. The challenge to the Christian of today is that he shall develop to the full both the social conscience that the radicals know, and the personal completeness that radicalism has ignored.

In our time the secular radicals still may confront the Church with charges of social ignorance, and, worse, of social indifference. Indifference may be countered only by new concern and renewed consecration. Ignorance must be met by new means of supplying information, so that social conscience shall be enlightened as well as inflamed. Some of the churches, and the Federal Council of Churches, have made admirable starts in the securing of data. As yet they have had little success in persuading general lay attention to the data supplied. Until the Christian makes full use of the radical resources of social concern and social knowledge, he can expect the continuing resistance of radical contempt for irrelevant sentimentalism.

Religion must not be the opiate of the people. It is challenged to provide the food of the people: to concern itself with all the food of all the people. True religion will join with the secular radicals in seeing to it that the people's bodies are fed. It will serve, beyond the radicals now but (we may hope) with them ultimately, in the nourishing of man's spirit.

FURTHER READING

MacMurray, John. *Christianity and Communism.*

Marx, Karl. *Capital.* Ed. by Frederick Engels. Tr. by Samuel Moore and Edward Aveling. New York: Modern Library, Inc. Giant Edition.

Periodicals:

American Federation of Labor. *American Federationist.*

Communist. *New Masses; Daily Worker.*

Co-operatives. *The Co-operative Consumer.*

I.W.W. *The Industrial Worker.*

Liberal. *Nation; New Republic.*

Trotskyist. *Fourth International.*

4

THE FASCIST MASQUERADE
Howard Thurman

*1. Definition of the term: statism, economic control, general
totalitarianism. The basic concept: inequality. 2. Three American examples: Christian American, The Nationalists, The Ku
Klux Klan. 3. The challenge to the Church: the appeal of
fascism, the failings of the Church.*

The purpose of this chapter is to analyze the basis of fascism
as it has developed in America during the last decade and to
delineate the challenge which it presents to the Church in its
commitment to an ethic which is at once revolutionary and
compelling. Special attention will be given to the aspect of
fascism which lends itself to the release of unrestrained passions
in human nature, causing the focusing of hatreds on individuals
because of race, class or religion.

1. DEFINITION OF THE TERM

There is a medley of confusion as to what fascism is and how
it operates in modern life. The indiscriminate use of the term
reveals that it is a "catchall" to describe individuals or movements with whom we are in disagreement or concerning whom
we wish to express contempt and disapproval. It is of critical
importance to define our terms as accurately as possible not
only so as to make clear what it is with which we are dealing,
but also, so as better to discriminate between the doctrine itself

and its concomitants, as we point up the true basis of the challenge which it represents.

Mussolini states:

> The foundation of Fascism is the conception of the State, its character, its duty, and its aim. Fascism conceives of the State as an absolute, in comparison with which all individuals or groups are relative, only to be conceived of in their relation to the State. . . . The Fascist State is itself conscious, and has itself a will and a personality—thus it may be called the "ethic State."[1]

Further he says:

> The State . . . is a spiritual and moral force in itself, since its political, juridical, and economic organization of the nation is a concrete thing.[2]

Concerning liberty under fascism, Mussolini affirms:

> The Fascist State organizes the nation, but leaves a sufficient margin of liberty to the individual; the latter is deprived of all *useless* and possibly *harmful* freedom, but retains what is essential; the deciding power in this question cannot be the individual, but the State alone![3]

As to the place of religion under the fascist state, he avers:

> Fascism respects the God of the ascetics, the saints, the heroes, and equally, God as he is perceived and worshipped by simple people.[4]

Ralph Robey writing in *Newsweek*, July 30, 1945, on "One Way to Identify a Fascist" defines fascism strictly in terms of economic theory.

> The distinguishing characteristic of Fascism is complete government control and direction of all production

[1] Benito Mussolini, *The Political and Social Doctrine of Fascism* (New York: Carnegie Endowment for International Peace, 1935), p. 13.
[2] *Ibid.*, p. 13.
[3] *Ibid.*, p. 14. Italics mine.
[4] *Ibid.*, p. 16.

and marketing, but this is accomplished, not through government ownership of the factors of production, but within the framework of a system of private property. And such complete government control and direction of what private owners shall do with their property is the only distinguishable characteristic of Fascism. It has no ideological relation to whether it persecutes the Jews, any more than Communism is philosophically related to the liquidation of the Kukoa or the denial of the freedom of religion. In other words both Communism and Fascism in their basic concepts, are strictly economic, and the curious quirks and antisocial traits that those who run the system may develop have no necessary relation to the underlying philosophy of such systems. To be specific, a person may be arrogantly intolerant and simply unspeakable in his attitude toward other races, and still not be a Fascist.

The War Department in a statement issued to members of the armed services under date of March 24, 1945, defines fascism more inclusively than as that which has to do only with the economic life:

Fascism is government by the few and for the few. The objective is seizure and control of the economic, political, social and cultural life of the state. Why? The democratic way of life interferes with their methods and desire for: (1) conducting business; (2) living with their fellowmen; (3) having the final say in matters concerning others as well as themselves. The basic principles of democracy stand in the way of their desires; hence—democracy must go! Anyone who is not a member of their inner gang has to do what he's told. They permit no civil liberties, no equality before law. . . . They maintain themselves in power by use of force combined with propaganda based on primitive ideas of "blood" and "race," by skillful manipulation of fear and hate and by false promise of security.[5]

[5] Quoted in *Time Bomb*, by E. A. Piller (New York: Arco Publishing Company, 1945), p. 12 ff.

Further, in the statement the War Department gives "Three Ways to Spot U.S. Fascists":

> Fascists in America may differ slightly from fascists in other countries but there are a number of attitudes and practices that they have in common. Following are three. Every person who has one of them is not necessarily fascist. But he is in a mental state that lends itself to the acceptance of fascist aims.
>
> 1. Pitting of religious, racial, and economic groups against one another in order to break down national unity is a device of the "divide and conquer" technique used by Hitler to gain power in Germany and in other countries. With slight variations, to suit local conditions, fascists everywhere have used this Hitler method. In many countries, anti-Semitism (hatred of Jews) is a dominant device of fascism. In the United States, native fascists have often been anti-Catholic, anti-Jew, anti-Negro, anti-labor, anti-foreign-born. In South America, the native fascists use the same scapegoats except that they substitute anti-Protestant-ism for anti-Catholicism.
>
> Interwoven with the "master race" theory of fascism is a well-planned "hate campaign" against minority races, religions, and other groups. To suit their particular needs and aims, fascists will use any one or a combination of such groups as a convenient scapegoat.
>
> 2. Fascism cannot tolerate such religious and ethical concepts as the "brotherhood of man." Fascists deny the need for international cooperation. These ideas contradict the fascist theory of the "master race." The brotherhood of man implies that all people—regardless of color, race, creed, or nationality—have rights. International cooperation, as expresssed in the Dumbarton Oaks proposals, runs counter to the fascist program of war and world domina-tion. . . . Right now our native fascists are spreading anti-British, anti-Soviet, anti-French, and anti-United Na-tions propaganda. . . .
>
> 3. It is accurate to call a member of a communist party a "communist." For short, he is often called a "Red." Indiscriminate pinning of the label "Red" on people and

proposals which one opposes is a common political device. It is a favorite trick of native as well as foreign fascists. Many fascists make the spurious claim that the world has but two choices—either fascism or communism, and they label as "communist" everyone who refuses to support them. By attacking our free enterprise, capitalist democracy, and by denying the effectiveness of our way of life they hope to trap many people.[6]

The basic concept

The three definitions have certain elements in common. In the first place, they agree that under fascism the State is not only central but supreme in its complete control and direction of the economic life. In the second place, the individual is always and in all circumstances subordinate to the State, and, what is more important, the significance of the individual is defined by the State. In the third place, the State is epitomized by that individual or those individuals who are able to speak on behalf of, or themselves to *personify*, the State. This means that the fate of the average citizen is in the hands of those who have taken onto themselves, or have had delegated to them, the power of the State. The peculiar character of such power or powers is that social responsibility that extends beyond the defined categories is reduced to zero. Such power has its own ethic, etiquette and ritual. Its major function is to keep itself fat and strong. To those who "belong," who satisfy the demands of the etiquette, there is given a priority in terms of privilege, security and status. This fact becomes the basis of a generalization as to equality and inequality. Therefore, it seems clear to the writer that fascism in the very nature of the case has to be committed to a fundamental inequality among men. This theory of inequality, a derivative from the basic fascist doctrine of the State, becomes a doctrine of inequality from which there flows a bloody stream of racism and terror. As Jacques Maritain says, writing in *Commonweal*, January 4, 1943, "Racist law is nothing

[6] *Ibid.*

but a secondary ideological process which aims at justifying a primitive criminal passion and freeing it of all restraint."

This concomitant of fascism, namely, racism is significant because it gives to any current doctrine of racial inequality or superiority a new dimension of dignity and respectability. Obviously, this particular concomitant of fascism is not new; it merely provides a fresh banner under which the same old warriors may parade. American soil is particularly fertile for this new facade. Already in solution in American mores and folkways there is the compound that recognizes, for all practical purposes, the basic "inequality" among men. This is evident in many of our statutes, our customs and in our social structure. It is not meant to ignore the ideal of equality as set forth in the Declaration of Independence or in the Constitution, for that matter; nevertheless, in Church and State any notion of equality that extends into the realm of rights has been constantly most bitterly fought and challenged. In Jefferson's original draft of the Declaration of Independence he makes the connection between equality and private rights unmistakable: "We hold these truths to be sacred and undeniable: that all men are created equal and independent; that from that equal creation they derive *rights* inherent and *inalienable* . . . ." In a further revision he says, "We hold these truths to be self-evident; that all men are created equal; that they are endowed by their creator with equal rights, some of which are inalienable and inherent. . . ." We draw the line at equality of rights.

We must hold steadily in mind the fact that an important part of the menace of fascism as defined here is its property as a catalyst. It crystallizes moods, attitudes and fears that are already in solution. Our country has a long and ignoble record in the Vigilante tradition. It is true, therefore, that in a wide variety of instances hate organizations spring up, flourish for a season, disappear, and reappear in another form without any formal ideological recognition of the existence of classical fascism, either as a political or economic doctrine.

2. AMERICAN EXAMPLES

It is now in order to examine a sampling of certain contemporary movements in American life in the light of our discussion up to this point. To get one's hands on facts relative to the so-called fascist movements in American life requires far more time and skill than were available to the writer. There is an abundance of materials on the various movements and individuals who were operating under the general classification of fifth columnists and whose records are now a part of public property. But these activities were largely directed against the government to hinder the successful prosecution of the war. For the most part they did not represent a direct challenge to the Church. But there are other movements that draw largely upon the church-going people and whose leadership defines their position within the framework of Christianity despite the fact that their appeal is to criminal passion, freed of all restraints. Again it is difficult to know accurately the numerical strength of these movements because of the inaccessibility of records and the potent tendency to exaggerate their strength and power.

I have chosen three organizations because they represent three different lines of attack: one is avowedly political in intent; one is definitely antilabor; one is woven into the social fabric of American life, walking upright under its own name and title. They present the challenge most clearly, and they crystallize attitudes that are ever present in American life, in the homes, the churches and the schools. They make the obvious appeal at the level of the average American's fear and mistrust of minorities, and do this in the name of authentic Christianity, patriotism or Americanism.

Christian American

The headquarters of the Christian American is Houston, Texas. The choice of the name is very significant. To call itself Christian is to announce to the unwary that the organization is not in opposition to, or is not to be contrasted with, the Church and that for which the Church stands. It is to symbolize in the popular mind the highest form of idealism and righteousness of which millions can conceive. It is a magic password. To be American is to appeal to pride of country, and, what is more important, pride of section that gives to the average individual a certain sense of separateness, making for a special category of distinctiveness owing to the accident of national origin. To be a Christian American is to be but a little less than an angel.

The Christian American came into national prominence by its sponsorship of the "Right to Work" Amendment. According to E. A. Piller in *Time Bomb* this group was actively at work on behalf of such an amendment in the State of Arkansas during 1943. On March 4, 1943, in the State Legislature of Arkansas there was a bitter debate on this particular amendment which resulted in its passage of the House by a vote of 62 to 29. This bill seeks to destroy unionism by abolishing the closed shop. Coupled with this is the "anti-violence in strikes" law which places a heavy penalty on any union that is accused of threatening to use violence against any individual in its effort to keep a man from going to work to break a strike. The Legislature of Louisiana passed the following resolution relative to the Christian Americans:

> WHEREAS Hitler has boasted and emphatically stated that it will be a simple matter in our country to set capital against labor, Negro against white, Catholic against Protestant, and Christian against Jew,
> WHEREAS recently in the Heidelberg Hotel, a public headquarters was announced for an association known as Christian American, which association is domiciled and located without the state of Louisiana, and has boasted and advertised the fact that they have come into the state of Louisiana for the purpose of seeing that our legislature would enact laws, which laws would create animosity, antagonism and unrest among the employers and employees of this state and interfere with the harmonious relations of capital and labor in this state,
> BE IT RESOLVED that the legislature of Louisiana do

request the FBI and the Dies Committee to investigate the source of revenue, general activities, and personnel and the objectives of The Christian American Association of Houston, Texas, to ascertain and determine whether or not said association is conducting subversive activities in the United States.[7]

The *New Republic* for July 20, 1942, quotes a spokesman for the Christian American as saying:

White men and women have been forced into unions with black African apes whom they must call "brother" or lose their cards and their jobs.

The sinister aspect of this movement is in the fact that it is backed by a group of skillful men who are adequately financed and who recognize that under the guise of their basic theory of inequality they can appeal to the fears and the frustrations of the rank and file of Americans without restraint. One of the sponsors of the Christian Americans, according to Harold Preece in a signed article in the August, 1946, issue of *NOW*, is the man who started the "Eleanor Club" rumor about secret revolutionary organizations of Negroes, sponsored by Mrs. Roosevelt. The organization is fascist because it is concerned with the control of production by a select few in whom all powers are resident and who in turn can determine arbitrarily the priority of privilege. This is the basis of the attack on collective bargaining; the appeal to racial and religious prejudice is the masquerade.

The Nationalists

During the summer of 1945, Eugene Segal, Scripps-Howard Staff Writer, published for his paper a series of articles under the general title, "The Nationalists Unmasked." Mr. Segal begins his first article, appearing in the San Francisco *News* under date of July 16 with these significant words:

[7] *Ibid.*, p. 54.

Capitalizing on prejudice and discontent, the Nationalists party of former U. S. Senator Robert R. Reynolds is seeking to weld the dissident groups of the country into an organization which he hopes will become a dominant force in American politics.

Mr. Segal states that the methods used are those employed by Hitler in his rise to power.

They have started a campaign of infiltrating the ranks of groups which may have a real or fancied grievance against the federal administration and its policies.

They have taken over a Midwest farmers' organization. Their henchmen are moving into key spots in labor unions. They have formed two veterans organizations. . . .

They have started a youth movement. . . . The Nationalists have won the affiliation of certain church groups and have the backing of the president of an old established theological seminary, who preaches a hate creed in the school's official publication.

The Nationalists are anti-Negro, anti-Semitic, and anti-Catholic, and anti-foreigner as situations demand, but apparently they will accept any convenient alliance.

Mr. Segal lists Robert Reynolds as leader of the movement, and sharing his leadership "is Gerald L. K. Smith, rabble rouser, founder of the 'American First Party' and idol of various 'mothers' groups." Continuing the listing of personnel the reporter says:

Around Reynolds and Smith moves a circle of satellites, such as Carl Mote, of Indianapolis, part owner of two small public utilities and president of the National Farmers Guild; Mrs. Lyrl Clark Van Hyning of Chicago, head of We, the Mothers Mobilize for America, Inc.; the Rev. Gerald Winrod, popularly known as the "Jay-hawk Nazi" of Wichita, Kansas; and the Rev. Harvey Springer, a Denver rabble-rouser who is called the Cowboy Preacher."

In the article under date of July 20, 1945, there is an account of a convention held at the Englewood Baptist Tabernacle,

Englewood, Colorado, January 6, 1944. There were 350 young people and pastors present, representing churches in seven Midwestern states. At that time an organization was formed of the "Christian Youth of America," with national headquarters in Englewood. Segal says, "A call was issued to 'all Christian youth organizations in America to join us in a united front against the flood of communism in the land.' One Kenneth Goff was named Chairman of the Youth Movement."

Writing about Goff, Segal says, "He formerly was on the advisory staff of the American Youth Congress and a member of the National Executive Committee of the Young Communists League. . . ." After coming into the Nationalist camp he wrote for Gerald L. K. Smith's, *The Cross and Flag.*

The movement, crystallized at Englewood, has taken in the youth group of the "Rev. Bob Parr's Church in Detroit and organizations in Buffalo, Los Angeles, and other cities." They distribute tracts among high school students and servicemen.

The Ku Klux Klan

The story of the Klan is familiar to any person conversant with the history of the country. The modern Klan presents a critical challenge to the Church because, as do the other organizations mentioned, it bases its position within the framework of Protestant Christianity. Occasionally one is reminded through news item or the public press that the organization, often in new dress, is a potent factor in American life. To set before us clearly how sharply defined is the issue which the Klan represents I quote at some length from the stated ideals of the organization:

1. This is a White Man's Organization, exalting the Caucasian Race and teaching the doctrine of White Supremacy. . . .

2. This is a Gentile Organization, and as such has as its mission the interpretation of the highest ideals of the White, Gentile peoples. . . .

3. It is an American Organization, and we do restrict membership to native-born American citizens. . . .

4. It is a Protestant Organization. Membership is restricted to those who accept the tenets of true Christianity, which is essentially Protestant. We maintain and contend that it is the inalienable right of Protestants to have their own distinctive organization. We can say to the world without apology, and say truly, that our forefathers founded this as a Protestant country and that it is our purpose to re-establish and maintain it as such. While we will energetically maintain and proclaim the principles of Protestantism, we will also maintain the principles of religious liberty as essential to the life and progress of this nation, and we will vigorously oppose all efforts to rob the American people of this right.

RACIAL IDEALS

1. We stand for White Supremacy. Distinction among the races is not accidental but designed. This is clearly brought out in the one book that tells authoritatively of the origin of the races. This distinction is not incidental, but is of the vastest import and indicates the wisdom of the divine mind. It is not temporary but is as abiding as the ages that have not yet ceased to roll. The supremacy of the White Race must be maintained, or be overwhelmed by the rising tide of color.

2. We must keep this a White Man's Country. Only by doing this can we be faithful to the foundations laid by our forefathers.

    a. This Republic was established by White Men.

    b. It was established for White Men.

    c. Our forefathers never intended that it should fall into the hands of an inferior race.

    d. Every effort to wrest from White Men the management of its affairs in order to transfer it to the control of blacks or any other color, or to permit them to share in its control, is an invasion of our sacred constitutional prerogatives and a violation of divinely established laws.

e. We would not rob the colored population of their rights, but we demand that they respect the rights of the White Race in whose country they are permitted to reside.

f. Purity of the white blood must be maintained.

CHRISTIAN IDEALS

1. We magnify the Bible—as the basis of our Constitution, the foundation of our government, the source of our laws, the sheet-anchor of our liberties, the most practical guide of right living, and the source of all true wisdom.

2. We teach the worship of God. For we have in mind the divine command, "Thou shalt worship the Lord thy God."

3. We honor the Christ, as the Klansman's only criterion of character. And we seek at His hands that cleansing from sin and impurity, which only He can give.

4. We believe that the highest expression of life is in service and in sacrifice for that which is right, that selfishness can have no place in a true Klansman's life and character; but that he must be moved by unselfish motives, such as characterized our Lord the Christ and moved Him to the highest service and the supreme sacrifice for that which was right.[8]

There are many other groups following the same general line to be found in various parts of the country. In the winter of 1945 Allan L. Swim, Scripps-Howard Staff Writer, published a series which he called "Merchants of Hate." One may find them in the morgue of any Scripps-Howard newspaper. The point of the series is to make clear that hate is a commodity for which there seems to be a ready market in American life. And one of the best counters is patriotism and religion—as witness the well-known activities of Father Coughlin and Father Terminiello.

There is something ominous about the totalitarian notion,

[8] From a photostatic copy appearing in *NOW* (semi-monthly) First half, August, 1945.

whether it is in a small, loosely thought-out hate organization, a large powerful organization like the Roman Catholic Church or an institution of higher learning. The matters of dedication, motivation and intent are in a sense irrelevant. The point is that given the acceptance of totalitarian theory, there is no other-than-self reference by which character may be determined. At any particular moment the organization may have social weal as its aim universally extended, but it stands ever in candidacy to be manipulated in terms of all that stands against social weal. As a case in point let us give a passing glance to technocracy.

William Russell writing in the *Annals of the American Academy of Political and Social Science* for July, 1935, says:

> The present situation is different from any that has gone before, because modern business enterprise for the first time is able to bring under one central control all necessary raw materials and fuel resources, the mechanism of transports and communication, the mechanism of fabrication and assembly of parts to produce the completed article of consumption.
>
> But say the technocrats, we can save this society. We can give everybody an equal treatment. We will provide everybody . . . with everything he could buy if they had an income of $20,000 a year (Howard Scott) or $4,000 (Goodwin Watson). . . . We will determine, by techniques, that we have mastered, the capacity for consumption of the American people, and we will plan production to match it. . . . We will tell people what work they are to do, and provide everybody with everything that is good for them to have. . . . There will be no depressions etc. . . .

Totalitarianism is a threat to, and the enemy of, liberty ever— it makes no difference whether the totalitarianism is benign or wicked, its power works inevitably towards the absolute and it cannot survive with any competitor. Watch for the signs in your community, whatever may be the banner or the masquerade.

3. THE CHALLENGE TO THE CHURCH
The appeal of fascism

The appeal of the organizations outlined and similar ones that are functioning sectionally and nationally, is in the fact that they meet a need in the lives of the people that is not being met by the Church. They provide three very important things for their followers:

1. Integrated action. There is a crisis dramatized which calls for action on the part of the individual. A sense of urgency is communicated and an assignment made well within the ability of the devotee. This was exemplified, for instance, in Father Coughlin's platoon scheme of organization. Each person was urged to gather around him twenty-five others to read *Social Justice*, to listen to the weekly radio address, to contact congressmen, etc. A job needs to be done; the job is defined within the ability of even the simplest person; there is a short distance from center to circumference. The strategy of this appeal is that when a person acts on an idea, he secures his stake in it.

2. They inspire a willingness to sacrifice. Here again, the extent of sacrifice is carefully charted. In most instances, it means a willingness to be counted on the "right" side even at the expense of separating one's self from former friends and even relatives. I have seen the Klan in western New York separate families, set brother against brother—in one instance it actually caused men who "belonged" to walk down a certain side of the street so as not to pass by the door of a particular shop owner who opposed the organization. In their most fanatical demands, even life may be forfeited. Here the symbol of the State as being the Highest Loyalty and the individual having his status defined only in reference to it, is on the point.

3. A sense of collective destiny that gives to the individual a validity and a profound sense of significance. The individual counts. He may be poor, ignorant, hungry or unemployed, but he is caught up in a movement that promises his redemption

from these things if he joins with others in removing the obstacles which are the obvious enemies of his security.

Further, these organizations exploit the active and latent prejudices that the average American has against non-white races on the one hand and against Jewish people on the other. They make it possible for a creative rationalization to provide a cloak for group hatreds which can be objectified as true Christianity or true Americanism. In other words, they provide for a legitimatizing of sadistic and demoniacal impulses of which, under normal circumstances, they might be ashamed. To appeal to anti-Negro sentiment in many sections, communities and among many groups is a "natural" for the would-be demagogue. It is sure fire.

The failings of the Church

The fact that these appeals are made in the name of Christianity is itself most revealing. It is no answer to the fact to say that it is a false interpretation of Christianity. Such a reply merely etches more clearly than ever that the Church has done a wretched job in making clear what the Teaching is, either about God or man. It is to the utter condemnation of the Church that large groups of believers all over the United States have stood, and, at present, stand on the side of a theory of inequality among men that causes the Church to practice in its own body some of the most vicious forms of racial prejudice. It often affirms separateness solely on the basis of race, which separateness it insists upon in worship, in organization and even in its graveyards. I remember hearing a Mohammedan say in an address before a young people's society in a Christian church, "Allah laughs aloud in his Mohammedan heaven when he beholds the Christian spectacle of the First Baptist Church White and the First Baptist Church Colored."

The bitter truth is that the Church has permitted the various hate-inspired groups in our common life to establish squatter's rights in the minds of believers because there has been no adequate teaching of the meaning of the faith in terms of human dignity and human worth. The same default is evident in the effectiveness of the appeal to anti-Semitism. The responsibility of the Church to teach Christianity and at the same time not to aid and abet anti-Semitism seems to the writer to be morally inescapable. The roots of anti-Semitism are much deeper than this statement would indicate. In essence, anti-Semitism is a form of protest arising from the fundamental rejection in our culture of the ground of Christian ethics which is to be found in the prophets of Israel. The presence of the Jew becomes the unconscious symbol of that rejection and the attack on him is the measure of the rejection of the ethic. Anti-Semitism is the result of the battle against the ethic.

The crux of the issue for the Church is this: The Church is irrevocably committed to a revolutionary ethic, but it tends to implement the ethic by means that are short of that which is revolutionary. The dilemma is to try to implement a revolutionary ethic without resorting to revolutionary means. The appeal of the fascist is in terms of that which is revolutionary by the standards to which the appeal is made. This was certainly true of fascism in Italy, in Germany, and is implicit in our own varieties. It was on the basis of the revolutionary character of fascism that it was the object of concern, observation and in some instances, indictment on the part of the federal government during the war that has just ended. The Church must be as revolutionary in practice as it is in the genius of the ethic to which it is dedicated.

One of the things that weakens the positive stand of the Church with reference to the position of inequality of men in fascism is the curious social result of the doctrine of salvation. The very categories of "the saved" and "the sinners" load the scales on the side of inequality in intrinsic worth. For whatever reasons, whether by election or by self-surrender, a man comes into "the fold" he at once is seen by himself as being in a basic category of superiority. This is the psychological fact—there is a desert and a sea that separates him from his fellows who do not "belong." There is just a step between this and the straight practice of the doctrine of superiority due to the fact of special grouping or racial origin. If I am saved by grace, it is without merit, ultimately, on my part, but by means of the operation of a divine Power whose purposes are beyond my apprehension or understanding. Unless that state is for all and enjoyed by all potentially, there is no fundamental difference between the spiritual arrogance arising from my state of grace and the spiritual arrogance arising from the incident of race. The issue is softened, somewhat, if my state of grace is on the basis of some measure of personal merit and achievement.

If it be true that God is the source of life, then it follows that each individual is grounded in God in a direct and primary manner. There can be no valid distinction between the God of religion on the one hand and the God of life on the other. The task of the Church then must include the conquest of the world, and in the fulfillment of that task it can rely upon the guarantee of God in whom life and all of the great potentials of mind and spirit are grounded. Such a position establishes the infinite worth of all individuals and denies that for which fascism stands in its regard for persons. The degree to which the Church stands for less marks the measure of its tacit support of such theories of life as fascism affirms. This places a great teaching responsibility upon the Church to give a growing, dynamic and intelligent content to the faith which it inspires men to have in Jesus Christ as Master and Lord.

FURTHER READING

BRYSON, LYMAN. *Which Way America? Communism—Fascism —Democracy*. New York: The Macmillan Company, 1939.

DENNIS, LAWRENCE. *The Coming American Fascism*. New York: Harper & Brothers, 1936.

MUSSOLINI, BENITO. *The Political and Social Doctrine of Fascism*. New York: Carnegie Endowment for International Peace, 1935.

PILLER, E. A. *Time Bomb*. New York: Arco Publishing Company, 1945.

SWING, RAYMOND GRAM. *Forerunners of American Fascism*. New York: J. Messner Inc., 1935.

THOMAS, NORMAN M. *After the New Deal, What?* New York: The Macmillan Company, 1936.

5

WELFARE WORK:
ALLY OR ALTERNATIVE?

Buell G. Gallagher

Introduction. 1. The historical perspective: the development of almsgiving: corruption and reaction; new conceptions: welfare work and the social gospel. 2. Organized social work: early beginnings, present scope. 3. Philanthropic foundations. 4. Agencies to serve agencies. 5. The Social Service State. 6. Falsehoods and fakeries. Resistance or resource: criteria of judgment. The challenge to the Church. 7. Resistance or resource? 8. The real question.

~~~~~~

"Quhate is cherite?" asks Archbishop Hamilton's *Catechism*. And the answer is: "It is lufe, quharby we lufe God for His awin saik . . . and our neichbour for God's saik, or in God."[1] Charity, says Paul, is greater than faith, greater than hope: the highest Christian virtue.

But the charity which the archbishop and the apostle are here talking about is not what modern usage imputes to the word Today, "charities" may be worthy objects of gifts of money, or of old clothing, or of discarded furniture. "Charity" in our vocabulary has taken the place of "almsgiving" in ancient times, probably because the common exordium used by preachers in appeals for money for the poor or for prayers for souls in purgatory, for many centuries, was, "Good Christian people, we

---

[1] *Catechism* of 1552.

pray you of your charity to give thus and so." Gradually it came about that a word which meant a consuming affection of God for man and of man for God and men in God's name—which in the Greek is *agape*, in the Latin (inaptly, because there was no Latin equivalent) *caritas*—was equated with the act instead of the motive. "Almsgiving" in the Christian vocabulary was re-placed by "charity," and the spirit of considerate sharing was replaced by the act of benevolence.

Worst than the degredation of the word is the final discourage-ment of the act to which it has been wrongly attached. We have today come into a period in which the act of benevolence itself is strongly questioned, both from inside and outside the Church. It is sometimes claimed that philanthropy is a substitute for justice—the pittance gift offered to the exploited working classes as a sop for inadequate wages. At other times it is argued that modern organized social work has replaced the personalized charities of the Church with the impersonal and professionalized heartlessness of "standards" and "tests." And from still other quarters comes the accusation that the ethical sensitivity of the Church has been blunted in permitting benevolence with its paternalism to be the moral equivalent of brotherhood with its egalitarian ethic. Still others, from within the Church, are alarmed at the displacement of much former charitable work of religion by social work under secular and governmental auspices. All of these contemporary questions and accusations can be more intelligently assessed in the light of history which has brought us to this moment. It is only as we see the present moment in historical perspective that we can rightly analyze our predicament.

1. HISTORICAL PERSPECTIVE

Let it be remembered that we are not here attempting a definitive history of Christian charities and Christian social service. In the hurried review we must here put down in skeletal form, there is not space to add the many qualifying clauses and adjectives or to note the exceptions. With this caution, and referring the reader to available histories of Christian philanthropy,[2] we here summarize the movements which have brought us to our present dilemma, in which churchmen are asking whether welfare work is an ally or an enemy of the Church, and in which there comes from outside the Church the counterquestion, Is not the Church itself standing in the way of human welfare?

The early church in Jerusalem is often described as communistic. To be sure, they "had all things in common." But this was not the common ownership of the means of production and distribution, with the elaboration of industrial and political mechanisms to administer economic processes. It was the complete sharing, within the brotherhood, of all consumers' goods. It was the practical expression of what the early Christians called *agape*, a Greek word which is poorly translated as "love" in English or *caritas* in Latin. First found in the Septuagint, this word is given the special meaning of God's love toward man and man's reciprocal love in God. It has no suggestion of sexual love or lust, no eroticism (*eros*). The early church was a community in which charity (as *agape*) abounded.

This impulse of mutualism was early corrupted and lost, principally because of two factors. On the one hand, the community of *agape* in Jerusalem was dependent upon gifts from Antioch, Galatia and the sister churches elsewhere. These churches in their turn were struggling under persecutions, and it must have been a considerable drain on their resources continually to raise contributions for the saints in Jerusalem. The frequent urgings of the Epistles, in which Paul shows marked

[2] See, for example, Helen Leland Witmer, *Social Work* (New York: Farrar & Rinehart, 1942), pp. 127-155, for an excellent short summary. See also: W. J. Ashley, *An Introduction to English Economic History and Theory* (New York: G. P. Putnam's Sons, 1910), Vol. II; H. O. Barnett, *Canon Barnett: His Life, Work, and Friends* (London: J. Murray, 1918); Helen Bosanquet, *Social Work in London, 1869-1912* (London: J. Murray, 1914); and Sidney and Beatrice Webb, *English Poor Law History* (London and New York: Longmans, Green and Company, 1927-29).

concern over the collections to maintain the community of *agape* in Jerusalem, give evidence that even during his lifetime the charitable urge was not too strong. And secondly, the impulse to share and share alike within the Christian community was subjected to the corroding influences of a prudential concern which prompted the individual Christian to covet the merit of his own almsgiving rather than to lose himself in the anonymity of institutional charity. In the Judaic literature from the third and second centuries B.C., almsgiving is enjoined on all pious Jews as a specially efficacious means of making atonement for sin and of obtaining divine protection from calamity; the merit of almsgiving is an unfailing possession; and it is lauded as a means of securing an enviable reputation.[3] The teaching of Jesus had de-emphasized the last named of these Hebraic teachings, but the *quid pro quo* of heavenly reward for earthly alms was retained.[4] Through this doorway, a strange and monstrous notion made its entrance into the Christian heritage. The idea that works of charity are spiritual currency enabled Simony, the revolting twin of Mercy, to take up residence in the household of the faithful, initiating a process which was to reach its climax in the practice of the sale of indulgences.

The development of almsgiving

For many centuries, the duty of almsgiving was encouraged by the Church, receiving great, and sometimes exaggerated, attention. Without reference to the debilitating effect of indiscriminate giving upon the recipients of alms, giving came to be encouraged as an expression of virtue which brought special spiritual benefits to the giver. In his famous sermon *On Alms*, the fourth-century father, John Chrysostom, says:

> God did not ordain the giving of alms only in order that
> the poor might be fed, but also that blessings might be

---

[3] See Tob. 12:8; 14:10-11; Ecclus. 3:14, 30; 7:10; 16:14; 29:12; 31:11; 40:17; 40:24.

[4] Matt. 6:2-4.

added to the givers, and even more for the sake of the latter than of the former.[5]

The preacher's logic led him to conclude that, since almsgiving is a Christian virtue, and there could be no almsgiving if there were no poor, poverty is ordained by God as a necessary condition of almsgiving.

> . . . For God condemned many to poverty, both for their own good and for yours. For poverty is more conducive to virtue than wealth, and for the sin laden no small consolation arises from works of charity.[6]

It makes no difference whether the recipient of the alms is "deserving" or not. Indeed, the donor is enjoined not to pry curiously into the pedigree, origins and private life of the beggar.

> Even as your Lord, although countless men blaspheme Him and practice fornication, steal, rob, dig up graves, commit sins without end, does not withdraw His universal bounty, but brings forth the common sunlight, the common rain, and the fruits of the earth, showing His loving-kindness toward men; so do you also, and when you have opportunity for showing mercy and kindness, then help the poor, satisfy their hunger, deliver them from wretchedness, and inquire no further. For if we investigate the lives of men too carefully, we shall never have pity on anyone. . . . Wherefore, I beseech you, let us cast aside this inopportune curiosity and give alms to all the poor, and let us do it generously, that we, too, on that day of judgment, may receive from God abundant pity and kindness.[7]

Gradually, the Church itself took over the giving of alms; and from the eighth century onward, it established a system of

[5] St. John Chrysostom, *Sermon On Alms, Delivered at Antioch After Passing Through the Market-Place in Winter-Time, and Seeing the Paupers and Beggars Lying There Neglected.* Trans. Margaret Sherwood, New York School of Philanthropy, "Studies in Social Work, No. 10." 1917, p. 15.

[6] *Ibid.*, p. 19.

[7] *Ibid.*, p. 24.

care for the poor which was paid for with tithe monies—a tithe levied more or less compulsorily upon members. With the growth of ecclesiastical endowments, the Church became the dispenser of alms, replacing the face-to-face relationships of an earlier day, and ultimately the alms were dispensed by bishops and prelates, replacing even the local parish priest. Secular rulers and men of means, jealously following the example of the spiritual overlords, established their own alms dispensaries. Thus monasteries, prelates, earls and nobles gave meals and doles indiscriminately to all who came, building up an enormous mendicant class which roamed from handout to handout, their position not greatly differing from the "industrious" poor who labored for the temporal and spiritual landlords to produce the largesse the princes of Church and State dispensed. "Foundations" were established by bequests of the wealthy to care for the aged, sick, crippled and infirm. The guilds set up institutions to care for their own aged and infirm.

Following the precept so ably enunciated by Chrysostom, and embalmed in canon law, much of this charity was indiscriminate, passed out to all comers as long as the supply lasted. In the later Middle Ages, the mendicant class had grown so large that the problem of poor relief became a major social issue. The wheel had come full circle: what had been encouraged as an ungrudging impulse of generosity (with a view, also, to one's own salvation) now became the root of a giant parasitical growth which not only sucked the lifeblood of a decadent economic system but also deprived great masses of persons of their self-respect, encouraging them in indolence and beggary (particularly when their lot was not much better if they labored), and creating a bobtailed proletariat which was a constant threat to the established order, calling for more bread and bigger circuses as the price of peace. It was time to call a halt to almsgiving.

Varied reactions

The first Statute of Laborers in England (1349) accordingly starts with these words:

Because many valiant beggars, as long as they may live
by begging do refuse to labor, giving themselves to idle-
ness and vice, and sometimes to theft and other abomina-
tions, none . . . shall, under the colour of pity or alms,
give anything to such . . . so that thereby they may be
compelled to labour for their necessary living.[8]

The subsequent developments in poor relief, "aimed at repres-
sion and deterrence" according to Witmer,[9] had their culmina-
tion in the institution known as the workhouse to which, by the
Act of 1723, all classes of paupers were condemned. Work-
houses were brutally massive studies in unpleasantness, deliberately made so by overcrowding, poor and insufficient food,
and general squalor.

As the inadequacies of this system of dealing with the poor
became apparent, there followed a period of using relief as a
means of supplementing inadequate wages on a sliding scale
which paid nothing to the able, employed workingman, and
increased with the incompetence or improvidence of the individual. It was bad psychology, and proved to be bad economics,
as it was accused of being bad religion. The history of English
Poor Relief from the *Report of the Royal Commission* in 1832
down to the *Reports of the Poor Law Commission* in 1909 is a
story of blind men attempting to march through quicksand.
They had no clear notion of where they were or where they
wanted to go; and every effort seemed only to sink the people
deeper into general impoverishment.

But other forces were at work. The Evangelical Revival had,
among other things, elaborated a theory of the stewardship of
wealth, in the famous dictum of John Wesley: "Make all you
can; save all you can; give all you can." Under this impulse,
the practice of private philanthropy began once again to make
its appearance, alongside the efforts of government and Church.
And by the time the Industrial Revolution had begun to work
its horrors of human exploitation in factory, mine and mill,

[8] W. J. Ashley, *An Introduction to English Economic History and Theory*
(New York: G. P. Putnam's Sons, 6th ed., 1910), Vol. II. n. 333.

[9] Witmer, *op cit.,* p. 133.

men like Lord Shaftesbury gave to this impulse of generosity a
new direction and intensity in demands for legislation to correct the grosser evils of economic slavery. Men began to talk
of democracy and to dream of building Jerusalem in England's
green and pleasant land. Humanitarian sentiments were nurtured.
The iron hold of the Poor Laws, with the "workhouse test," was
bound to break under these pressures. It broke at two points
during the nineteenth century.

One of the movements was expressed in an interest in making
the administration of government relief more humane, and
possibly supplanting government relief with private philanthropies. Somewhat more radical was the second development
of the nineteenth century, an inchoate and unco-ordinated con-
geries of humanitarian and reformist impulses generally aimed
at preventing poverty and utter destitution by strengthening
educational and medical institutions and improving the functioning of economic processes: agitation for factory legislation
and for old-age pensions, the beginning of free public schools,
the improvement of medical services, with various utopian or
radical schemes and ventures such as Robert Owen's Utopian
Socialism. None of these efforts pointed toward the Church as
the instrument to be used, and (with certain notable exceptions)
none of them drew heavily upon religious sentiments for support. The Church was being by-passed. Social work and social
reform began to replace government relief, just as the latter had
replaced ecclesiastical charity. Indiscriminate doles, the practice
of the medieval church, continued to be good church practice;
and countless helping-hand agencies continued to copy this
practice. Private charitable institutions continued to carry on
the tradition of the medieval "foundations." Private agencies
were created to hand out relief to supplement inadequate wages.
The workhouse, with its punitive purpose and deleterious effects
survived well into the twentieth century. Outdoor relief, soup
kitchens and bread lines, flophouses and rescue missions continued to operate. And poverty continued. Of charity there was
much; of *agape*, little or none. The displacement in vocabulary

had come to correspond to the displacement in fact. Charity had sunk to almsgiving.

New conceptions

Christian sentimentalists, reacting against this situation, indulged their emotions at the expense of their intellects, and launched the great series of "social uplift" movements, establishing a multitude of institutions and agencies best characterized by the sentimental, if militant, good intentions of the selfless Christians who labored in them, asking nothing in return.

Christian radicals, stirred by the seething unrest of the poor, launched the series of movements which began with the Christian Socialism of Frederick Dennison Maurice, Charles Kingsley and J. M. Ludlow, progressed through the Guild of St. Matthew and the Industrial Christian Fellowship in England and the Church League for Industrial Democracy and similar movements in America, to prosecute an educational campaign which, while it has partially leavened the great lump of the Church, has done little to affect the position of the poor or to modify the course of social welfare work.

Christian revolutionary thought has thrown itself into movements which have carried it even farther afield, and which lie beyond the scope of this chapter.

Beginning in the late nineteenth century, and carrying with increasing force through the first third of the twentieth, the social gospel gave a new slant to the whole development. Under its aegis, the task of religion came to be seen not as an ambulance service for the human wreckage of the existing economic and social order, but as the champion of the rights of the oppressed, the enemy of injustice. Philanthropy was seen to be the worst enemy of justice; paternalism was condemned as the worst enemy of brotherhood. Amos, with his demand that justice roll down as waters and righteousness as a mighty stream, became the major prophet of an emboldened religion. The kingdom of Heaven was to be realized here and now, through the consecrated and adventurous idealism of dedicated and enterprising men and women. All forms of amelioration were looked at askance: these were designing substitutes for necessary basic reform. If essentially ethical adjustments could be made in the basic pattern of economic and political life, "charity" would be a thing of the past, unknown because it had become unnecessary. The theological student who prepared himself to promote this gospel commonly felt that he would be ejected from at least two or three pulpits for steadfastly proclaiming the Truth of religious revolution—and not infrequently his feeling became father to the fact.

Within the Church there were three great groups who opposed the social gospel: (1) those who believed that the kingdom is not of this world and that the duty of the Christian is to watch and pray and prepare himself for the coming of a kingdom which is not brought in through human effort or participation; (2) those who believed that voluntary poverty, as a precondition to the exercise of Christian generosity, was a necessary part of a world in which Christian virtues were to find expression; and (3) a great group of the solid middle-class membership and their ministry who had a stake in the established order, and a great tradition of genuine piety to support their position.[10] All three of these groups agreed in believing that the "Philanthropy of God"[11] was neither social welfare work nor social reform, certainly not social revolution. They believed in charity as almsgiving, not as *agape*.

2. ORGANIZED SOCIAL WORK

With the Church divided within itself as to what expression ought properly to be given to the impulses of Christian affection and brotherly love, secular movements, and movements with religious impulses under secular auspices, have moved into the field of social welfare and social work. In so doing they have

[10] See R. H. Tawney, *Religion and the Rise of Capitalism* (New York: Harcourt, Brace and Company, Inc., 1926), especially ch. iv.

[11] Titus 3:4.

largely taken over an area of service which, a millennium ago, was pre-empted by the institutions of religion and copied by such men of means as were able.

Early beginnings

The beginnings of modern social work are seen in the London Charity Organization Society, established in 1869 on a pattern which had been advocated by a Scotsman, the Reverend Thomas Chalmers, demonstrated effectively in his own parish, but unaccepted outside his bailiwick. Its general ideas were of two kinds: (1) that all relief was to be orderly and businesslike, with the eliminating of indiscriminate charity, the investigating of all applicants to determine their need, the co-operating of all agencies to prevent an applicant from milking several at one time, and no more supplementing of public charity by private agencies, thus fixing the responsibility for the client and fixing the client's responsibility as well; and (2) that one of the purposes of social work should be that of re-establishing the applicant as a self-supporting breadwinner, through job placement, medical aid where necessary, education of children, and other forms of personal and family counseling and aid. But the Charity Organization Society in rightfully stressing the need for rehabilitation tended to lose sight of the place of necessary relief. Seeking to avoid the evils of dependence upon charity, it failed to win the support of relief authorities and philanthropic agencies whose sole reason for being lay in providing relief. Whether it is putting the matter too strongly to suggest that the administrators of relief had a vested interest in the continuance of their philanthropies, must be judged by those who will take the trouble to look at the facts which we do not here have space to present or discuss. It is at least an open question.

In any case, the Charity Organization Society planted a seed which was to germinate and eventually bring forth a forest of growth. The basic ideas back of the C.O.S. are the foundations of present-day social work and social case work. The individualization of service, the elimination of overlapping of agencies and clients, the combination of necessary relief and constructive rehabilitation—these are values which have been fruitful not merely in poor relief but in other fields of social work.

The present situation

For our purposes in this chapter, there is no need to trace the development and growth of the social work and social service agencies and institutions. They have gone through a period in which the bright star of economic determinism suddenly ascended to fascinate their bewildered gaze. Recovering from that, they have gone off on a tangent suggested by the first, feverish, partial assimilation of psychology and psychiatry. They are now recovering their balance and beginning to see that they do not stand as embattled and embittered champions of the rights of the proletariat nor *in loco parentis* to society's stepchildren. They are increasingly acquiring the conviction that their job, as distinct from the helping-hand agencies on the one hand and the revolutionaries on the other (both of whom may have, in their own turns, legitimate functions to perform), is to help people to help themselves. In so far as this means an attempt to help the individual or the family to "adjust" to conditions as they are, social work tends to take on a conservative character which, in its net effect, is not altogether different from the bread and circuses of ancient Rome. In so far as it means the integrating of disorganized personalities and families so that full release of latent strengths is obtained, without necessarily adapting the client so completely to the iniquities and inequities of his situation that he ceases to rebel against what is essentially immoral, it is not altogether unlike the social gospel expression of Christianity. This same line of analysis applies *mutatis mutandis* to other areas of social welfare work; and we shall return to it at the conclusion of our review.

The list of social service and social welfare and social work agencies is fart oo long to be given even in outline here. We can, however, suggest something of the scope of these institutions and agencies by citing various types. The social work agencies may be illustrated by the public and private agencies concerned with individual welfare: the private agencies usually concerned with a particular category of persons such as the orphans of sailors lost at sea or the residents of a particular city slum, the victims of a particular disease such as leprosy or infantile paralysis or tuberculosis, or the members of a disadvantaged racial group; the public agencies tending to be less specialized, but to deal principally with the financial aspects of clients and to care for dependent or neglected children. Attached to many welfare institutions, such as hospitals, schools and recreational programs, are auxiliary social case work activities, calculated to meet the special needs of persons who might otherwise become increasingly maladjusted and ineffective members of society. Some agencies make wide use of volunteer and semiprofessional services, while others have exacting professional standards for all staff members.

The tremendous spread of social welfare, social service and social work agencies may be suggested by a random listing: settlement houses; international institutes; group work agencies such as the Boy and Girl Scouts, the Hi-Y Clubs; low-cost residential centers for youths, indigents and transients; clinics; public health services; visiting nurses associations; camps and other recreational organizations; employment offices and vocational guidance bureaus; public housing administrations; vocational rehabilitation bureaus; workshops for the physically and mentally handicapped; day nurseries; homes for the aged, the blind, dependent children, the chronically ill; correctional institutions of many kinds. Many of these agencies are under church auspices or enjoy church support; some are adjuncts of particular local churches; by far the greater proportion are at least nonsectarian in character, and most are free of any suspicion of religious affiliation.

Organized social work is, in our day, one of the careers bidding for the most competent and idealistically inclined young college graduates. For persons who are interested in working with people and helping to meet human need, the variety of activities and interests provided in the field of social work appear enticing. Whether it be physical or mental illness, unemployment, death, desertion, emotional instability, financial reverses, or almost any other precipitant of difficulty, the social worker is called on to help, in much the same fashion that the parish minister was once appealed to. And preventive social work, in recreational, vocational and avocational training and supervision, as well as in a number of allied fields, is increasingly being recognized as a legitimate field of operation for social workers.

Schools of social work have been organized in all parts of the country to train professional persons to fill these jobs. The standards are comparable to those for entering law, medicine, teaching, nursing or the ministry. There are thirty-nine such schools on the accredited list of members in the American Association of Schools of Social Work.[12] There are several specialized associations: of social workers, of medical social workers, of psychiatric social workers, of church social workers, and for the study of group work. The salaries paid compare favorably with those paid in the ministry, ranging from $1500 to $2500 for workers in the lower brackets to $2400 to $5000 a year for the better trained and abler persons in executive and supervisory positions. There are upwards of twelve thousand persons now holding membership cards in the American Association of Social Workers.

3. PHILANTHROPIC FOUNDATIONS

Another important development in the general field of work once pre-empted by ecclesiastical charities is the foundation or fund. The exact number of such organizations now in existence is not ascertainable; but it is somewhere in the neighborhood

[12] As of March, 1942.

of fourteen hundred, according to the best estimates.[13] In recent years, there has been a marked increase in the number of "family foundations," which usually bear the name of the donor and whose trustees include members of the donor's family. Many of these serve as a reservoir into which the donor may annually put the whole percentage of his income for which he is allowed tax exemption by the government for charitable contributions, thus permitting more leisurely and more careful donation, and incidentally exempting the subsequent security transactions of the endowment from taxation. There has also been a great increase in the number of "industrial foundations," established by an industry, by a company, or by groups of companies or groups of industries. Many of these have philanthropic purposes, concerned with the welfare of employees and their families, with the provision of scholarships and educational grants-in-aid for study in fields closely allied to the industry, or with the welfare of the community in which the industry operates. The function of taxation laws in encouraging these foundations is also apparent.

Thirty-four of these foundations have capital assets in excess of five million dollars each; and together these thirty-four make up more than 85 per cent of the total assets of the one hundred and sixty-two foundations covered in the Rich study. Total annual disbursements for the foundations listed run in excess of fifty million dollars, with the capital assets exceeding a billion.

Whether the donors and trustees of these foundations wish it or not (and not all of them are frankly committed to an announced social policy), the policy decisions of foundations have a tremendous effect upon the policies and activities of hopeful votaries. Their effect upon educational institutions, medical facilities and programs, and many other fields of

[13] Raymond Rich Associates, for example, report in *American Foundations and Their Fields*, *Vol. V.* (1942) that they had on file more than thirteen hundred foundations and funds, of which 314 were included in their study.

organizational and institutional activity is incalculable, although the officers of not a few foundations openly bemoan the alleged lack of tangible movement in directions which they desire. These foundations have made giving, on a large scale, into a science, and transformed philanthropy into a billion dollar business which is one of the forces with which religion must increasingly reckon. The day of vast fortunes accumulated by the captains of industry may be past (or in eclipse), but the foundation no longer depends on individual fortunes. It feeds on corporate income directly. For the foreseeable future in the American scene, the foundation is one of the most important determiners of the policies and programs of social service and social work agencies at all levels and in most areas of endeavor.

If now the scope of our recording be expanded to include not only the foundations and funds established for philanthropic purposes, but also the educational institutions (other than tax supported), hospitals, and other eleemosynary institutions supported by endowments, we reach the staggering total of more than twenty billions of dollars.[14] Philanthropy, if considered only as an industry, ranks fourth among all American industries in the size of its investment. Only agriculture, railroads and public utilities, with forty, thirty-one and twenty-eight billion respectively, outrank private philanthropy in the size of the capital investment. This sum is nearly twice the total amount on deposit in all the savings banks and mutual savings banks of the nation. At 3 per cent interest, the income on these funds of private philanthropy is one hundred and fifty million dollars. The United Stewardship Council estimates that the best year for twenty-two principal American Protestant denominations showed a total income for these denominations combined at five hundred and six million dollars, a little over three times as much as private philanthropy's annual income from its own funds. But if the donations of individuals to these same private philanthropies be added to the income from their endowments,

[14] *Yearbook of Philanthropy*, 1940, by John Price Jones (New York: The Inter-River Press, 1940), p. 3.

the average annual expendable funds of private philanthropy in America over a seventeen-year period which included both prosperity and depression reaches one billion six hundred million, or more than three times as much as the twenty-two leading denominations reported in their best year on record.[15]

In assessing the organized forces in American life which cooperate or compete with organized religion, organized philanthropy must be given an important place on the list, if for no other reason than the magnitude of its operations. The further reason that the field and function of philanthropy is one which once belonged almost exclusively to the Church, obligates both philanthropy and religion to examine the record and see what has happened to religious purposes as *philanthropia* (lamely translated "lovingkindness") has become Philanthropy.

4. AGENCIES TO SERVE AGENCIES

The growing complexity of the whole field of philanthropic endeavor is evidenced by the fact that there are now in existence agencies whose sole or primary purpose is to render service to other social service agencies. They are principally known as community chests or councils of social agencies.

The original purpose of the community chest was to eliminate a multiplicity of competing drives for funds which were necessitated when each separate agency solicited in its own behalf. The united drive undoubtedly reached a much broader base of support in the citizenry than did the former separate drives. It also made it possible for the individual donor to settle the community's claims against his conscience (and pocketbook) at a somewhat lower figure than he might otherwise have done—a fact which has led some commentators to observe that the community chest is a polite form of blackmail in which some wealthy donors pay a smaller sum to be rid of the repetitive nuisance of giving a larger total to a series of appeals; while others probably pay more, under the pitiless glare of publicity.

[15] Based on Jones, *op. cit.*, pp. 13 and 16.

Every American city of five hundred thousand or more has a community chest or a council of social agencies; and most of the cities of one hundred thousand have such an agency. There is a noticeable tendency for the organizational movement to spread into the smaller population centers, and even into rural areas. In addition to correlating the fund-raising activities of the several social welfare and social service agencies in the community, these chests and councils also function in the area of social welfare planning, which entails considerable research and evaluation. This evaluation usually covers not only the work and performance of existing agencies which are members of the chest or council, but also extends to agencies which are hopefully anticipating getting "on the chest," or which are brought into purview as proposals for new work. There appears, however, to be very little broad-gaged, overall planning and programming of social services by these chests and councils, in terms of basic social planning: most of them appear to be concerned with gaining the co-operation of existing agencies in a program which, by compromise of the interested agencies, is accepted from year to year.

Nevertheless, the agency-serving agencies wield an influence which, to the individual member agency, or to the local churchman and minister, is formidable. They serve to establish standards of performance for adequacy and competence in the field in which each agency operates. Unpopular causes, or agencies somewhat off the accepted highways of respectability (concerned with interracial fellowship or not subscribing to economic orthodoxy, for example), are sometimes given budgetary cuts to encourage them to return to the community norms. Rivalries between various branches of Christendom have been known to influence apportionment of community chest funds. And the institutional church which tries to maintain its own social services without benefit of chest support often feels disadvantaged by its more opulent competitors.

Whether the standards set by councils and chests, or the pressures directly and indirectly exercised, are correlated with or in contravention of the intentions and purposes of religion is a question which can best be answered specifically in each instance, although some general comments will be in order at the conclusion of this chapter. Not infrequently it is charged by church-affiliated agencies that the standards are discriminatory with reference to them; and not infrequently it is replied that the churches have for too long permitted good intentions to be a substitute for adequate preparation and professional performance in social welfare work.

5. THE SOCIAL SERVICE STATE

However short our list might be, we could not omit mention of the Social Service State, the newest and most robust of the agencies of philanthropic purpose. With the Federal government moving aggressively into the field of old-age pensions and unemployment insurance, operating employment agencies, subsidizing day nurseries and school lunch programs, and operating administrative units such as the Tennessee Valley Authority, the thinking and programming of Christian charity and philanthropy will inevitably be reoriented. If federal public housing develops as a large-scale pattern of permanent peacetime policy, and if some form of socialized medicine and co-operative hospitalization be added to the already substantial governmental activities in the field of personal and family security, the *need* for private "charity" will be sharply curtailed. If the newer developments in the direction of a Social Service State continue, and if they are consolidated in fiscally sound practice, the net effect upon the status and psychology of American people generally will be profound. As the State takes over an important segment of individual and family life, removing it (at least partially) from the realm of insecurity, the scope of private charities is sharply restricted. Whatever prestige value and attracting power the Church has gained in these areas is quite certain to dwindle if the Social Service State becomes a full blown reality.

The great depression of the 1930's made the need of governmental aid so apparent that none of the private agencies, secular
or religious, raised an effective voice to protect its vested interests
in philanthropy. The fevered flush of wartime prosperity suddenly reversed the picture; and once again, the abnormal needs
of uprooted populations in industrial centers, seen in the light
of the war itself as a national government concern, served to
cushion the shock of the new governmental departures in their
impact upon the charitable inclinations of American Christianity.
In the immediate postwar years, the eyes of churchmen are turned
toward relieving the dire distress of Europe and Asia. The full
effects of the emergence of the Social Service State will be
realized only as the decades pass. It is a nice question whether
the Social Service State should be listed as "competing" with
the Church, or as merely superseding it in this entire area.

6. FALSEHOODS AND FAKERIES

We must also mention the fake philanthropies: activities
which masquerade as benevolent ventures, but which actually
exist for purposes quite different. Numerous lotteries, bingo
parties, horse races, ball games and similar activities are adver-
tised as "benefits." Some "worthy charity" (it may even be a
church!), usually an orphanage or a school for unfortunate
children or fresh air and milk for babies fund, is named as the
beneficiary of the proceeds of the scheme.

It is questionable whether sufficient protection against this
form of racketeering could be secured by requiring promoters
to publish full details of their financial take and the percentage
which finally dribbles through to the "worthy charity." In some
cases this has been known to be as little as 2 or 3 per cent of
the *net* proceeds. In other cases, it may be much better. At any
rate, the objection to publicity could come only from those who
have something to hide. The legitimate activities in this field
(and there appear to be some) ought to welcome the clear
light of public knowledge. They would then be included in our

list as those who ride the coattails of organized philanthropy; while the illegitimate operators would be exposed as the frauds they are: not competitors, not co-operators, but parasitic chameleons, using the protective coloration of respectable philanthropies to promote their gambling rackets.

Before leaving the point, it may also be added that full publicity as to the purposes and performance of all philanthropies, large and small, might do much to discourage that type of operator who uses weasel words to hide his real purposes. It might also expose the tarnished tinsel of not a few enterprises under ecclesiastical auspices. There are various levels of fakery and fraud. The less obvious and more subtle varieties lack the merit of robust racketeering. They are jackals in Santa Claus whiskers.

7.   RESISTANCE OR RESOURCE?

On the basis of this all too inadequate summary and review, what now can be said about the questions and accusations noted at the beginning of this chapter? Does organized social work compete with the Church, or is it a co-operating ally? Does organized philanthropy tend to replace the Church, or to complete its activities? Are philanthropy and social work properly to be thought of as extensions of religious interest and activity under secular auspices, or as enterprises which drain off the idealism and radical content of true religion to fritter it away on activities which, while they may be useful in reducing the crime rate or the death rate, may not necessarily elevate the spiritual level of the nation? And finally, is the cream of the financial interest and voluntary leadership and support of the American people being siphoned off into social work and philanthropy so that the Church is reduced to a skim milk diet?

These are questions which cannot be answered in generalities, but which must be answered with an exact assessment of each specific enterprise. All that can be done in this review is to suggest a few of the criteria by which judgments may be made, encouraging readers to revise and add to this listing as they make their own assessment. As this writer now sees it, religious concern would ask of each institution or agency of social service and welfare work, and of each person engaged in such work, a series of questions among which the following are important.

(1) *Questions having to do with progress of the client.* The primary test is the effect of the philanthropy, the social service or the agency, upon clients. Our test is pragmatic. By "client" we mean to indicate the individual or group or organization or institution served by the social worker or agency or foundation.

Religion is not alone in insisting on the pragmatic test; but there is no test which supplants it in religion's standards. "By their fruits ye shall know them. . . . Not everyone that saith, Lord, Lord; but he that doeth. . . ."

This test, however, is not a Procrustean bed on which every passing agency is to lie, and either lose its head or be stretched in every joint until it conforms. Religion's test is best stated in a series of antitheses, indicating opposing directions of movement, the undesirable and the desirable. The question to be asked is whether the client actually moves in desirable directions under the influence of the particular social worker or agency.

Some of these antitheses (others will suggest themselves to readers) are: (a) passiveness *versus* initiative; (b) imitativeness *versus* creativity; (c) dependence *versus* self-reliance; (d) independence *versus* interdependence; (e) selfishness *versus* mutualism. One important index which clearly distinguishes religious social work from nonreligious or antireligious social work is presented in the fourth and fifth antitheses in this list. Many a piece of otherwise acceptable social work will pass the first three tests with ease, but will fall short of the last two, thereby exhibiting a net resistance to religious purposes. Many naïve persons are perplexed when religion criticizes an apparently efficient and valuable piece of social work. "The work is 'good,'" they protest. "It makes 'better people'; it 'meets professional standards.' What more can religion ask?" Religion can ask that welfare work not only give the client increasing confidence in his own developing abilities to care for himself, but that this be matched (or surpassed) by an increasing confidence in his fellows and concern for the common welfare, and that both of these be climaxed in an increasing confidence in the moral order and in its Orderer. There is a great gulf between the sort of busy-ness which is concerned with running about and doing good to people, and that sort of creative labor which takes on the character of high religious purpose. The great danger is that what is merely helpful and good will be accepted as satisfactory, when what is needed is that which is radically revolutionary in its transforming character. It goes without saying that social service under the name and aegis of the institutions of religion must pass the tests which are also applied to work under secular auspices.

Wherever social work, welfare work or philanthropy, under whatever auspices, tends to answer our questions affirmatively, such work may rightly claim to be a resource for religion. Where the answer tends to be negative or equivocal, we are confronted with resistance.

(2) *Questions having to do with social policy.* Religion is concerned not merely with the Christian individual, but also with the Christian community. The series of antitheses suggested in the foregoing section are stated in terms of social values as they come to a focus in personal characteristics. Another dimension is added to our measuring process when we examine the social policy implicit or explicit in the work we are examining. Here, again, we state the matter in terms of more-or-less of a series of qualities, indicating opposite directions of movement: (a) totalitarian statism *versus* democratic freedoms; (b) rugged individualism *versus* a co-operative society; (c) materialism *versus* ethical values; (d) "charity" *versus* justice; (e) paternalism *versus* brotherhood; (f) secular ethic *versus* religious ethic. Here, again, as we go down the list, we discover the manner in which seemingly "good" pieces of welfare work fall short of the growth demanded by the standards of high religion. There

is little question raised by any socially minded person in the choice between that social policy which is concerned with getting a quart of milk daily to every child in the world and that social policy which is aimed at smug self-sufficiency. (Yet many philanthropic or welfare agencies would fail on this elementary test.) But when the question is pushed to a deeper level, and we inquire whether the milk of humankindness is also to be freely available to all, we introduce qualities of the spirit which sharply distinguish nonreligious from religious values.

(3) *Questions having to do with institutions.* It might be supposed that this third category is included in the materials suggested in the other two; but we have here in mind specific questions to be addressed not toward the work of the agency or agents as seen in the effects upon clients, nor toward the examination of the social policy implicit in their operations, but toward the actual (as distinguished from the stated) purposes of the institution or agency itself.

Using the same method of stating antithetical directions of movement, we ask the agencies of philanthropy, social work and social welfare in which direction they are facing on the following scales, and whether there is actual movement in the directions they are facing: (a) agency self-advertisement *versus* agency modesty; (b) jealous competition with other agencies for prestige, contributions or kudos *versus* effective performance in a co-operative team; (c) vested interest in continuance of the agency *versus* the effort to work itself out of a job.

When, for example, a minister objects that the scoutmaster takes his boys on Sunday hikes instead of bringing them to church, and the scoutmaster retorts that he is teaching the boys more religion than they would get in a formal service, does this reveal that the two agencies are working at cross purposes? And which is serving the purposes of religion? Or let the government initiate a comprehensive system of old-age pensions. Does this undercut the religious purposes of homes for the aged under

Church auspices? Or when agency *A* and agency *B*, both concerned with character building in service to youth, project competing and overlapping programs in the high schools of a city, are there sufficient differences in the qualities of the services offered (as measured by our standards) to justify the loss of energy and time and the waste of money occasioned by the competition and the friction? And is the residue of community ill will not to be considered in assessing the two programs? Or when a settlement house proudly advertises that it has maintained itself in the heart of one of the nation's worst slums for fifty years, is it exhibiting a decadent sense of values? Has it shown a vested interest in the continuance of the slum which, if removed, would put the settlement house out of business? Again, as the scale of operations of philanthropic and service agencies outstrips the magnitude of institutional religion, and as many able persons are diverted from the ministry of preaching to the ministry of service and of social engineering, is the Church justified in concluding that it is encountering resistance and competition? Or does this mean the discovery of resource?

None of these questions can be answered except in terms of specifics. And none of them can be answered except as the measures of institutional purpose include those here suggested.

Our listing is far from complete; but it is sufficiently long to indicate the sort of analysis which is necessary if we are to judge whether the enterprises under review in this chapter are to be catalogued as resistance or resource in religion's ledger. Wherever one finds movement in desirable directions, one is inclined to believe that the enterprise in question is of the essence of religious values—whether it appears to compete with the institutions of religion or not. Indeed, if the institutions of religion are found to be in competition with such agencies of society as are moving in desirable directions, it is fair to inquire whether these institutions of religion are religious in anything more than name. This brings us to the final question toward which this chapter has been leading.

8. THE REAL QUESTION

The answer to our most important question must be sought on a level deeper than this chapter has yet suggested. The real question before us is not whether social welfare agencies and institutions of philanthropy and social work compete with or co-operate with the Church. The real question is whether these agencies *or the Church*, separately or together, are serving the purposes of religion in contemporary life. The writer has a suspicion that some of the attention among churchmen which is now devoted to critical comments and condemnation of the activities of the so-called "secular" agencies which are "invading the province of the Church" might legitimately be directed toward the institutions of religion. If the Church had been doing a satisfactory job in binding up the wounds and setting the captives free, men would not have looked for another physician or welcomed another liberator. Nor given their money to these others in quantities which dwarf the resources of the institutions of religion. Perhaps organized social work and organized philanthropy are neither co-operators nor competitors with religion. Perhaps they are a challenge.

If much of organized philanthropic social work in our day does not proceed on the basis of religious assumptions, if it does not promote religious values, if it tends to become secularized and to operate with secular purposes and methods, whose fault is it? Can religion feed into these far-reaching social developments the essential stream of Christian personnel, to give religious direction and religious values to social work and philanthropy? If, under secular auspices, social service tends to become the moral equivalent of social reform, and social reform stands in the way of necessary revolution, what can the Church say about its own efforts of charity? Are theological seminaries ready to train men and women of religious purpose for desirable social service and social engineering? Is the Church able to break the confining bonds of its narrowed horizons, discard the outmoded notion of "charity," and recover the flaming purposes of *agape*?

It was the fourth century pagan Emperor, Julian the Apostate, who tried to revive the dying institutions of paganism by throwing over them the robe of Christian charity. Here are his words, addressed in earnest exhortation to the remnants of paganism:

> Let us consider that nothing has so much contributed to the progress of the superstition of Christians, as their charity to strangers. I think we ought to discharge this obligation ourselves. Establish hospitals in every place. For it would be a shame for us to abandon our poor, while the Jews have none, and the impious Galileans provide not only for their own poor, but for ours also.

Sixteen centuries later, the positions are approximately reversed. In 360, paganism pointed to Christianity as the exemplification of virtue. In 1946, the Church finds the secular agencies giving expression to many values for which it once labored. The result of this reversal of positions has been partly to infuse a Christian spirit into much secular work (as, indeed, most social service efforts historically root in the Christian heritage), and partly to dilute the peculiar quality of work remaining under church auspices, so that there tends to be very little difference in purpose between the better enterprises under secular auspices and the better pieces of social work supported and managed by religious groups. But, as we have seen, the *quantity* of work done under non-church auspices has by now so far outreached the quantity of work done by the churches themselves, that we begin to inquire whether it may not be that the Church has accepted a position which substantially reverses that noted by Julian the Apostate.

There is, of course, another side to the matter. We cannot overlook the way in which secular social work sometimes leads to moral and religious cynicism—a pattern hardly less objectionable to high religion than sentimental moral optimism. Here, again, generalizations are dangerous. All we can do is to comment in passing that where the social workers show a lack of affirmative religious insights, or are equivocal and hesitant in adherence to religious values, these lacks are evidenced when the series of tests are applied by men of religion. And, on the other hand, where the fruits of social work are in fact the fruits of the spirit, who shall say that the Spirit has not been at work? "Professionalizing" of the vocation of social work may be disastrous, just as it may be in the ministry or in teaching. But this is not to say that a high sense of vocation cannot carry one into the professions named, transforming them with ethical purpose to serve religious goals.

The real question, then, is one which must be answered both within the Church and within all phases of philanthropic social service, if either the Church or the secular agencies are to be measured by religious values. *What has become of the flaming purposes of* agape? Is it not true that Christians have largely lost sight of the consuming passion for human welfare which was at the heart of their religion? And may this not be, at least in part, due to the failure of the Church to proclaim or to practice the radical ethic of brotherly love?

Earlier in this chapter, we spoke somewhat critically of John Chrysostom. Let us give him his due. It is true that his emphasis on almsgiving as *the* expression of *agape* laid the groundwork for the degeneration of *agape* to charity and charity to almsgiving. But it is also true that, in his day, to preach almsgiving to a congregation of comparatively well-fed Christians was as offensive to his listeners as to preach social revolution to a contemporary congregation. Repeatedly and heavily, Chrysostom laid upon his listeners the radical demands of *agape* impelling them to almsgiving. When they grumbled, objected and remonstrated with him, he retorted that he would preach charity and never cease to preach it, that alms, alms, and more alms was the burden of his message. If his listeners too readily assumed that they were discharging the full obligations of *agape* by dispensing alms, that was only partly the fault of his preaching. He, at any rate, did not stand in awe of their wealth so that he hesitated to lay upon them the obligations of Christian brotherly affection for others. He preached radical *agape* to the wealthy in terms which demanded compliance.

But this is not commonly done in the modern church. Preaching of charity today is so commonplace a matter as to be boresome to churchgoers. Charity is an accepted part of even the common secular mores of our day. To press the claims of *agape* today means utterance and action equally radical with that of John Chrysostom's time, under circumstances demanding specifics which go much deeper. Aside from a dwindling remnant of the social gospelers, this is not done today. To do so would alienate parishioners and donors. Stained glass costs money. Vested choirs and adequate professional salaries for ministers do not get paid without contributions. To be unduly exercised over the demands of *agape* as something more than almsgiving is to run the risk of defection in the ranks and red ink in the ledger. After all, a man can give handsomely to some secular agency, without having his sensitivities bludgeoned. Therefore, reasons the cautious churchman, why should we run the risk of losing such support for our worthy church charities merely in order to increase the demands of the Christian ethic beyond the point of tolerance? And thus it comes about that the Church ceases to be able to comfort the afflicted because it is afraid to afflict the comfortable.

If, then, the Church is genuinely concerned whether philanthropy, social service and social work are properly to be called competing or co-operating agencies, the question returns: *competing or co-operating with what?* With an institution which is more solicitous of its own continuance than of the plight of mankind? Or with a courageous fellowship which knows that life is found only in being lost? Christian love is not "charity": it is a crusade. It is not almsgiving: it is revolution.

FURTHER READING

CARNEGIE, ANDREW. *The Gospel of Wealth.* New York: Doubleday, Doran & Company, Inc., 1933.

Buell G. Gallagher

COON, HORACE. *Money to Burn*. London and New York: Longmans, Green and Company, 1938.

DOUGLASS, H. PAUL, and BRUNNER EDMUND DE S. *The Protestant Church as a Social Institution*. New York: Harper & Brothers, 1935.

HART, HORNEL H. *The Spiritual Dynamics of Social Work*. New York: Russell Sage Foundation, 1916.

LINDEMANN, EDUARD C. *Wealth and Culture*. New York: Harcourt, Brace and Company, Inc., 1936.

NIEBUHR, REINHOLD. *The Contribution of Religion to Social Work*. New York: Columbia University Press, 1932.

6

THE CHURCH AND
ORGANIZED FRATERNALISM

Dwight C. Smith

*Introduction. 1. The facts of the case: the churches, the fraternal
organizations. Summary data. 2. Elements of resistance in
organized fraternalism: competition in finances and time,
substitute religion, secularization. 3. Elements of resource in
organized fraternalism: fellowship, service, world-wide interest,
accepted standards. 4. Conclusions.*

When the Nobel Prize Commission selected Sinclair Lewis to
receive the award in literature, it endorsed the assumption that
Mr. Lewis reflects the mood of middle-class America in his
stories of Zenith and other American small towns. So the world
takes it for granted that the average American citizen belongs
to at least one fraternal organization.

The resident of a large metropolitan city may not be convinced of this. In the great cities, the proportion of the population
actively interested in exclusive clubs and lodges may not seem
very impressive. But as one considers smaller communities, the
importance of fraternal organizations appears to be in inverse
ratio to the size of the city.

The same thing may be said about churches. An occasional
big-city church will exert notable influence upon its community;
but in general the Protestant churches of this country are relatively more influential in smaller towns. Indeed, the yearbook
records of almost any Protestant denomination will show not

only that the majority of congregations are in small towns, but that in aggregate membership they form the bulk of national church strength. Nor is this surprising. Despite the economic and political importance of the big cities, more than half of our national population is to be found in communities of ten thousand inhabitants or less. It is to be expected, therefore, that churches and fraternal organizations alike should thrive in the small-town environment.

There are further similarities between these two types of organization. By nature, fraternal groups are limited in size. So, in fact, are the churches. They seldom exceed a membership of a few hundred. Except at Easter, and perhaps Mothers' Day and Christmas, the ordinary Protestant congregation does not greatly exceed three hundred.

There are also comparable limitations in type of members. In fraternal groups one does not expect to find significant variations in type. In the case of the churches, however, it might be supposed that the only limitation would be in terms of religious convictions and attitudes. But where church membership is determined by voluntary choice rather than by geographical parish divisions, there develops a definite trend towards a common level in economic, cultural and social standards. This social stratification in churches is not commonly a matter of intentional policy, but it is a phenomenon easy to observe, and it is almost universal among Protestant churches, to which members are drawn by personal inclination rather than by geographical location.

In view of these external resemblances, it should not surprise us to find that churches and fraternal groups tend to enlist their members from the same community groups. How much duplication of membership there may be is not easy to discover, but it is certainly common. Overlapping will not often occur between churches. One selects a particular church to join. But fraternal membership is not restricted in this manner. And membership in a church is so seldom regarded as incompatible with fraternal membership that the typical "joiner" usually claims church affiliation as well as membership in perhaps half a dozen clubs and lodges.

This overlapping develops tensions not so much in the claiming of identical names on membership rolls as in demands made upon the time, the interest, the resources and the loyalty of members. Furthermore, this tension is not always a detriment to the groups concerned. It is possible for a member to contribute to the life of one organization some of the ideas, experiences and training in techniques which he learns from another. Whether this happens frequently or not, the very possibility indicates that the Church may find resource as well as resistance in the experience of rubbing shoulders with organized fraternalism.

1. THE FACTS OF THE CASE

An indication of the extent to which this close contact exists in the ordinary community may be seen in the results of an informal survey of a specific community. The 1940 census credits this city with less than fifteen thousand inhabitants. The population of the residential community, including suburban developments, is now approximately twenty thousand. The city has nineteen congregations which are neither Roman Catholic nor Jewish. There is also one Roman Catholic parish and one Jewish congregation.

Without attempting strict scientific accuracy, an inquiry was made as to the approximate membership and total budget of each congregation. Similar information was sought from the fraternal organizations. Such information makes it possible to compare the numerical strength and also the relative financial evaluation placed upon these respective groups by their own constituents. The interpretation of these facts and figures may be subject to various qualifications, but they should offer a certain rough-and-ready basis for comparison.

Facts and figures about the Churches

NAMES OF CONGREGATIONS

Assembly of God (Pentecostal)
Baptist
Christian and Missionary Alliance
†Christian Scientist
†Church of God
Church of the Brethren
Church of the Nazarene
Disciples of Christ
†Foursquare Gospel
Free Methodist
†Jewish
†Latter-day Saints
Lutheran (Augustana Synod)
Lutheran (Missouri Synod)
Methodist
Protestant Episcopal
Roman Catholic
Seventh-Day Adventist
United Churches (a federation of Congregational and Presbyterian)
United Presbyterian
†Unity Truth Center

† *Indicates congregations from which information was not obtained.*

In most instances, the person able to give information was not available when the inquiry was made. One church alone refused information, citing a rule against doing so.

CHURCH MEMBERSHIP

Total for 15 congregations reported................6,350
Estimate for remaining 6 congregations.............. 650
    Estimated total church membership 7,000
Estimated number of non-member adherents (including Sunday-school children) 3,000
    Estimated total church constituency 10,000
Proportion of church constituency to total population.. 50%

CHURCH FINANCE

Total budgets reported........................$172,250.00
Estimated budgets for churches not reported.... 27,750.00
    Estimated total church budgets...........$200,000.00

Average contribution per member in churches reported....$27.12
Average per individual entire church constituency.......... 20.00
Average per Protestant member reported.................. 33.60
Average per member 5 largest Protestant churches........ 21.61
Average per member 9 other Protestant churches reported.. 43.57

Two possible reasons account for the smaller per capita giving of the larger churches, which represent the larger denominations:

(1) Members may take their church obligations less seriously.

(2) They may acknowledge more outside interests as having legitimate claims upon them.

Facts and figures about fraternal organizations

This study includes all lodges and clubs which seem either to compete with the Church in program and activity, or to conflict in the effort to claim time, interest and loyalty. A complete list is almost impossible to achieve. Certain organizations should obviously be included. Others may be discovered by careful inquiry. There being no accurate listing available for these organizations, there are undoubtedly omissions in this survey. Organizations reported upon are listed under five general headings.

(1) FRATERNAL LODGES

Lodges for Men Only

Free and Accepted Masons (2 lodges)
Scottish Rite Masons (4 lodges)
†York Rite Masons (4 lodges)
Nobles of the Mystic Shrine
†DeMolay (Junior Masons)
Benevolent & Protective Order of Elks
Fraternal Order of Eagles
Loyal Order of Moose
Independent Order of Odd Fellows
†Junior Odd Fellows (boys)
Knights of Pythias
†Princes of Syracuse (Pythian boys)

Lodges Partially or Entirely for Women

Order of Eastern Star (2)
White Star of Jerusalem
†Order of Amaranth

Order of Rainbow (girls)

†Women's Auxiliary of Eagles
Women of Moose
Rebeccas

†Theta Rho (Girls of I.O.O.F.)
Pythian Sisters

† *Indicates lodges from which information was not obtained.*

Knights of Columbus   †Catholic Daughters of America
†Columbian Esquires (K. of C.
  boys)

Lodge Membership

Total membership of 20 lodges reported.................5,356
Estimated membership of remaining 12 lodges 1,000
                                                        ———
    Total estimated lodge membership....................6,356

Lodge Finances

Total dues in lodges reported......................$44,442.00
Average dues per member...........................   8.29

Lodge members also pay initiation fees.

Two lodges, (Elks and Eagles), having 41 per cent of the
total membership reported for 20 lodges, maintain club houses
as well as lodge halls. The major cost of upkeep for these
clubs is met by profits from liquor sales and the operation of
slot machines, both forms of activity being publicly forbidden
under State law, but permitted in private clubs. It is impossible
to tell the proportion of members who contribute to club costs
in this indirect fashion. Some members abstain entirely; others
plainly look upon these features as the primary attraction in
their clubs. The total amount of money involved is so large that
the clubs could not operate on the present basis without this
revenue.

(2) SERVICE CLUBS

Men's Clubs

†Active

Kiwanis
Lions
Rotary
Young Men's Business Club
Y's Men's Club (Y.M.C.A. spon-
  sored)

Women's Clubs

†Business and Professional
  Women
Kiwanis Ladies
Soroptomists
Venture Club
Zonta

† *Indicates clubs from which information was not obtainable.*

SERVICE CLUB MEMBERSHIP

Total membership of 5 Men's clubs reported...............378
Total membership of 4 Women's clubs reported.............173
Estimated membership of remaining 2 clubs................ 50

Total estimated Service Club membership.............601

SERVICE CLUB FINANCES

Total dues in clubs reported.........................$7,078.00
Average dues per member............................ 12.84

Service club members also pay initiation fees.

Men's Service Clubs add to their revenue by charging fines for various trivial offenses. This is done in the spirit of fun, and constitutes a social as well as a financial practice.

Service Clubs meet at mealtime, and members therefore have an additional expense for meals. It is proverbial that members always complain about both the quality and the price of the food they are served.

(3) VETERANS' CLUBS AND AUXILIARIES

American Legion
Disabled American Veterans
Veterans of Foreign Wars
†United Spanish-American War
  Veterans
†Grand Army of the Republic

American Legion Auxiliary
Army Mothers' Club
†Navy Mothers' Club
†Spanish-American War Veterans'
  Auxiliary
†G.A.R. Auxiliary

† *Indicates organizations from which information was not obtainable.*

VETERANS' CLUB MEMBERSHIP

Total membership for 5 organizations reported.............1,673
Estimated membership of remaining 5 organizations........ 100

Total estimated veteran organization membership......1,773

VETERANS' CLUB FINANCES

Total dues in organizations reported...................$5,281.00
Average dues per member............................ 3.10

(4) WOMEN'S CLUBS

American Association of University Women

Daughters of the American Revolution

P.E.O. (2 chapters)

Women's Club

Junior Women's Club

No attempt was made to include Bridge Clubs or other purely social groups.

WOMEN'S CLUB MEMBERSHIP

Total membership reported.................................368

WOMEN'S CLUB FINANCES

Total dues.. $1,168.00
Average dues per member............................   4.53

(5) COUNTRY CLUB AND YACHT CLUB

CLUB MEMBERSHIP

Total membership reported.............................650

A Women's Auxiliary and a Junior Yacht Club are also being organized.

CLUB FINANCES

Total dues... $10,190.00
Average dues per member............................   15.68

Initiation fees are charged by both clubs.

There are also incidental fees and charges for various activities. The Country Club raises a considerable amount of maintenance costs from revenue on slot machines. Participation in either of these clubs obviously requires initial outlay for the appropriate equipment. One may then maintain membership without paying anything more than regular dues, but active participation in club events requires additional payments according to what one chooses to do.

Summary comments

Total number of organizations listed.................   61
Total estimated membership of all fraternal groups..... 9,748
Total dues of 42 organizations reported............... $68,059.00
Average annual dues per member reported............. $ 7.72

There is a considerable amount of overlapping membership. The gross total estimate of membership corresponds closely to the total estimated church constituency. The actual number of individuals involved is probably more nearly the 4,850 membership claimed by the fourteen Protestant congregations reported above. If this approximate figure is right, the average per capita expenditure for dues is $14.03. If, as is possible, the number of individuals is less, then the average payment is larger. To this figure, whatever it is, must be added the average initiation fee as well as those various direct and indirect payments mentioned above.

While these figures are only approximate, they offer substantial support to the assertion that in the small-town environment in which their greatest strength lies, churches and fraternal groups are strikingly similar in numerical strength and also in their financial claims upon their respective constituencies. The total amount of overlapping membership is difficult if not impossible to determine. Anyone who is familiar with local situations knows, however, that a very large percentage of church people have at least some fraternal relationships as well as their church connections.

2. ELEMENTS OF RESISTANCE IN ORGANIZED FRATERNALISM

Financial competition

This being the area of competition for which statistical evidence is most easily secured, it may seem the most obvious, although it is probably the least important. Figures already cited suggest that the average contributions of church adherents and fraternal group members are about equal. Presumably, many individuals belong in both categories. Still, this does not prove that if it were not for the fraternal organizations each of these individuals would contribute that much more to the church. It may fairly be assumed that each church adherent gives to his church the amount of financial support which he believes its program deserves from him in his particular circumstances. If this is not flattering to the church, the challenge is not so much to the fraternal groups to modify their zeal as to the church to make its appeal more convincing.

Fraternalism has an initial advantage in the fact that its financial demands are clear and unequivocal. Payment of minimum dues is a basic requirement for membership. By contrast, the church often seems not to know its own mind. In a society accustomed to the price mark as a criterion of value, this raises the question of what estimate of worth the church sets upon itself. There are certain notable exceptions. Some churches have definite rules in regard to tithing, and leave no room for doubt in this respect. Most churches, however, refer to tithing as an ideal without establishing rules about it. On principle they oppose the practice of compulsion, believing that a trained conscience is a better incentive than an inflexible rule. This reliance upon a developed sense of moral obligation may offer greater values for the training of character, but it also requires education and habit training in stewardship if it is to be effective for the needs of the Church or the growth of Christian character.

The competition offered by fraternalism in the financial field is, then, not so much a resistance as a challenge to the Church. It may even turn out to be a resource. The Church, undertaking to set a higher estimate of worth for its program, may use the fact that fraternal organizations expect a specific amount of support from their members without any question.

Competition for time

Every minister of a small-town church knows that overlapping memberships in fraternal organizations and churches create problems in the working out of activity schedules. If a large number of church workers are active lodge members, for instance, it is folly to plan church functions on lodge night. Throughout the week, the same rule holds in regard to other organizations as well.

Sometimes it may seem as though a large proportion of

church people are willing to put any other appointment ahead of the claims of the church. Yet the case is seldom so extreme as this. Church members may acknowledge obligations from other commitments without being disloyal to the church. The simple fact is that we no longer live in a time when the church is the one center of social life. This fact may, indeed, offer genuine resource to the deepest purposes of the church. Membership in fraternal groups, cutting across denominational lines, offers experienecs in fellowship and co-operation which can be a definite asset in building the mood of mutual understanding on which the ecumenical program depends.

The problem of getting members to give time adequate for carrying on a full program is not peculiar to the church. Any lodge officer will admit that the maintaining of attendance is always a problem. Service clubs are the only fraternal organizations that usually show a good average on this score. Nor is this an accident. In the average service club the most consistently hard-working group is the attendance committee. Members who let their attendance lag are interviewed to give reasons. Those unable or unwilling to improve are invited to drop out so that their classifications may be filled by applicants who will participate more actively. It may be that the average club meeting scarcely warrants such persistent effort. But each member is made to feel that his active interest is essential to the health of the club. Because he feels that it makes a difference whether he attends, he arrives at the meeting with a mood of expectancy and interest which contributes to the group morale. The way in which this affects the church is indirect. The man who knows he will find most of his fellow club members at their meeting, looks about him at church and may be pardoned if he wonders what has become of the men whose names are on the membership roll.

It is interesting to speculate on what might happen if this same technique were used by churches. If members were bluntly asked to give evidence of interest or else drop out, would the result be a permanent reduction in membership? Or would the list of really active members grow, once the initial losses had been sustained? Even if not carried to such extremes, this pressing of responsibility to support the church with active participation might be undertaken in a tactful way by an attendance committee, with positive results.

As a matter of fact, this question of attendance at church services is of more significance to the Church than just a question of numbers might suggest. Perhaps some congregations are so over-organized that unfair demands are made upon the faithful few, throughout the week. But any church must believe that attendance at its services of public worship is important. Corporate worship is not just a social gathering. It is an appointment not only with one's fellow worshipers but with God. This is why the Church exists. Attendance at worship is, therefore, a matter of incalculable value to its members, and not a thing to be left to casual convenience or whim. The Roman Catholic Church, with its well developed system of authority, leaves no room for doubt as to what not only is expected but demanded of those who would be in good standing. Protestant churches, avoiding such compulsion on principle, run the risk of seeming to have no convictions on the subject. Some members, therefore, regard attendance at worship as an issue of secondary importance. If current pledges to the church budget are paid, they feel little personal responsibility to keep up regular attendance. So they give haphazard personal support to the church, in contrast to their faithful attendance at fraternal groups which seem to have more sharply defined policy in this matter.

Most fraternal groups are not in active conflict with the church at the hour of public worship. The country club type of organizations, with more or less elaborate Sunday schedules, are the outstanding exceptions; others only occasionally arrange functions on Sunday, with scant regard for any church programs. The real competition occurs during the week. Then the church is thrown into the arena in a free-for-all contest. If it hopes to hold the loyal interest of its members, it must contrive to justify its claims upon them. Some communities seek to bring order out of this chaos by a common agreement that certain afternoons during the month shall be kept free for meetings of church women, with one evening a week recognized as church night. A church thus situated is well advised to show its good faith by co-operating with such a plan. For there is a valuable resource in this tacit assumption that church people should support the programs of their respective churches on the designated days.

Fundamentally, this question of giving time to church affairs is a matter of accepted attitudes. If the program of the church is regarded as just one more addition to community social life, the evaluation of the church which this implies may be a positive resistance to its genuine purpose. If the inherent difference between the meaning of the church and the fraternal groups is not recognized, it may be because the church does not demonstrate that difference. Yet such failure to discriminate is usually due in at least some measure to the secular mood fostered by fraternalism. This point is so important that we shall discuss it in greater detail later.

Substitute religion

Fraternal lodges in particular offer what is often accepted as a substitute for the Church in religious terms. Lodge ritual, which one may hear at funerals or other occasions, is full of Biblical or pseudo-Biblical language. Various circumlocutions, such as referring to God as "The Great Grand Master," or to heaven as "The Great Lodge on High," seem to infer that the routine of lodge activities is somehow the equivalent of membership in a divinely appointed society. An occasional lodge member will insist that he finds all the religion he needs in his lodge. Even church members will sometimes indicate that the spiritual aims of their lodges seem to be fundamentally as religious as anything the church has to offer. Granting that one should not belittle the honest religious feelings of any person, it may still be pointed out that there is a basic difference between a vaguely religious attitude and that which is specifically and avowedly Christian.

The resistance offered by fraternalism to the Church by means of quasi religion appears, for one thing, in the reckless use of language normally reserved for religious devotion. The ponderous, over-flowery wording of lodge ritual may strike the nonmember as being only amusing. Consider the titles assumed by lodge members without even a self-conscious blush! When a person of merely average capacity, spiritual or otherwise, is called Worshipful Grand Master, or some equivalent title, one may well ask what has happened to the meaning of language. It is an elementary fact in economics that debased currency tends to destroy the value of that which is good. The inflationary spiral may also be observed in speech. Superlatives used without regard for relative values make it impossible to give adequate expression to genuine feelings. So, by devaluating the language of religious devotion, fraternalism impairs the proper understanding of truly religious expression.

Again, fraternalism offers a synthetic product in place of genuine religious experience. With empty superlatives and meaningless terms of reverence and devotion, it imparts a vaguely religious inference to esoteric symbolism which has little or no intrinsic worth. One is reminded of the lady who felt so very religious whenever she heard that blessed word *Mesopotamia.* Anyone with college fraternity experience will understand the frank lodge member who confesses that he cannot remember the secrets which he learned under the most binding and sacred oaths. Indeed, there is no reason why he should remember them. The association of secrecy with religious implications is very old. The Orders of Knighthood in the days of chivalry, the fugitive secrecy of the catacombs, the secret rites of the mystery cults, the secret Orders of King Solomon (if they ever existed)—all have their psychological roots in the initiation ceremonies of primitive tribes through which the youth enters the sacred brotherhood of the tribal elders. Such vestigial remnants have no useful meaning in modern life. When otherwise mature individuals dress up in the gaudy tatters of a historic memory from which all real content has vanished, it may seem harmless make-believe, however silly. But the person who is satisfied with such quasi-religious mummery thereby rules out the possibility of comprehending the tremendous, transforming, revolutionary significance of the real gospel of Jesus Christ.

Competition through secularization

Fraternalism offers most serious resistance to the Church by giving the momentum of common consent to an easy acceptance of a secular attitude towards life in general and the Church in particular.

When fraternal organizations treat the Church as just another social organization, on a par with themselves, it is with no intention of either injury or insult. Yet this assumption does injury by helping to cut the nerve of church loyalty, particularly in the case of members whose understanding of the Church is somewhat confused at best. As for the insult, that is so unintentional that it seems almost churlish to mention it. Note what happens when a lodge or service club decides to do Brother So-and-So the honor of attending his church as a group. Sometimes the plan falls through and, even if a handful come, the conspicuous absence of the majority of the group is so eloquent as to be almost deafening. Perhaps all goes well, and the majority attend as agreed. The regular congregation is then aware of the fact that something unusual has transpired to tear these visitors away from the activities which ordinarily absorb their attention on Sunday. In either case the baffled minister is acutely conscious that the moral support given to his church by his fraternal brothers is usually expressed *in absentia*. Like the prosperous family who wish their impecunious relations well, but would rather not be bothered, the fraternal groups mean no offense. They simply offer unconscious evidence of the secular view which regards religion as essentially irrelevant to normal, healthy life.

More directly, fraternalism resists the purpose of the Church through a matter-of-fact acceptance of standards which the

Church generally seeks to discourage. The clubs which actually sponsor liquor sales and gambling devices as sources of revenue are an obvious obstruction to the Church in its effort to raise social standards. Even those which do not engage in such business usually assume that these are normal, legitimate activities, though the Church is expected to regard them as at least socially harmful if not worse. It may truthfully be protested that such silent assent merely reflects the common attitude of our time, and that there are some churches which give even more direct approval in their own practices. Still it is a fact that such standards are crudely secular, and that the general weight of fraternal opinion gives them at least tacit approval.

Fraternalism further hampers the aim of the Church by encouraging a smug sense of self-satisfaction. The ideal of service, which is highly important in the Christian view of life, is much diluted in the loudly acclaimed efforts of many fraternal groups. Its least worthy form is nothing but mutual back-scratching. Its best results may, on the other hand, deserve much praise. Most commonly, however, what happens is that a social event, arranged with great extravagance and display, is sponsored in the name of some charitable purpose. The trickle of benefits which finally emerges is often a pitifully small proportion of what was spent in a primarily self-indulgent affair. Let it be confessed that this sometimes happens also in activities which are called "church works." The implications then are equally regrettable, if not more so. But our concern at present is with the fact that fraternal groups have an almost habitual way of treating actual extravagance as though it were something very generous and virtuous. Such uncritical self-satisfaction means that the real meaning of the Gospel can only fall on deaf ears. The oft-quoted assertion that Jesus Christ was the first Rotarian is simply an exaggerated instance of the way in which essential secularism, expressing itself in uncritical self-congratulation, distorts the very essence of the Christian message.

Most devastating because it is most subtle is the inherent snobbery of fraternalism. The naïve suggestion of the membership committee chairman of one club who said, "We are going to build up our membership to seventy-five, and then we'll be exclusive," illustrates the hold which this ideal may have upon the unwary imagination. Basically, all fraternalism is founded on the notion of exclusiveness, which usually finds expression in social, economic, religious or racial superiority attitudes. It is true that such qualities permeate our whole society, and may all too often be found among good church folk as well. Still the tendency is a serious impediment to the Christian spirit; and it is in the very structure of fraternalism. The fellowship developed in small social groups may have creative results in personal development and self-expression. But when they are gained at the price of deliberate cultivation of attitudes of superiority and exclusiveness, they confirm the social injustice which the Church must always strive to resist. Knowledge that membership in the charmed circle of the elect is evidence that one has arrived socially, produces a subtle complacence toward the system which so properly brings the cream to the top. So fraternalism helps to paralyze any vital concern for those ideals of universal brotherhood and equality which are inherent in the Christian gospel. It raises instinctive barriers against any radical effort for racial or social equality. Fraternalism implies brotherhood, but it is generally on a very limited scale. This veneration for conventional success in economic and social terms constitutes a strong spirit of reaction toward the essential implications of the gospel of Jesus Christ.

3. ELEMENTS OF RESOURCE IN ORGANIZED FRATERNALISM

The resource of fellowship

Granting all that has been said above, there are still positive values for the Church in the spirit of comradeship fostered by fraternalism. Secrets that are not worth knowing and stereotyped phrases of brotherly affection may have little real worth; but the attitude of concern for one another's welfare, which is an

integral part of lodge life, is wholesome, even if it operates in
a very restricted area. In theory, the ideal of brotherhood which
the Church professes is far more significant. Yet, in practice,
the lodge even with a lower aim may produce more real brother-
liness among its members than does many a church. If the
Church would deliberately cultivate such comradeship it might
then communicate to its members a sense of concern for others
which would not only enrich their lives, but might help to open
wider horizons for the lodges as well.

The spirit of comradeship in service clubs is the very lifeblood
of the organization. Anyone knows there is much which is banal,
not to say vulgar, in the adolescent habits of many service clubs.
But the friendly atmosphere which permeates the typical service
club does not depend upon the elements which violate good
taste. The relaxed, informal spirit provides an opportunity to
develop mutual appreciation and understanding in ways often
impossible in the more reserved contacts of ordinary, casual
relationships. It is often in marked contrast to the stiff, un-
natural attitude so frequently assumed to be necessary for church
functions. To say that the Church might well learn from these
clubs does not mean that it should imitate the horseplay and
noisy exhibitionism which they often practice. But it does mean
that the good-natured friendliness which is their outstanding
characteristic might well be cultivated by church groups. Put
to the purposes of Christian brotherhood, it might help to re-
capture for the Church some of the mood so plainly reflected
in the gospel stories of Jesus and his associates.

Service

The shortcomings of many fraternal service projects should
not obscure the fact that many fraternal members have learned
through them some sense of the satisfactions which come from
giving practical help to others. Of course this lesson could and
should be learned through church activities having a sounder
basis in principle and purpose. Yet the church often appears to
lag in organizing such training in unselfishness. This should

not be so. The ideal·of service at which the Church aims goes far beyond what any fraternal group attempts in both scope and purpose. Perhaps the very magnitude of that effort makes it difficult for the ordinary member to comprehend. In contrast, the undertakings of his fraternal group are usually immediate, personally appealing, and easily visualized. The Church, then, needs to educate the imaginations of its members in order to enlist their enthusiastic co-operation in its world-wide program.

The proclaimed purpose of all service clubs, and the common readiness of any fraternal group to assist in service projects which capture their sympathetic interest, constitute a potential resource of much value to the Church. The primary task of persuading men and women to appreciate the value of helping others is being done on a wide scale by these groups. The Church faces the task of harnessing this good will to the great tasks of Christian brotherhood. This means both interpretation and organization; but in preparing the groundwork, organized fraternalism offers a significant resource to the Church.

World-wide interest

Most service clubs are, or hope to become, international in scope. Some fraternal lodges are likewise international. Most other clubs have a definite and avowed interest in promoting international understanding and good will. Indeed, fraternal groups which profess no world interest at all are rare exceptions. In these postwar days even the most provincially minded organization has members who have learned by experience that we live in a world which is interrelated, whether for good or ill.

In the case of service clubs, the international interest is explicitly stated in aims and objectives which every club is expected to adopt. A local club may make little of these purposes, but the original incentive towards them is energetically presented by the international officers. Thus the way is opened for the presentation of the Christian ideal of world brotherhood with the powerful backing of the highest officials of these clubs.

One may protest that the incentive came in the first place from the Christian leaven at work in world life, and that it therefore needs no such endorsement. But a realistic approach to the matter makes it clear that the avowed international interest of almost every fraternal group is a positive resource to the Church as it strives to promote the ideals of peace and brotherhood throughout the world.

Wisely used, this may be a leverage to combat within fraternalism itself the exclusive, snobbish, race-conscious, reactionary attitude which has been mentioned as a serious factor of resistance. It uses the very authority which the fraternal groups are most committed to respect. To say this does not mean that the struggle is already over, and the battle won. But it does mean that the prestige enjoyed by fraternal groups in many communities may be used to this purpose outside fraternalism as well as within it. So, in the task of building a world community, the Church may find a resource in the leadership of fraternalism.

The resource of accepted standards

Having pointed out that the common standards of fraternalism are often crudely secular, we should observe that the tendency to accept certain standards may also be of value to the Church. Judged by the highest Christian ideals, the behavior taken for granted by fraternal groups may seem low; but it is only fair to remember that fraternalism does not claim to be ideal in this sense. Its area of interest is essentially social rather than religious. Not claiming to be models of spiritual life, fraternal groups do attempt to reflect a better-than-average standard of common decency. If the average level is below the highest standards of some members, it is also above the level which might otherwise satisfy others. Standards of speech and conduct in fraternal groups do, therefore, represent a gain for what the Church seeks to do as a leavening influence in soicety.

This may sound like damning with faint praise, but it signifies more than that. Remembering the prevailing standards of language, thought and conduct in the army and navy circles which have recently involved so many of our younger men, we must agree that the setting of better standards of taste and decency is a contribution not to be scorned. Considering the gains accomplished rather than the unattained ideals, we must concede a positive contribution in the maintenance of a decent quality of group conduct by fraternalism.

4.   GENERAL CONCLUSIONS

In seeking a fair balance of judgment as to the relationship between the Church and fraternalism, we need to bear in mind the basic distinctions between the two. The church, as a contemporary institution, is part of the social scene, and competes with fraternal groups in some ways. Nevertheless, it has aims and inherent resources which give it quite different implications. This is not to say that fraternalism is unworthy. The social relationships fostered by fraternal groups within their particular spheres may be generally quite wholesome. The encouragement of decent standards, the cultivation of service ideals, and a broad interest in world affairs, are all constructive assets in promoting the type of citizenship which can support the Church in its concern for a Christian world community. Even those organizations which aim at nothing but recreation may perform a useful service in a day of increasing nervous tension. To point to their limitations is merely to underscore the fact that they do not function in the field which is the Church's main concern.

On the other hand, this does not signify that the Church has no interest in such programs. The well-rounded Christian life involves the full development of personality in every wholesome way. The institutional church, with its broad program of activities and interests is a legitimate expression of the conviction that Christian ideals and attitudes are relevant in all phases of normal life. To the extent, then, that fraternalism performs its functions in ways that do not obstruct the purpose of the Church, it serves as an ally, and deserves to be so regarded. But one need not be blind to the shortcomings of an ally, particularly if they imply serious conflict with one's true purposes. The Church has every right to examine fraternalism so as to discover the areas of basic conflict as well as those of agreement.

Furthermore, the Church should examine itself, to see not only where it differs from fraternalism in basic intent, but also where the distinctions lie even in the areas of agreement. The fact that both types of organization stress the ideal of fellowship does not mean that their treatment of that ideal is equivalent. There are different levels of comradeship. The service club level does not, as a general rule, touch very profound issues of life. It is a fairly superficial, good-natured fellowship. As a start towards a deeper understanding it may be highly significant; but within the sphere of service club life it seldom goes beyond the preliminary stage of breaking down ordinary reserves. The same thing may be said of most club life, which is socially pleasant, and may involve certain aspects of co-operation capable of further extensions if the parties involved choose to make them. In theory, lodge relationships are supposed to have a deeper basis of mutual concern. It often happens that a truly fraternal spirit is developed among those lodge members who take their organization seriously. Such a feeling of personal responsibility for one another's welfare is perhaps the greatest element of strength in the lodges. At least in theory, the sense of Christian fellowship has within it an orientation much more significant than any other. The Church in its early experiences demonstrated this fact very clearly. If churches today do not make of this quality what they should, then they are falling short of their own finest purpose.

The same thing holds true of every other quality which the Church and fraternalism have in common. Christian service involves a commitment of heart and mind far more significant than the more or less sporadic undertakings of good will in which fraternal groups engage. Furthermore, its ultimate objective is the regeneration of the one served, and the transformation of an unjust world. In thoroughness of purpose it far transcends the palliative results of even the best efforts of those who are not moved by the deepest Christian motives. The church member who gladly supports the service projects of fraternal organizations should not, therefore, imagine that he has done his whole Christian duty. "These things ye should have done, and not left the others undone" may well be his motto as he balances fraternal service and the tasks of the Church.

At the same time, the Church should never forget that real Christian experience implies a genuine joyfulness. If church members do not enjoy church life, but feel that they look elsewhere for such satisfaction, they are either deficient in their comprehension of the Christian spirit, or unfortunate in their church connections. The Church may learn techniques and methods from fraternal groups, but it should never have to learn the basic purpose of life together in mutual fellowship and joyful service.

How, then, shall the Church deal with these organizations which are so characteristic a part of the contemporary environment? There are three possible attitudes.

One extreme is for the Church to denounce fraternalism as an unfair competitor, and to make every effort at resistance to it. Some churches do this, insisting that no member may remain in good standing and be involved in any fraternal life. The result is most unfortunate. The church deprives itself of every potential gain that might come from contact with this significant part of modern social life. Its members develop an unhealthy feeling of moral superiority. Such social asceticism leads to extreme forms of piety and self-righteousness, either of which is hard to reconcile with the spirit so clearly illustrated in the gospel accounts of Jesus and his associates. This otherworldly emphasis produces individuals profoundly lacking in adjustment to ordinary, healthy life in the world in which, as a matter of fact, they ought to strive to live as instruments of God's purpose.

The other extreme takes fraternalism at its own, exaggerated self-evaluation, treating it as though it were a genuinely religious institution, on a par with the Church in this respect. Some

ministers, for instance, throw themselves with abandon into
fraternal life, paying court to various fraternal groups, arrang-
ing to have them come as honored guests to church services, and
giving the unmistakable impression that they regard them as
being practically the equivalent of the Church. The result cannot be satisfactory. Those who imagine that fraternalism is an
adequate substitute for the Church accept this evidence that the
Church itself endorses their view. Others infer that the very
leader of the church considers the more colorful and snobbish
lodge or club as a sort of inner circle of the elect. Either way,
the church appears to approve of the least meritorious aspects of
its presumed competitor.

The third approach is to look at fraternalism as it really is,
a limited and often inadequate social phenomenon, which
achieves many successes in its restricted sphere. From the standpoint of the Church, fraternalism is a mixed blessing. The
Church may gladly approve certain of its inherent qualities,
and may make every legitimate effort to strengthen them, using
them as resources both in its own program and in its approach
to the community at large. Where it can do so without compro-
mising its own nature, the Church should welcome the aid of
such an ally, offering co-operation in meeting whatever issues
can be faced with honest agreement. Such co-operation, however,
must have definite limitations. The Church must never cease to
be discriminating in its evaluation of fraternal groups. The
ways in which they offer resistance to the true meaning of the
Church and its purposes are too serious to ignore. The Church's
own integrity demands that it shall never seem to approve or
to condone those aspects of fraternal life which conflict with
Christian standards and aims. This requires constant vigilance.
If the Church too readily assents to the shortcomings of fraternalism, the result may be a subtle corruption of its own
standards.

Co-operation within proper limits is not always easy. It involves possibilities of misunderstanding and friction, which is
true of any attempt to follow a line of discriminating choice.

At the same time, it holds possibilities of a truly creative relationship from which both parties may benefit. The Church which holds true to its own high purpose may discover in its contacts with organized fraternalism real qualities of resource as well as problems of resistance.

FURTHER READING

LYND, ROBERT S. and HELEN M. *Middletown*. New York: Harcourt, Brace and Company, Inc., 1930.

————*Middletown in Transition*. New York: Harcourt, Brace and Company, Inc., 1937.

Also such periodicals as:

American Legion Magazine.

Elks Magazine.

Kiwanis Magazine.

The Rotarian.

7

CHRISTIANITY AND ORGANIZED EDUCATION

Frederick West

Introduction. 1. Scientism: the expansion of science, the claims for "scientific" precision, naturalistic histories in scientism, movements of scientism, scientism and Christianity. 2. Humanism: pragmatic and ethical humanism, the new humanism. 3. Vocationalism: teacher training institutions, public institutions, Church-related institutions and movements, religious leadership. 4. Conclusion.

~~~~~~

Convinced that the knowledge of God is the beginning and end of wisdom, Christians are charged to love God with all their minds. Assured that the truth will make them free, Christians confront current movements of organized education which are enslaved in their self-conscious knowledge and conceptions of objectivity. Modern education poses before its traditional Christian sponsors intermittently as a skeptical witch and a believing wizard.

Prior to the nineteenth century, American educators sought no breach between Christian education and general education. Both involved the common responsibility of the Church and the State. A knowledge of God and of moral obligations was requisite for a universal understanding of physical nature and good citizenship. Thus, unity and consistency were possible in educational objectives.

For decades the Bible, the Psalter and the New England

Primer were the only elementary schoolbooks in early New England. Over five million copies of the Primer were published between 1690 and 1830. With it the child was taught to spell through an alphabet of religious rhymes, as the letter *A* indicates: "In Adam's Fall We sinned all." Then the child was instructed in his "Duty" and encouraged in his "Learning": for example, "I will Love my Friends. I will hate no Man. I will forgive my Enemies, and pray to God for them." Regardless of archaic methods of instruction and Puritan propaganda, moral and religious values were fundamental both in the intent and content of the educational program.

Nevertheless, today, according to the *1940 White House Conference on Children in a Democracy* report, about "one-half of the children and youth in the United States receive no religious instruction outside the home." Of the 29,805,259 children of public school age in July, 1940, 85 per cent were enrolled with an average daily attendance of 22,042,151. Yet 357 public school systems, three-fourths of those releasing pupils for weekday religious instruction, had an average attendance of only 164,013 pupils in January, 1940.

The oldest institutions of higher learning in America were founded primarily to train religious leaders. Christianity pioneered in higher education until after the Civil War; of the 246 colleges founded by 1860, only 17 were State institutions. But, now, the State or publicly controlled institutions train more than half of the American college students.

In spite of the alleged separation of Church and State in American education after the Revolutionary War, religious liberty did not mean religious license. Nor did it mean the freedom of a secular few to thwart and dwarf the Christian faith of many. Religious liberty meant religious obligations with freedom of conviction. The founders of the Republic assumed that religious and moral needs were basic for the welfare of the national life. This commitment was made manifest by provisions for chaplains in the armed services, national thanksgiving days, and the exemptions of both colleges and churches from taxation.

Today the Church is obligated to come to grips with the spiritual problems of the national life as reflected in the entire sweep of education, private and public. Granted that the mantle of formal education has been placed largely upon the shoulders of the government, no heavenly chariot has lifted the Church out of the educational world. The Church is involved in it and in the movements, from the National Association of Manufacturers to the Army, which would control it. Churchmen support the public educational system with a large proportion of its students, staff and taxes. Most of the leaders and laymen of the Church are educated, in part, by publicly controlled institutions.

In spite of efforts to appear young and experimental, American education now is like Thoreau's "half-witted" State which was "timid as an old woman with her silver spoons" not knowing "its friends from its foes." This confusion has been unveiled by Robert M. Hutchins, Frederick S. Breed, William Adams Brown, Theodore Greene and others. It was confessed by the National Society of College Teachers of Education in 1933. It was recently studied by such universities as Stanford, Harvard, Chicago, Yale and North Carolina.

Three movements have been instrumental in the secularization of American education: scientism, humanism and vocationalism. We shall examine them in relation to Christianity.

1. SCIENTISM

Christianity must distinguish between modern science and scientism in organized education. Modern science is a potential ally of Christian truth, but scientism is a rival. Science is an accumulated knowledge systematized and derived by experimental methods in reference to conceived general laws or probabilities. "Scientism, as all other *isms*, is a faith. It is a faith in the universal adequacy of scientific procedures."[1]

The modern scientific and Christian spirits have much in com-

[1] William L. Patty, *A Study of Mechanism in Education* (New York: Bureau of Publications, Columbia University, 1938), p. 155.

mon in the quest and the respect for truth. Both require the greatest humility as servants, not as masters, in seeking, interpreting and using truth for the welfare of all men. Science and Christianity have a meeting ground in the degree of faith, assumptions, tolerance, self-sacrifice, disinterest, honesty, self-criticism, discipline, labor and co-operation required for significant achievement. Neither the scientist nor the Christian, as such, can absolutize or deify his knowledge or contribution to society without ceasing to be scientific or Christian, respectively.

Scientism, however, absolutizes science. Scientism assumes that science is the natural savior of mankind. Appealing to freedom and objectivity in thought, the orthodox teachers of scientism allow no other gods before them. Heretics, denying the scientific method as the ultimate means of human deliverance and as the arbitrator of all knowledge and values, are branded as "superstitious," "subjective" and "traditionally minded." The scientific method and the rational control of applied science are regarded as the only instruments adequate to serve disinterestedly the common salvation of all.

Characteristic of scientism is its love of modernity and its hostility toward tradition. In organized education scientism has arisen in proportion to the decline in emphasis upon classics and Christianity. Scientism comprises a mixture of movements enthused with the expansion of pure and applied science, the relative exactness of the natural sciences, and naturalistic philosophies of history claiming scientific foundations.

The expansion of science

Science had a small academic place when classical and Christian studies dominated American education. It became popular during the second quarter of the nineteenth century after Benjamin Silliman and others aroused New England with lectures upon the new sciences of chemistry, geology, medicine and biology. During the next few decades many American students studied in Germany where natural sciences were advanced and the scientific method was used and abused in other specialized studies. This methodology, admired for its exactness, and the specialized Ph.D. degree, were imported.

Meanwhile, the new sciences did not obtain full academic standing in America until independent scientific schools were opened. The Morrill Land Grant Act of 1862 enabled public institutions of agricultural and mechanical arts to be founded; this brought public schools closer to state universities. Cornell College was founded in 1867 upon a basis of equal credit for both "practical" and "required" courses.

Two years later, President Charles Eliot introduced the elective system at Harvard. This allowed full academic credit for the new social sciences without requiring new schools for them. But the elective system became so widespread and flexible that anarchy prevailed in liberal arts subjects. Over-specialization often gave students great scientific knowledge, but scanty religious and ethical information for other than a naturalistic view of life. This tended to make organized education a process of learning "more about less and less about more until life was meaningless." A greater premium was placed upon scientific facts than upon moral and spiritual insight.

At the outbreak of this gold rush after material facts and things, the idealistic Emerson warned Americans against "the half-sight of science" and "penny wisdom." The "scholar" needs to merge "know thyself" and "study nature" into one maxim. Emerson declared that "the best read naturalist rarely sees his relation to the world," for scientific exactness may "lose the end in the means and miss the wonderful congruity which subsists between man and the world." To balance this half-sight, Emerson said that men need Plato's insight into poetic truth and to know that the foundations of man are "not in matter, but in spirit."

After the Civil War vast systems of industry were based largely upon new inventions in the realm of applied science. The age of steam, steel and gadgets produced material results and comforts of life—a telling triumph for believers in scientism.

The claims for "scientific" precision

As a result, specialists in exact and applied science modeled the fashions, curriculum and vocabulary of American education. The physical sciences became the ideal standard of exactness and objectivity in studies. Scientific courses were supposed to deal with sure knowledge—"the provable facts." Ethics, philosophy and religion dealt with the unessential guesses of the race. Classical literature became only an indoor recreation for the new naturalistic intellectuals rather than important and imperishable accounts of the life and insights of society.

Therefore, social, philosophical, religious and literary pursuits either had to become "scientific" or risk being intellectual outcasts. In their efforts to be scientific, they became both. Social studies became "sciences" with all the precision of physical science. Theology, the old queen of the sciences, dressed up as a twentieth century "empirical science." The scientific method of the natural sciences was fancied to be the means of rigid exactness for studies in sociology, government, economics, ethics, history, literary criticism, psychology and education.

Consequently, courses in religion in both secular and church-related schools often jettisoned their uniqueness in behalf of the safe spirit of detachment. Religious history, comparative religion, Christian thought and Biblical literature became "sciences" and were coldly taught, while courses in natural sciences were taught with commitment and enthusiasm. The former have not emerged from this scientific sacramentalism.

In short, although it is hard for us to see our own provincialism, our veneration for the modern scientist "can only be compared with the superstitious regard which the medieval peasant paid to his priest. . . ."[2]

Naturalistic histories in scientism

In addition to the expansion of physical, applied and alleged sciences and the popularity of their precision, naturalistic views

[2] Arnold S. Nash, *The University and the Modern World* (New York: The Macmillan Company, 1943), p. 41.

of history gave prestige and a philosophical basis for scientism in organized education today. In fact, they added an almost eschatalogical note of urgency to the faith of scientism. These views are typified in the systems of Robert Owen and Auguste Comte.

Owen's socialism of the 1820's pictured the near arrival of the third and final stage of history—a scientific millennium which would bring Utopia when men rationally discovered the "facts" about society and its environment which conform to the "laws of nature." Society, for him, had already advanced beyond the historical stage of sectarian religion to the second or transitional stage approaching the era of the scientific use of intelligence. Comte's view of history was similar: the first historical stage was magic or religious supernaturalism; the second, metaphysical reasoning; and the final approaching stage was "Positivism" or Science in which sociology would be as exact as any physical science. For our purposes there is no need to describe these completely naturalistic views of history further or to analyze similar influential views held by Herbert Spencer and Charles Darwin. The important thing is to note the part truth which they offer under the guise of the whole truth, and how kindred they are to modern scientism in education. In many respects they were the ideological parents of our naturalistic social sciences and scientism.

In modern American education John Dewey and George H. Mead are outstanding leaders in scientism, particularly in their influence upon "progressive education." As Owen, Comte and Spencer, Dewey projects three similar stages of history with the final one being completely naturalistic. In the final stage of history religious values are "capable of verification" and "expansion" by the "same experimental method" by which "all natural facts are established." Dewey foresees what he calls "the science of man." He regrets that "physical science and its technological applications" are "highly developed while the science of man, moral science, is backward." The basis for this moral science of man is the development of physical science, especially "chemistry, biology, physiology, medicine, and anthropology." The emergence of this new science is now evidenced "in the movements in the clinical behavioristic and social (in its narrowest sense) psychology." There is only one "sure road of access to truth—the road of patient, co-operative inquiry operating by means of observation, experiment, record and controlled reflection."[3]

In short, Dewey, like Mead, while formally rejecting the dogma of mechanism and positivism in his naturalistic view of history, interprets the modern scientific method as an all-inclusive "sure road" to all truth.

Movements of scientism in education

The John Dewey Society and the American Progressive Association, especially, are composed of distinguished disciples of Dewey who influence American educators with their versions of the plea against traditionalism in behalf of scientism. Both movements have conferences and publications to implement their programs. Furthermore, for decades the Teachers College of Columbia University has been the educational mecca for the training and the propagation of the Dewey faith in the schools of the nation.

At the present scientism in progressive education is divided into two camps. William L. Patty describes them in terms of those who follow rigidly the empiricism based upon Newtonian science, stressing exact laws, and those influenced more by newer conceptions of science, stressing probabilities. The former group thinks in terms of pure science based upon the assumption of "mechanistic change" in a "static world"; the latter group thinks in terms of "organic change" in a "dynamic world." Patty lists men like Bobbitt, Charters, Peters, Waples and Thorndike in the mechanistic emphasis; and Dewey and Bode in the dynamic emphasis.

[3] John Dewey, *Human Nature and Conduct* (New York: Henry Holt and Company, Inc., 1922), pp. 72-73, 295-325; *A Common Faith* (New Haven: Yale University Press, 1934), pp. 32, 72-73.

Generally the mechanistic group tends to disregard "the implied but often forgotten philosophical doctrines which involve definite restrictions and limitations." The curriculum-makers Bobbitt, Charters and Peters, of this "narrower type of scientism in education," have the "faith that the methods and principles of scientific thought and of technology can and will some day serve education as they have already served other phases of knowledge, notably physics, business management, and engineering."[4]

However, sometimes both emphases of the two camps of scientism overlap. Then one often views the world in terms of dynamic change, yet defines the scientific method in terms of Newtonian exactness for the study of society and values.

Scientism and Christianity

Regardless of the changes developing between the narrower and the broader types of scientism in education, Christianity cannot compromise with the faith of scientism. Christianity can cherish the scientific method as a valid way to obtain needed truth, but not all truth. Although science is a potential ally of Christian truth, scientism, new or old, is basically a rival claiming exclusive loyalty. Any scientism is rooted in an ultimate faith in the adequacy of modern scientific procedures for all truth. This makes the "responsibility for human affairs lie solely with man."[5]

Thus, scientism strikes at the roots of Christian faith in God's continuous revelation as a method of man's receiving essential divine truth and power which are not invented and fully known by human reason, but confronted in events within human history. Christian revelation is based upon man's faith in a God of and beyond history who adequately reveals or discloses Himself through history, and especially in the person, mission and mes-

[4] William L. Patty, *op. cit.*, pp. 2-7.

[5] Alfred Stafford Clayton, *Emergent Mind and Education* (New York: Bureau of Publication, Teachers College, Columbia University, 1943), p. 172.

sage of Jesus Christ as verified by the experience of the community of believers in Him. God's revelation is

> not primarily to *enlighten the minds of men*, but to *bring*
> *them into fellowship with His own life and obedience to*
> *His will.* . . . It does not provide answers to all our prob-
> lems, it bestows life upon us. In short, revelation is for
> the sake of liberation, redemption, salvation.[6]

Christian faith in the importance of revelation is rooted in
the conviction derived from the Hebrew-Christian experience
that man cannot live at his best as an ultimate law and power
unto himself. Man needs to be transformed as well as informed;
this is not what man's unaided reason requires, but it is what
is required of the man of faith as he confronts and interprets
God disclosed in history and the moral struggles of the race.

The scientific method is an inadequate instrument for obtaining the variety of truth needed in its own realm of life. Faith is
required in a being and sovereign only partially disclosed in
history. Faith and mystery, basic to religious experience, are as
involved as human reason. In this sense part of the task of
Christian witness to revelation is to point out where the most
valid and eternal mysteries of life are and *what the man of faith*
can know and must do about them. Scientism, positing a completely naturalistic and knowable universe, recognizes the validity of no such faith or mystery at the heart of religious or any
other experience in history. Consequently, scientism absolutizes
the scientific method with an unlimited authority for universal
truth, rather than as a partial instrument in the quest.

Nevertheless, modern science and its objective spirit in seeking
truth can be of considerable aid to the Christian experience of
revelation, and *may become a means, but not the only means, of*
further revelation. The more adequate the Christian knowledge
of science is, the less are the chances for false and superstitious
interpretations of revealed truth. Since man's interpretation of

[6] Henry P. Van Dusen, ed., *The Christian Answer* (New York: Charles
Scribner's Sons, 1945), p. 97.

divine action is always partial, he needs every available check upon his inner religious experience. Also, it is conceivable that God discloses himself, in part, in history by means of the scientific method when religious faith is involved. But this is a far cry from the faith of scientism which holds that the scientific method "forms for the modern man . . . the sole authentic mode of revelation."[7]

An encouraging trend today is the attitude of the modern scientist, himself, in his new concern for ethics and for more than science to help solve the problems of civilization. This is dramatized by the plea of scientists for moral and spiritual resources to control the use of atomic energy for the welfare of all. The trend is developing among science teachers in America.

In 1942 Dr. Ira Davis, the chairman of the National Science Committee (supported by the National Education Association), reported on conferences for a new science program in education. Meetings were attended by administrators, supervisors and heads of departments connected with more than eleven thousand teachers. As a result, there was a growing conviction that "science must help solve the social problems which it has been instrumental in creating," and science teachers must not teach subject matter "merely for the sake of subject matter." According to the questionnaire-answers of over nine thousand teachers, one third of whom were classroom teachers of science, little was being done about it yet, but there was an opinion that pupils "would acquire more desirable outcomes from a study of these controversial issues than they are now getting from the study of our present subject matter."[8]

Another potential resource for Christianity in facing scientism in education is the symposiums being conducted by scientific and religious leaders. This makes possible a mutual and humble

[7] Albert Einstein, and Others, *Living Philosophies* (Cleveland: The World Publishing Company [Towers Books Edition, 1943]), p. 24.

[8] *Education*, Vol. 62, January, 1942, pp. 260-263.

understanding of what both science and religion offer civilization.

2. HUMANISM

Humanism in organized education is a man-centered philosophy. It believes in the rational dignity and power of natural man as the ultimate hope for progress on earth.

There are three main types of humanism, each of which may be religious or secular: the *classical*, the *humanitarian* and the *pragmatic*. Classical humanism centers its interest upon the durable arts, learning and the institutions of mankind. The humanitarian is marked by an ethical concern for the welfare and destiny of man. These two humanisms can be combined, and they may conceive of God as a necessary aid for advancing human culture and welfare. Erasmus, for example, cherished both the classics and human welfare, but believed in God as a reality essential for adequate human welfare and culture.

Pragmatic humanism is concerned primarily with the practical welfare of man. It treasures any value or thing which appears to favor human welfare temporarily, but resents traditional judgments and practices as unnecessary obstacles in the way of intelligent progress. *Pragmatic religious humanism* stands, in part, as a resistance to traditional Christian faith. It rejects an objectively real God, but often projects the subjective idea of God as a great value for man. God becomes the instrumental product, not the ultimate object, of human experience. The idea of God is desirable, for it helps man to work out his own salvation with faith and power.

Pragmatic humanism

Of the three types of humanism, naturalistic pragmatism is the most widely organized in American education largely because of the Mead-Dewey influence upon educators and teachers. John Dewey's religious credo is pragmatic humanism, stripped of both theism and any institution of religion in the effort to divorce "the religious attitude" from "religion" and from a defined religious object, content and community.

Christianity faces resistance from the denial of an objectively real God in history, of the necessity of an institution like the church for religious attitudes and life, and of the existence of lasting values in a world of change. However, in other respects, tremendous resources are available for the program of Christianity in Deweyite influences upon organized education in general and progressive education in particular.

Their greatest resource for Christian education is methodology. This methodology is built around the conception of "learning as a process by which experiences are changed so as to become more serviceable for future guidance."[9]

Christianity can welcome the slogan that learning involves "the reconstruction of ideas through experience."

Many emphases based upon this conception of learning are highly favorable to Christian education. Among these are: respect for the individual, freedom from authoritarianism and rote memory, growth, interest, self-activity, "maximum development," democracy, developing habits of co-operation instead of habits of competition, learning by doing, life-situation problems and the nature of change as dynamic in an organic world as against atomistic change within a world of static mechanism. If the Church is to be more effective, it must use the lasting contributions of progressive education in its own educational program. Progressive methods are a resource for the church school, especially in training children.

Another potential resource for Christianity is the present self-criticism within the progressive movement which makes for a more adequate philosophy of life and education. Able leaders of the movement are not only aware of its lasting contributions, but also of its misinterpretations and the overemphasis of some good aspects of its program. These leaders acknowledge that liberty in learning is of little value apart from helpful disci-

[9] Boyd H. Bode, *Progressive Education at the Crossroads* (New York: Newson & Company, 1938), p. 41.

pline; projects, from subjects; interest, from wise guidance; and growth, apart from direction according to an integrating plan for life. Also they confess that intelligence does not mean either anti-intellectualism or the lack of convictions.

Harold Rugg, for example, represents the prophetic spirit within the movement by questioning its scientism in terms of the nature of man and his variety of needs. He stresses the human need for meditation, feeling and the attitude of the artist who sees life as a whole—these are as important as "success," problem-solving, doing and making, conformity to society and a mere analysis of the parts of life.

Ethical humanism

Humanitarian humanism in organized education represents chiefly the efforts of liberals to stress the good works wrought by the ethical ideals of religion. Growing social problems have uncovered the urgent human need of moral standards for the welfare of all. These liberals tend to scrap traditional theology in an attempt to soften the intellectual conflicts between a spiritual Christ and a secular culture. Students respect Jesus Christ, if not because of his divine mission, for his works and humanity's sake. This humanism often uses religious moralism without the resources of religious faith, and fails to recognize the impotence of religious ethics apart from its theological content.

In spite of the tendency toward Christian atheism in giving loyalty to "the moral and social ideals of Jesus without the faith of Jesus in a Heavenly Father,"[10] this humanism offers resources for the Christian program. Christians have a common meeting ground in any high moral and social idealism. If these humanists are not seeking first the kingdom of God, they are at least seeking its righteousness in a one-sided emphasis upon Christian truth which stresses the worth of all human beings and social welfare. Christianity can strengthen ethical humanism by co-operating with it in a witness to the power of God in

[10] E. S. Brightman, *The Future of Christianity* (New York: Abingdon-Cokesbury Press, 1943), p. 88.

reform and in causes making for human welfare. Christianity can find resources in the intelligence, the honesty, the courage, the sensitive conscience, the respect for individuals, the sense of community and the aggressiveness which characterize this movement.

The new humanism in education

American education now faces a revival of humanitarian and classical humanism. These resurgent humanisms are combining to challenge the orthodox domination of pragmatic humanism in organized education. The movements are notably expressed in conferences and in the symposium publications of Stanford, Harvard, Chicago, Yale and North Carolina. Their common concern is for commitment and integration of American education in terms of the democratic faith and tradition of Western civilization. They demand a balanced general education in the humanities, the natural sciences and the social studies. Without making a philosophy of education from a methodology, they would allow content and teaching abilities to determine methods of instruction. No longer would students be enslaved in their own freedom and the provincialism of the present, but freed to tap the entire heritage of humanity. *The scientific method is not upheld as the only objective and scholarly approach to knowledge and life.*

So far, this trend is favorable to Christianity, but not necessarily committed to it. It is a new humanism in education which is a timely critique of both scientism and pragmatic humanism, and a potential resource for Christianity. Especially is this true when it stresses the responsibility for integrating educational experience and knowledge in terms of the democratic faith, tradition and morality of Western civilization. The way is open for Christianity to stress the abiding Christian contributions to Western civilization, and to show that many of its most desirable fruits depend upon Christian roots. The acknowledgment that the scientific method is not the only valid, objective approach to essential knowledge is all to the good as far as Christian faith in revelation is concerned.

As a result of the First and Second Annual Conferences in 1943 and 1944 of the Stanford School of Humanities on "The Content of Humanistic Education" and "The Humanities in the War and Post-war World," respectively, two important books appeared. Although interest is revealed in the need for educated morality, no specific concern is shown for a definite religious power and faith to sustain it.

The Harvard Committee on "The Objectives of a General Education in a Free Society" made the most extensive study in decades of the program and needs of American education. It reveals a concern for ethics and a faith to empower educated peoples to use their knowledge wisely for the welfare of all, but makes no provisions for them as a direct responsibility of the school or college. Although the Committee sees that "good education" is not in conflict with good religious education, it leaves religious and moral education to the family. Yet the school and college are responsible for teaching the role that faith and ethics have played in the Western democratic tradition through secular subjects. Here, the task of Christianity, particularly, is to show that religious and ethical information *and guidance* are as essential for grownups as for children, and that this hush-hush policy in organized education will disallow an adequate integration of all of life. And, surely, the family cannot perform this educational task adequately in view of its lack of training and opportunity, especially at more advanced levels of knowledge.

President Hutchins of the University of Chicago holds that organized education is responsible for both moral and religious education. This should be done through an integrating background of metaphysics. St. John's College is experimenting with his theory in tradition with the classics as the basic guide. However, the metaphysics of Hutchins is a particular kind of metaphysics—the classical realism of the Catholic Schoolmen of the Middle Ages. To an extent Hutchins is closer to the more extreme progressive educator than is often realized, although one reveres tradition and the other experiment. One tends to make an orthodox philosophy of education out of a particular kind of traditional metaphysics; the other, out of a particular kind of modern methodology. Genuine freedom of thought, conscience and provincialism are not provided in either philosophy of education when overemphasized.

The North Carolina and Yale studies reflect a greater interest in the need for unprovincial moral and religious education. This is more hopeful as a resource for Christianity. For example, a Yale faculty committee, surveying the postwar needs for religion in the university, "was unified in its common concern for the vitality of religion at Yale 'both as a body of knowledge to be dispassionately appraised and as a way of life to be passionately expressed.' "[11]

3. VOCATIONALISM

The crucial problem which Christianity faces in organized education today is vocationalism. It often becomes a substitute for religious vocation, rather than a part of religious vocation. Vocationalism is the calling of only a part of human living, namely, a profession or an occupation. However, religious vocation is the calling of all of human life. The tendency is for vocationalism to become secularized and to lose its meaning in relation to the calling of all of life in the service of God.

Vocationalism actually involves only the training and skills of man for his daily work. Vocation involves the total orientation of a man's life and work in terms of his ultimate sense of mission. Vocationalism is based upon daily employment, but vocation is based upon ultimate faith.

Religion, as a divine vocation, is the "*calling forth of a person's entire range of capacities and skills to worship and devoted work for the common good, by a power not only greater than*

[11] *Report of the President of Yale University to the Alumni* (New Haven: Yale University Press, 1944-45), p. 21.

himself but greater than the whole world in which he lives.
Such a view, instead of splitting up men's experience, can undergird the whole of it."[12]

The tendency of vocationalism as a resistance to Christianity
is to split up life so as to deify one's trade, business or daily
work as an ultimate end in itself. As a resource for Christianity
vocationalism provides the skills and training needed in daily
work to glorify God and serve mankind with a faith which
deprives man's employment of deadly routine or selfishness.
Vocationalism is a breeding ground for scientism and naturalistic humanism, for it produces the specialists, teachers and
leaders who apply those doctrines to daily work and living. But
it also molds the Christian ministers, teachers and laymen whose
work is an expression of their worship.

Especially is vocational training a problem of Protestantism
because of its mission to extend religious calling beyond the
narrow and exclusive sense of specialization in religious leadership. It involves the Protestant's effort to teach the sacredness
of all work and walks of life which are beneficial to society as
an expression of love to the human neighbor. Religious calling
adds common dignity and divine mission in all helpful daily
work from the clerk to the parson, the teacher to the pupil, the
farmer to the machinist, and the newsboy to the legislator.

Today vocational training in specialized knowledge, skills
and occupations is inevitable, and the religious vocation is all
the more urgent. It is increasingly easy for courses such as
cooking, auto mechanics, journalism and medicine to become
so departmentalized in vocational education as to lose their
meaning and mission in relation to life as a whole. Consequently, vocational training must be consciously related to the
religious calling of all of human life, unless man's daily work
is to become secularized and without the challenge of service
to God and man.

Vocational training, then, particularly in specialized teach-

[12] Robert L. Calhoun, *God and the Day's Work* (New York: Association
Press, 1943), pp. 1-2.

ers' colleges, junior colleges, institutions of technology, advanced professional schools and the armed services, becomes a Christian problem and a social crisis. Especially is this true when religious insight and worship are omitted from these disciplines. If vocational training is not related responsibly to all of life, but only to making a living, no sense of Christian mission through that living is possible.

Dr. George L. Carrington recognizes part of this problem in professional medical training:

> To understand and treat men adequately, the practitioner is beginning to find again that he needs to draw upon all the spiritual heritage of the ages. . . . Most of all, perhaps, he needs to understand religion. In the study of these things the student acquires an understanding of others, and himself takes on stature.[13]

Teacher training institutions

Christianity's greatest threat and hope in vocational education is in the training which teachers receive. This is crucial in professional schools and institutions of higher learning in which so many teachers are chosen only because they are regarded as specialists by other specialists without respect for greatness of character, perspective or a sense of mission in teaching. Norman Foerster notes that the 1933 report of the American Association of University Professors acknowledges "that their own profession is failing to attract to itself 'a sufficient number of broadly cultured young men and women' because the 'examples are so bad that they are not worthy of imitation.' "[14]

Foerster describes four types of teachers: (1) The "pedants" —the "dead wood" of the large part of the "academic forest." (2) The "dilettanti"—popular clowns posing as scholars. (3) "Career-builders"—the successfully cynical "yes-men" usually

---

[13] Loren C. MacKinney, ed., *A State University Surveys the Humanities*, (Chapel Hill: The University of North Carolina Press, 1945), p. 166.

[14] *Ibid.*, p. 248.

rewarded by administrations, but seekers of power and money. (4) "Man-Thinking"—the few who are "great in what they represent," people of character and perspective.[15]

The importance of a well-rounded education, including character, perspective and a sense of mission, is especially crucial for teacher training institutions. Particularly is this relevant for the training of public school teachers, since three-fourths of the students in public schools today never enter institutions of advanced learning, but go to work or unemployment. There were 918,715 public school teachers and officials in the United States in 1939 and 1,196 institutions of higher learning were qualified by the state departments of education to grant teacher education certificates.

The Church can help convince the state departments of education of their task to require public school teachers to be trained, at least, with an adequate knowledge of religion and a tolerant attitude toward Christianity. Otherwise, most of the public school teachers of the nation will continue to be incompetent to teach their students with an academic perspective that integrates knowledge and total living with meaning, power and mission.

Public institutions

The Church has the same task with State and publicly controlled institutions in regard to staff and curriculum. To condone a program which omits a background in religious insight and atmosphere on a tolerant and academically respectable basis, is to rob scholarship of its spiritual insight and force. Such education is not guidance into a grasp and appreciation of all realms of culture and knowledge; it is partial. It compels "educated" people to have a knowledge of fine arts, sciences, government, economics and other realms of universal social experience, but to be uneducated on the same academic level in religion which is a part of normal group experience throughout human history and all over the world.

[15] *Ibid.*, pp. 248-249.

The secularist usurps the law of the land when he makes timidly patriotic educators withdraw a religious education and atmosphere in the name of freedom from sectarian conviction. Conviction and ignorance are never identical. As J. Paul Williams observes, many citizens have only a freedom for religious ignorance in education, but not freedom for intelligent choice based upon religious knowledge. The secularist, however, is free to indoctrinate pupils with scientism and pragmatic naturalism. Since religion influences all of human culture to some extent, religious convictions are not actually omitted from classrooms although they often are amateurish because of the teacher's lack of religious information.

In the public schools Christianity has a growing resource for teaching religious vocation through weekday education. Over forty states have granted religious forces the opportunity to try the experiment.

Church related institutions and movements

The greatest resource for Christian vocationalism in education is the church-related colleges and universities. Over three-fourths of the Church leaders with college training come from church-related colleges. Here the resistance is not so much the world outside the Church, but the world inside the Church. These institutions have unlimited opportunity for Christian teaching, worship and administration. But many institutions, which are not over-dosed in dogmatic sectarianism and unbalanced in general education, are losing their unique Christian function by imitating secular neighbors in administration, staff and curriculum. Especially is this seen in competitive drives toward expansion, nonchurch donors and students. Recently, much money has been raised by church-related schools on the basis of the hatred of the wealthy for the government and the "painless giving" of funds which would ordinarily be taken in taxes.

The Church is well equipped with organized movements to promote Christian vocation in education, if used with courageous statesmanship. For example, the Council of Church Boards of Education seeks to promote Christian education, the religious development of students in publicly controlled institutions, to strengthen church-related higher education and to arouse public concern for religious education. It helped to promote the National Commission on University Work and the National Conference of Church-Related Colleges which recently merged with the Association of American Colleges to help induce religious and moral values in higher education over the nation. Five representatives of the Council's voting membership of 117 persons are representatives of the American Association of Theological Schools. The student Christian movements and church foundations help to stimulate the inspirational life and the sense of Christian mission and community among students.

Religious leadership

However, the Church is outmaneuvered in recruiting its share of leaders among highly intelligent students. About half of the American ministers are neither college nor seminary graduates. This plight is not merely because denominations are lax in academic requirements for leadership, but because other vocations are more attractive and selective. In 1932 the average salary for lawyers and consulting engineers was $4,170; the average for ministers was $1,701. Now, the federal government through the Civil Service Commission hires select college science majors as junior professional assistants at $2,000 a year; and puts the picked science major through school as a student aid with summer work. In 1939 only one out of four of the 38,976 students who took examinations for junior professional assistants passed. Similar offers are made for junior engineers, meteorologists and physicists. Such governmental trends in the field of vocational education will continue, not to mention the attractions of military commissions.

Furthermore, the Church meets competition for talent in big business. For example, 16,000 examination papers were sent to high schools in the Fifth Annual Science Talent Research.

The forty top students will receive Westinghouse Science Scholarships. Two hundred and sixty others will be recommended for scholarships in advanced institutions of learning. This search, held by the Science Service Clubs of America, is given nation-wide publicity.

But the Church is not asleep in this draft of choice talent for leadership. As an illustration, the National Council on Religion in Higher Education was organized to promote improved religious education and counseling in higher learning. Now more than 130 of its Fellows have been assisted in aid and placement in administrative, teaching and personnel work in the United States and Canada. Among these Fellows are many present-day leaders of the Church.

It is important, nevertheless, to note that economic comfort is not the basic reason the Church fails to draw its share of talented leaders. On the basis of a thorough study of 176 of the 224 institutions training the ministry in 1929, it was concluded that most of the intelligent talent choose vocations because of their creative challenge, and even hazard, but not security. The leftovers tend to choose the ministry (as well as teaching, farming, salesmanship and retail business), because it is easier to enter than other vocations.

4. CONCLUSION

An increasingly secular trend in American education is implemented by scientism, humanism and vocationalism. Yet these movements offer potential resource as well as resistance to the Christian hope.

Christianity must be a friendly and mutually humble ally of science in the quest after universal truth and power without yielding to the exclusive claims of scientism which is a rival faith. Wide resources are available for Christianity in humanistic movements which cherish the dignity, worth, learning and practical welfare of man. The Church can undergird these tendencies with a witness to the power and goodness of the God of history without deifying man, his wisdom or his desires, as the ultimate source of adequate human welfare.

The crucial Christian problem in organized education is vocationalism which tends to become a substitute for religious vocation. When secularized, vocationalism makes a part of life, one's occupation or skill, an end and ultimate knowledge in itself, rather than a part of the calling of all his life in the devout service of God and the human neighbor. The task of the Church is to use its organized movements with courageous statesmanship in the entire sweep of education to renew the sense of creative religious vocation in all helpful walks of life, including its own leadership. Without religious insight and mission, educated people cannot live adequately or know sufficiently that allegiance to God is the beginning and end of all wisdom. Through its organized movements, the Church must teach and witness that "he who worships the great King milks heaven and drinks it day by day, his food is never exhausted."[16]

FURTHER READING

BODE, BOYD H. *Progressive Education at the Crossroads*. New York: Newson & Company, 1938.

CALHOUN, ROBERT L. *God and the Day's Work*. New York: Association Press, 1943.

Christian Higher Education. Washington, D.C.: Council of Church Boards of Education, 1940.

General Education in a Free Society. Cambridge: Harvard University Press, 1945.

MACKINNEY, LOREN C., ed. *A State University Surveys the Humanities*. Chapel Hill: The University of North Carolina Press, 1945.

NASH, ARNOLD S. *The University and the Modern World*. New York: The Macmillan Company, 1943.

PATTY, WILLIAM L. *A Study of Mechanism in Education*. New York: Bureau of Publications, Columbia University, 1938.

[16] *Ibid.*, p. 67.

8

THE CULTS

Pierson Parker

Introduction. 1. Classification of the cults: the non-Christian, metaphysical, quasi-orthodox and neo-fundamentalist types. 2. Non-Christian movements, especially Astrology. 3. Metaphysical cults, especially Christian Science. 4. Quasi-orthodox cults, especially the Church of the New Jerusalem. 5. Neo-fundamentalist cults, especially the British Israel Movement. 6. Elements of resource. 7. Elements of resistance. 8. The answer of the Church.

~~~~~~

Who today would think of calling the Methodist Church a cult? or the Seventh Day Adventists, or the Society of Friends? Yet when they began, these and countless other of today's most respected denominations were regarded in just that way. They arose out of the recognition that one or another aspect of the Christian revelation had been neglected by the existing churches —neglected to humanity's hurt. The very name of "Protestant" means one who *testifies, on behalf of* a forgotten truth. That was the meaning of the Reformation, and in turn has been the motive behind the rise of every Protestant denomination since the sixteenth century.

The same process is going on today. Christian truth is never embraced in its totality by any individual, nor by any group however large. Something is almost certain to be overlooked. When the neglect grows too glaring, voices will be heard in protest and, especially under today's religious freedom, groups will withdraw to form their own institutions wherein to promulgate the newly recovered emphases. True, such a movement nearly always overstresses its particular teaching. That is why we call it a cult. Always, however, the cult stands as a reminder to the Church at large of a task which the Church ought herself to be about.

It follows that there is bound to be difference of opinion regarding the proper classification of not a few religious institutions of our own time. Many movements have flowered in the past, only to fade and drop into the limbo of forgotten things. Others, however, not only persist but in many cases have developed into churches that take their place alongside denominations of older standing. With respect to the movements to be named in this chapter some readers—and not only adherents but outsiders too—will feel that one or another of them does not belong in such a list. Let it be understood, therefore, that in calling any movement a "cult" we do not by that fact disparage it. We simply indicate that it stands to one side of the great central stream of Christian thinking; and that it has not, or not yet, taken its place among the regularly recognized denominations.

1. CLASSIFICATION OF THE CULTS

The various cults and quasi-religious movements of our day may, for convenience, be considered under four main heads:

(1) *Cults having a non-Christian basis.* Excluding minor variations, the representative movements are: Alchemy, Astrology, Baha'ism, Ethical Culture, Father Divine movement, "I Am" movement, pseudo-Mohammedanism among American Negroes, pseudo psychologies of various sorts, Rosicrucianism, Spiritualism, Theosophy, Vedanta. While these are termed non-Christian, it must be said that, so far as their American propaganda goes, nearly every one of them tries to relate itself in some way to Christianity. Either it (a) claims support from the teaching of Jesus, or (b) lists him as one of the great prophets,

or (c) teaches that one can belong to a Christian body and to
this group too, since the latter but clarifies and enriches Christianity. In particular, the "I Am" movement, Rosicrucianism
and Theosophy have teachings closely resembling those of the
second group to be noted. Nevertheless, none of them is really
Christian, or claims to be. Alchemy, Astrology and Spiritualism
assert a basis in empirical science. Baha'ism, Theosophy and
Vedanta are demonstrably rooted in non-Christian religions.
Ethical Culture avows equal kinship with all faiths. The "I Am"
movement asserts the deific authority of each individual. Father
Divine teaches that he is himself God. Rosicrucianism traces its
origins to the Jewish Essenes and, further back, to Amenhotep
IV of Egypt.

(2) *Cults calling themselves "metaphysical Christianity"* and
having a *mentalist* basis. This group includes many small organizations, most of which, however, are offshoots from one of the
following: Anthroposophy, Christian Science, New Thought,
Science of Mind, Unity School of Christianity, the Mysticism of
Gerald Heard.

(3) *Quasi-orthodox cults* which retain numerous features of
traditional Christianity, yet *blur the distinction between God
and man.* The two chief representatives of this type of religion
in the United States are The Church of Jesus Christ of Latter-
day Saints (Mormonism) and The Church of the New Jerusalem
(Swedenborgianism).

(4) *Neo-fundamentalist movements* which, unlike the gener-
ality of fundamentalist bodies, tend to place extreme emphasis
on one or two doctrines of supposedly Biblical origin: Assemblies of God, British Israel Movement, Foursquare Gospel,
Holiness bodies, Jehovah's Witnesses, various Pentecostal movements, Youth for Christ. In the nature of the case, this fourth
list cannot be exhaustive or even, perhaps, representative. It is
typical of many of these bodies that they cross and recross, and
that they break up into ever smaller units over differences which,
to an outsider, seem trivial—though no doubt they are of crucial import to the parties involved.

In the space of a single chapter it is not possible to describe, much less to examine in detail, most of the cults just named. We shall select for special attention one typical representative from each group. The principles governing the choice in each case are (a) that the movement is of widespread importance nationally or internationally; (b) that it does not appear likely to disappear, or, contrariwise, to become a regularly recognized denomination within the foreseeable future; (c) that the information given here may not otherwise be readily accessible to the general reader.

Following these examinations, we shall notice some elements of resistance, and of resource, which these movements supply; and then shall try to suggest what ought to be the answer to them from the Church at large.

2. GROUP (1): NON-CHRISTIAN MOVEMENTS

Of the movements named in this group, the two having the widest appeal are Astrology and Theosophy. Theosophy is the less distinctive: it stems from the ancient religion of Buddhism; it shares many features with cults of Group (2); and it has had considerable influence on at least one of the latter, viz., New Thought. Astrology, on the other hand, is not only more distinctive. It is also a major element in one other member of Group (1), viz., Rosicrucianism. We therefore give attention to Astrology.

Popular interest in Astrology has grown rapidly in recent years. This is due in part, of course, to what has been characterized in America as "the neurotic personality of our time." But much of its success is due also to the popular misapprehension that it is a science, like astronomy. This confusion is fostered by the use, on the part of astrologers, of a pseudo-scientific vocabulary, and by the practice among some news-dealers of placing astrological magazines with those on science.

The fundamental tool of the astrologer is the *horoscope*. This is a circular diagram showing the positions of stars and planets on the celestial sphere at the instant of the individual's birth. Standard astrological manuals provide rules for interpreting the configuration thus depicted. The horoscope is divided into twelve equal parts, called "houses," each of which is associated with some phase or subject of human experience. The position or "aspect" of a planet in any house at the moment of birth plays a critical role in indicating the course of one's life.

Efforts reminiscent of the Middle Ages are made constantly by modern astrologers, to persuade the public that horoscope reading is a scientific procedure. Newspapers, and particularly those in large cities or near centers of learning, carry regular columns on the subject. Other journals, though excluding horoscopes from their news columns, yet accept astrological advertising. Weekly and monthly periodicals, devoted wholly to Astrology, pervade the newsstands. Horoscopes for the month or the day are on sale in department and "dime" stores and in some of the better-class bookshops. Yet on the astrologers' own admission such forecasts are worthless for, to quote the standard astrological code to which most of the profession adhere, "A precise astrological opinion can not honestly be rendered with reference to the life of an individual unless it is based upon a horoscope for the year, month, day and time of day plus correct geographical location of birth of the individual."

Moreover, Astrology has failed completely to offer a workable scientific hypothesis, to account for the supposed influence of stars and planets upon human destiny. For example, the gravitational effect of the moon, the *nearest of all* the heavenly bodies, is far less than that of the body of the attending physician at birth. We are not told why the instant of *birth* is selected as critical rather than, say, the time of conception. The "signs of the zodiac" are supposed to have major influence so that, e.g., more musicians ought to be born under Libra than at other times. Yet available statistical evidence shows no correlation whatever between the month of birth and the profession adopted. Furthermore, the fact is ignored that these signs have shifted (because of precession of the equinoxes) and are now 25°, or nearly a month, different from what they were in ancient times!

Astrology is actually much younger than astronomy. In Babylonia, for example, astronomy had reached a high development in lunar and solar theory long before the appearance of Astrology in the sixth century B.C. Similarly in Egypt and in Greece, for all their scientific achievements, Astrology did not come into its own until Hellenistic times. In fact, the only important ancient Greek treatise of the subject was by Ptolemy, whose *Tetrabiblos* became the standard work for Islamic and Western Astrology just as his *Almagest* was for long the foundation of astronomical science. In Rome, despite attacks from Cicero and edicts by nearly all the early emperors, popular interest in the matter was widespread until after the fall of the Empire.

A revival of Astrology came with the advent of Moslem civilization in A.D. 900-1100, when the Arabs took it over along with the science they had inherited from the Greeks. It is probable that Arab observatories, erected during this period, were intended not for astrological purposes, but to determine the direction of Mecca. Nevertheless, along with alchemy, astronomy, mathematics and medicine, Astrology was reintroduced into Western civilization by the Moslems. From the thirteenth century on it was widely regarded as a science. Despite official protests from the Roman Church, it was tolerated, and even encouraged by individual ecclesiastical officials.

With the Renaissance, opposition to Astrology by scientists and mathematicians again became intense. Still its practices did not abate to any appreciable extent. Tycho Brahe seems completely to have fused it with astronomy. Kepler, his successor, kept the two subjects distinct but was forced, for his livelihood, to add the casting of horoscopes to his scientific pursuits. Finally the Reformation dealt an almost mortal blow to Astrology breaking its power and depriving it of much public interest. It never disappeared altogether, but it is only in our day that it has again begun to flourish.

And flourish it does. Fortunately, however, its present successes are not unaccompanied by strong and growing opposition. Several popular magazines have recently published articles exposing its unscientific and fraudulent character. The subject is banned from the air by the Federal Communications Commission. Its legal status is more than questionable, many states classing its practice with all forms of fortunetelling, as a misdemeanor. Still, because of lax law enforcement, astrological literature continues to be sold, and its practitioners continue to make a very good living.

From what has just been said it is apparent that, although Astrology has contributed next to nothing to genuine human knowledge, it has tended to flourish in times of scientific advance. Another and to us more disquieting fact is that the strength of Astrology has in the past been in almost inverse ratio to the strength of philosophy and of real religion. That it is at a peak again today constitutes a challenge and a summons for the Church to rediscover and apply its own tremendous resources for private religious living.

3. GROUP (2): METAPHYSICAL CHRISTIAN CULTS

The reasons that impel many people to try Astrology lead large numbers of others to take up one of the so-called "metaphysical" Christian cults. Christian Science is by all odds the most important of this group. So many features are shared in common by them all, however, that we shall first describe some of these, before noting one or two peculiarities of Mrs. Eddy's faith.

Ideologically, the metaphysical cults stem from Hegelian idealism and from New England transcendentalism. Like the religions of India, they make a sharp dichotomy between the world of sense or matter, and the world of Spirit or Mind. (Nouns referring to the latter are customarily capitalized.) Spirit or Mind is God, and He (or It) is variously called the

Absolute, Divine Mind, Cosmic Principle and the like. He or It is suprapersonal, and mental in character. The life of man is happy or otherwise in proportion as man uses or ignores, in his consciousness, the powers made available to him by this Absolute Mind.

The logical result of this is a strong tendency to condemn the historic Christian faith. The latter is characterized as "dead dogma," the cruel God of which capriciously punished His Son for others' errors, sends poor humans to unending torture for the sins of a few tired years, and cannot control His world. All such "dead dogma" is, of course, eliminated by the new religion, which is able to see behind the absurdities of the churches, to the spiritual truth which the Bible really contains. The Bible itself is comprehensible only to the initiate, who has learned its hidden meanings as these are developed by stressing particular passages apart from their contexts, or by allegory.

All these cults insist with one voice that they hold to the divinity of Jesus. When the claim is examined, however, we discover that Jesus' divinity is identical with the divinity, real or potential, of all men. Jesus' prerogative consists simply in this, that he demonstrated the divine character of every one of us. Thus the proper and true religious life of man is comprised in his "realizing" his own divinity to the point where this consciousness becomes *externalized* in worldly experience.

The way is thus open for complete reinterpretation of most of the historic Christian affirmations. For example, the Immaculate Conception means that every conception, or state of mind, ought to be immaculate. Hell is the *error* in which man finds himself (or believes himself to be) when he is cut off from Divine, Absolute Mind. The Second Advent is the coming of Truth (i.e., the teachings of the cult) to our age. Judgment is this Truth acting upon false mentality with its cleansing purge.

Evil is unreal. It is false belief, or else it is good misplaced. Thus evil is inherently self-annihilating, its one virtue being that it drives man from itself. It has no Principle or rationale of existence. It is destroyed, "returns to its native nothingness," to the degree that man realizes its unreality. Heaven, on the other hand, is another name for Reality. It is the true, therefore the actual, state of man's mind. It is also conceived as the external effects produced by that state of mind.

Evil includes moral obliquity, pain and deficiency of any sort. Since all evil is unreal though believed absence of good, it follows that what will abolish sin will also, and with equal certainty, destroy lack, sickness and death. These all must vanish when the Truth is realized, just as darkness disappears when the light is lit. Similarly, since all reality stems from Divine Mind, therefore the unity of society consists simply in our all being part of that Mind. Hence any social advance must accrue through each individual improving his own mental state.

Most of these movements decry or specifically forbid the use of set formulas for dealing with human ills. One does not at all make use of anything savoring of magical incantation. Instead, one endeavors by study and meditation to appropriate, into one's own consciousness, the Truth about oneself and one's neighbor. This brings about healing of body and amelioration of circumstance.

The foregoing characteristics apply with little change to all the mentalist cults. Christian Science, however, has two special features. First, it is far more precise than the others, in saying what *constitutes* all this unreal human experience. (In this faith, the words "human" and "personal" have nearly always a bad sense.) Unreal, human, personal experience is particularized as the expression of *mortal mind* or *malicious animal magnetism*. All experience is mental: the difference between spiritual and physical phenomena is that the former come from Divine Mind and are true, whereas the latter are from the untrue (therefore unreal) human or mortal mind. Thus Christian Science is thoroughgoingly idealist, and at the same time quasi-dualist. While mortal mind is actually nonexistent, it has in the world of human belief a potency that is very great, accounting for all our woes. Within this sphere of unreal mentality it is possible, moreover, to engage in "mental malpractice" or the injuring of one's fellow by harmful thoughts. Christian Scientists are directed to protect themselves from such eventualities by daily mental prophylaxis.[1]

The second distinguishing mark of Christian Science lies in its attitude toward its founder. We quote from five anonymous articles, issued in 1939 by the Christian Science Publishing Society under the collective title, *A Prophet with Honor.* We give the page numbers of this booklet, and the title of each article:

> Mrs. Eddy's . . . character . . . is above human praise or criticism ["The Discoverer and Founder of Christian Science," p. 7].
>
> Mrs. Eddy's leadership is the most vital problem of today . . . and she represents the highest visible idea of God concerning leadership ["Mrs. Eddy as Leader," p. 15].
>
> I turned to the chapter on Fruitage in our textbook. . . . The cases of healing there recorded are so similar to those healed by Christ Jesus, that the same Mind must have healed them all. It is by such means that we learn the real nature of Mrs. Eddy's mind or consciousness [*Ibid.*, p. 17].
>
> If ever I should find myself at variance with her statements, I would drop that erroneous belief immediately. That is my sense of true obedience, and it exemplifies Jesus' words, "If ye love me, keep my commandments" [*Ibid.*, p. 22].

[1] In her message to the Mother Church (June, 1898) Mrs. Eddy defended her faith against the charge of pantheism. This, she said, is the doctrine that universal physical causation is God. Since Christian Science denies the very existence of physical causation, it cannot be pantheistic. Technically, of course, Mrs. Eddy was right. Pantheism is defined, in Funk & Wagnalls *College Standard Dictionary* (1925) as "the form of monism that identifies mind and matter, the finite and the infinite, making them manifestations of one universal or absolute being." So far from *identifying* mind and matter, Christian Science regards the latter as the "manifestation" of *unreal* mortal mind which is utterly at variance with the Mind of God. In popular usage, on the other hand, pantheism implies the belief that all that really exists, whatever its nature, is God or His manifestation—and Christian Science certainly says that.

Christian Science, the Comforter promised by Christ Jesus, is thus the final revelation of Truth to men. We should not have a trace of doubt about this. And more, we should understand and acknowledge Mrs. Eddy's rightful place in religious prophecy as in religious history. The Christ has never been absent from the world: . . . Christ Jesus demonstrated the fact. But the Comforter had yet to come; and in the fullness of time it did come, and through a woman. Religious prophecy has thus been fulfilled ["Christian Science: The Final Revelation," p. 25].

What I would emphasize now is that the Christ has been revealed in all its perfection by our Way-shower, Christ Jesus, and our revered Leader, Mary Baker Eddy. I am certain that if we hold to this correct view of our Master . . . and of our Leader . . . together bringing to the world the full revelation of God and His Christ—then we are equipped to carry on successfully the work of our movement [*Ibid.*, p. 26].

The problem, then, which he faced was to convince his disciples, and as many others as possible, of his status as the Son of God. His purpose was in no sense to exalt his human personality. . . . Mrs. Eddy was in no wise actuated by the desire to exalt her human personality. She invariably urged her students to follow not her human self, but the Christ she so effectually revealed ["Whom say ye that I am?" pp. 28, 30].

God spoke through her as surely as He spoke through the Founder of Christianity, for Christian Science supplements and completes the revelation of Jesus [*Ibid.*, pp. 30 f.].

Only through prayerful study of the Scriptures in their relation to the second appearing of the Christ will an adequate understanding of Mrs. Eddy's revelation be gained. And it follows with no degree of uncertainty that the revelation will not be understood in the breadth and depth of its precious import without an understanding and recognition of the Discoverer and Founder in her relation to prophecy [*Ibid.*, p. 31].

As Mrs. Eddy's status as Revelator, Discoverer, Founder,

and Leader of Christian Science is generally recognized, her place in the divine economy will be acknowledged [*Ibid.*, p. 32].

4. GROUP (3): QUASI-ORTHODOX CULTS

The Church of Jesus Christ of Latter-day Saints (Mormonism) and the Church of the New Jerusalem (Swedenborgianism) include among their devotees some of the world's most outstanding and productive citizens. Both are among the most highly respected churches of our time, and both have, to some degree, begun to take their place among the regular Protestant denominations.

Some readers may therefore question the inclusion of these two in a treatment of cult movements. Yet each of them claims to offer a new revelation to our age, which is set forth supremely in the writings of its founder, Joseph Smith and Emanuel Swedenborg. Each places paramount reliance on the visions and esoteric experiences of that founder. Each supplements, modifies and frequently sets aside essential elements of the historic Christian faith. Finally, each tends so markedly to reject the distinction between human and divine nature as to come under the charge that it deifies man and humanizes God. In the often quoted words of the Mormon faith, "What man is, God was. What God is, man shall become." In these respects, both Mormonism and Swedenborgianism stand to one side of historic Christianity, relating themselves to the cults, and especially to those of Group (2).

Of the two, Mormonism is more familiar to Americans, at least in the western part of the United States. However, it has had a great deal of notice in the press of recent years, so that information about it will be readily accessible to most readers. In accordance with our principle of endeavoring to supply less available material, and also because of the world-wide importance of Swedenborgianism, we give special attention to the latter.

Emanuel Swedenborg was a noted Swedish scientist of the early eighteenth century. In middle life he became interested in religion, and sought to apply to it the same rigorous logic as he was accustomed to use in physics and biology. So enthralling did he find his new interest that he left off his scientific pursuits and went to London. There, subsisting on a pension, he spent the rest of his life in studying and writing on theology. He tried to give to religion a complete, logical system, to which were added the results which he claimed to have received through revelation. He did not intend to start a new denomination, but only to lay down basic principles. The institutionalizing of these was done by his followers.

Swedenborg's religious writings were even more numerous than his many scientific works. The main points in his formulary are as follows:

(1) The universe is divided into two sections or aspects, natural and spiritual. While these are mutually distinct, there is a one-to-one correspondence between them. From God there emanates a divine sphere, which appears to man as a spiritual Sun and is the source of love, intelligence and life. From the spiritual Sun proceeds the physical sun, the source of all nature. All material objects are receptacles of their corresponding spiritual objects. The spiritual and physical worlds both have atmospheres, waters and earths.

(2) The consummation of all things is in the Divine Mind. The causes of all phenomena are spiritual, the effects are natural.

(3) In God there is no Trinity of Persons, but there are three infinite and uncreated degrees of being—a Trinity of aspects. Corresponding to these, there are in man and other creatures three finite, created degrees, viz., love, wisdom and use; or end, cause and effect. By attaining a love of each degree in turn, man comes into conjunction with them and the worlds of nature, spirit and God. The end of all creation is that man shall have this conjunction, thereby becoming the image of his Creator.

(4) In man there are two receptacles for God, the will for

Divine Love, and the understanding for Divine Wisdom. Only when love and wisdom flow into both receptacles does man become human. Hence complete humanity is equivalent to complete divinity, and hence

(5) *God is human.* He is the Divine Man. His essential quality is infinite love, and His manifestation or form is infinite wisdom. Self-subsisting Love, therefore, is the life of the universe.

(6) Rejection of the Trinity of Persons does not mean rejection of the divinity of Jesus. On the contrary, *Christ Jesus was Jehovah Himself* who, occupying a human body, came to exhibit His love more fully than had ever been done before.

(7) The doctrine of Redemption is taught as follows: At the beginning of creation, the influx of Divine Love and Wisdom into human receptacles had been free and unhindered. Creation was complete, and the nexus of man with God was complete. With the Fall this connection was broken, and God was obliged to interpose by successive dispensations. Finally, the power and influence of the spirits of darkness, with whom man by sin associates himself, became so great that human existence was threatened. Jehovah must therefore descend into the natural world to do battle with these evil powers, or "hells," thus restoring the connection. To come in His unveiled divinity would have been to destroy the hells, whereas His purpose was not to destroy but to subjugate them. Therefore He came in human form. But He is a Unity.

(8) On returning to heaven, God left the Scriptures as a successor to Himself. These are His eternal incarnation in the threefold aspects of the natural, spiritual and celestial. Swedenborg, the paraclete of the new dispensation, was divinely appointed to expound these Scriptures. Therefore he received immediate, but complete, revelations from Jehovah. In the revelations, he witnessed the Second Coming and the Last Judgment. They, therefore, are contemporary events.

On his death-bed, Swedenborg reaffirmed the revelatory character of his teachings. Belief in their divine character is essential in the Church which now enshrines them.

In driving a dichotomy between spirit and matter, with matter an emanation or manifestation of spirit, and in its tendency to equate divine and human nature, Swedenborgianism resembles the mentalist cults. Yet it teaches the plenary authority of the Bible, the doctrines of the Fall, Redemption by God in Christ, Second Advent and Final Judgment, and the hierarchies of angels and demons. These beliefs are not shared by either the non-Christian or the mentalist bodies, and place the faith of Swedenborg in line with Christian fundamentalism.

5. GROUP (4): NEO-FUNDAMENTALIST CULTS

Virtually all the neo-fundamentalist bodies named above hold an important series of beliefs in common: the plenary, verbal inspiration of the Bible in its original tongues; the full personalities of the Father, the Son and the Holy Spirit; the personality of Satan; Jesus' Virgin Birth, and physical Resurrection; the doctrines of Sin and Redemption; the early, physical return of Jesus Christ as Judge; the resurrection of the righteous to everlasting joy, and of the sinful to everlasting damnation. Also, most of them exhibit strong antipathy to the older denominations, and especially to the Roman Church which is frequently identified with the Antichrist. Despite this large common core, however, these groups differ sharply. Some hold that the dead are now asleep, others that they are awake and awaiting the Judgment. Some, not all, teach that the "coming of the Holy Ghost" is an independent, almost physically discernible event in the life of the individual. Some practice faith healing. Some believe in the gift of tongues. So great are these disparities, that it is not possible to regard any one of the movements as generally typical.

Among the neo-fundamentalist bodies, an important place is occupied by such Pentecostal movements as the Assemblies of God. These stress the "Second Blessing" or coming of the Holy Ghost, with effects which include speaking in tongues, ecstatic

behavior, healing and the like. Many of these cults are highly
unstable, and disappear after a short time. Those which abide,
on the other hand, are exceedingly likely to become regular
fundamentalist denominations, just as the Free Methodists,
Church of the Nazarene, and Church of Christ have done in the
past. Since, moreover, information regarding Pentecostalism is
readily available elsewhere, it seems best to give particular
attention here to a neo-fundamentalist movement of different
sort.

Almost more important than Pentecostalism, in its widespread
influence, is the British Israel (or Anglo-Israel) movement.
Holding to most of the fundamentalist tenets listed above, this
cult is characterized by the doctrine that the Nordic races of
Europe, and particularly the *Anglo-Saxons, are descendants of
the "lost ten tribes" of Israel*. This is regarded as proven by the
following Biblical prophecies and their fulfillments:

(1) The ten Israelite tribes were deported to Assyria
[1 Kings 8:9-12]. Later, the prophet Micah reported that
they had "broken up, and passed through the gate and
are gone out of it." By the gate is understood the head-
waters of the Euphrates, indicating that these tribes had
begun to move northwestward.

(2) Josephus says that at the time of the Return of
the Jews from exile, the Israelites were also given the
opportunity to return but refused, saying that they were
headed for the "far off isles" and the "great waters."
These mean the British Isles and the Atlantic Ocean.

(3) The traces of the tribe of Dan are discovered in a
path across Europe. Of this tribe it had been prophesied
that it would be like a "lion" and would "leave its mark
as the trail of a serpent in the sand." Marks of the tribe
are indeed found in geographical names from the Near
East to the British Isles: DarDANelles, DNieper, DONets
[they must have gone both ways around the Black Sea],
DANube; then DANark; then in England, DUNbar, DON
river, LonDON; and in Ireland, DANlough, DANegal,
DANsmore, LonDONderry. The prophecies about a lion

and a serpent are fulfilled in the national emblem of Norway, which shows a lion with a serpent's tail, proving that the tribes were there; and in the British lion.

(4) In Judg. 12, members of two nations are distinguished by their ability or inability to say "shibboleth." The Ephraimites, who said "sibboleth," were ancestors of the British who also drop their h's.

(5) Scotch plaid demonstrates descent from Ephraim, for Joseph's coat was of many colors.

(6) The stone of Bethel, on which Jacob slept, he later took with him to Egypt. Moses brought it back, and this was the rock he struck to get water. Also, it was the "pillar rock" of the later Temple. At the time of the exile, Jeremiah took the stone to Egypt again. He started out from Egypt to "visit his old friends" among the lost ten tribes, but stopped in Spain. Then, on the way to Denmark, Jeremiah was shipwrecked and thrown up on the coast of Ireland. The daughter of Zedekiah, who had accompanied him, met and married the Irish king. When Ireland conquered Scotland, the stone was removed thither, and now rests in the coronation seat of Westminster Abbey.

(7) America was not discovered by Columbus the Catholic, but by Leif Ericsson the Protestant, who was himself a descendant of Israel.

(8) The eagle, the emblem of the United States, was likewise the emblem of Israel. So were the olive branch and the thirteen arrows, which the eagle now holds. The reverse of the Great Seal shows the pyramids of Egypt, a reminiscence of our ancestors' sojourn in that country.

(9) The British coat of arms shows the harp of David, the lion, the unicorn, and the sphinx, all of which indicate Israelite origin.

It is further held that, while the people of the British Isles are of the tribe of Ephraim, America is from Manasseh for

(10) Manasseh was older than Ephraim, and in all pictures Uncle Sam is seen to be older than John Bull.

(11) "The daughters of Manasseh had an inheritance

among his sons" (Jos. 17:5f.) and it is in America that women have equal rights.

(12) Manasseh was a thirteenth tribe, and 13 is America's number.

(13) When crossing into Canaan, the tribe of Manasseh asked to be divided. Such requests typify the history of Manasseh's American descendants, for the exiles to Holland divided themselves, and America later divided itself by the Mason-Dixon Line.

If we smile at the lengths to which an uninformed Biblical literalism can go, let us not forget what British Israel does for its believers in Britain and America. It tells them that unschooled and underprivileged, spent and weary as they may be, they have a brighter vision: for they are none else than the chosen people of God.

6. ELEMENTS OF RESOURCE IN THE CULTS

There are two sides to religion. It is because, among the established churches, both sides have not always received their just due, that we find Christian history peppered with the rise and fall of movements that have stressed now this, now that neglected aspect of the total Christian claim.

The two sides are variously named. One may call them the *subjective* and *objective* aspects, since some thinkers are impressed chiefly by the inward values of religion, others by its external authentication. Or they may be described as *pietism* and *activism*. Again, since the difference has found expression in denominational divisions, one may speak of the Catholic and Protestant sides; for Catholic Christianity often tends to be more objective and externalistic than Protestant. Whatever names are chosen, the distinction is plain. One man will feel that religion is first of all a matter of experience, providing awareness of divine guidance and direction. He may, indeed, become so sensitive to the power of the divine Spirit, or to the transcendence of

God, as to deny that human capabilities or the material world
have any significance at all. Another, however, will with equal
sincerity reject all that as meaningless if not repugnant. For him,
religion must be rooted in "Reality"—in history, and action.
To borrow William James' phrase, he is the "tough-minded"
Christian; whereas the other, who is more concerned for spiritual
consciousness or the exclusive power of God would be called
the "tender-minded" Christian.

Now there can be little doubt that, for most of the egregious
religious cults of our day, the support has come mainly from
people of the "tender-minded" type. The stress of personal circumstance, and more recently the cracking apart of civilization
itself, leads multitudes to seek superhuman reassurance, whether
from the stars or from one or another sort of religious "gnosis,"
to enable them to meet life confidently and with inward peace.

The haven thus provided, it must be recognized, is often a
real defense against vicissitude. On all levels, physical, intellectual, moral and spiritual, some of the movements we have
named offer values of no mean importance, which are at the
same time challenges to what has often been regrettable laxness
and negligence in the Church at large.

Healing

Sometimes there is real healing of physical disease. While
the whole subject of psychosomatic medicine is in its infancy,
we know enough to be sure of the relationship between spiritual
and bodily well-being. There can be no doubt whatever that
genuine, even permanent, physical betterment sometimes accrues
from Christian Science and from forms of faith-healing, just as
from Roman Catholic healings at Lourdes. Such phenomena
almost certainly follow genuine psychosomatic laws. Danger
arises, of course, when a principle, of undoubted value in
selected types of illness, is by cult teaching made to apply to
diseases for which it is not effective, so that proper medical
care is deferred too long.

Morale

More important than physical healing is the value of the cult in promoting morale. Devotees of neo-fundamentalist movements, so many of whom are uneducated and poorly privileged, are given a new sense of importance: they have, so they are told, an insight and a promise that their more comfortable contemporaries do not share. In a different way, the mentalist cults often inspire the individual's confidence in himself, and in Divine Power, and thus eliminate much fear of the future.[2]

World view

The cult offers a unified world view. Its teaching is regarded not simply as *a* truth, but as *the ultimate* truth of the universe. Few cults would hold, to be sure, that no further knowledge can come to man. But such increase will be in the nature of the unfolding of ideas already latent in the cult teaching, which itself will never be supplanted. Hence the devotee is *now* in possession of the key to the riddle of the cosmos, all of whose phenomena are to be interpreted in its light.

Interest

It is not surprising, therefore, that the cult makes religion very interesting. Christian Scientists often say that when two or three of them get together, the conversation nearly always turns to Christian Science. The same could be said of most of these movements. Discussion of the religion is thus socially fashionable and, especially among the mentalist groups, sophisticated.

The religious life

The cult fosters and nurtures the religious life. The periodicals of movements like Unity and Christian Science, and similarly those of neo-fundamentalist bodies like Jehovah's Witnesses,

[2] It may be questioned, however, whether the movements of Group (2) impart much genuine stability. In the face of death, for example, adherents of these cults are notoriously *less* assured than the usual member of an ordinary Christian denomination.

treat almost exclusively of specific cult teachings and their application to the individual; and do not, like so much literature of the regular denominations, run the gamut of social and political comment, ecclesiastical structure, ecumenicity and the like. Besides periodical literature, intensive study of official cult books is strongly encouraged. Especially among the mentalists, adherents are usually expected to spend from a half-hour upward in daily study, and in the type of meditation which, in such circles, goes for prayer. Thus the individual is confronted constantly and almost exclusively with the application of religion to his own daily round. If this narrows, it likewise greatly intensifies his religious thinking.

All these resources combine, in the cult, toward *making religious activity a primary concern* for the adherent. Giving him so much that is immediately useful, the cult is able in turn to make drafts upon his time and money which, in comparison with results in older denominations, sometimes seem enormous.

7. ELEMENTS OF RESISTANCE

Yet the advantages which cult practices provide are balanced by most serious deficiencies. These too must be noted if the Church is to answer intelligently the challenge of these movements. Not all the shortcomings are shared, of course, by all the groups; nor by all the cults listed under any one group. Broadly speaking, however, the following characteristics do hold good of the groups indicated:

Deficiencies characterizing Groups (1), (2), and (4)

There is a marked tendency in many of these cults to be *ill-informed* and even *to make a virtue of ignorance*. Of course few of them would admit this charge. By and large, however, we find a strong disposition to deprecate scholarship, and to attribute unholy motives to the scientist, the theologian and the clergyman. This is an inevitable result of the fact that both the non-Christian and the neo-fundamentalist movements draw largely from people of limited schooling. In the mentalist bodies also, there is a tendency to disfavor painstaking research, and to prefer knowledge gained through spiritual intuition. Furthermore, almost none of the cults stems from what could be termed a real acquaintance with the Christianity of history.

The cult offers *a short cut to the good life.* Astrology and Spiritualism, in their several ways, claim to draw back the curtain of the future. Theosophy, like Buddhism, solves the problem of evil: it is regarded as punishment, if not for sins of this life, then for those of previous incarnations. The "I Am" movement, like the mentalist bodies, tells its adherents that they can acquire life's good things by affirming that these are already present. The neo-fundamentalist bodies teach, as we have said, that their followers are exclusive possessors of a truth, a hope or a heritage.

Most of these movements *lack social vision.* We search in vain for any organized, conscientious grappling with the outrageous public evils of our time. When problems of race, industry or war are mentioned at all, the answer of non-Christian and mentalist bodies is usually that social salvation comes exclusively from individual salvation, through each man appropriating for himself the teachings of the particular movement. Since many adherents of these two groups are already in comfortable circumstances, the effect is to desensitize them to widespread human need. On the other hand, cults of Group (4) are disposed to regard the social situation as irremediable, and to be *replaced* by supernatural intervention. "There'll be pie in the sky by-and-by." Adherents are thus persuaded to be content with their lot, awaiting a reward in the next world, and ill-disposed to agitate for present betterment.

There is much *commercialism.* Large sums of money are extracted from the devotee through fees for private consultations, sale of literature at prices considerably higher than is customary among the regular denominations, and emotionally powerful financial appeals. Nor do we deprecate this simply out of envy at the cults' financial successes. The condemnation arises from the fact that most of these movements are *not* known for widespread benevolences nor, except among a few neo-fundamentalists, for overseas missions. The money is kept at home, and goes to build the wealth of the institution or, far too often, the wealth of its leaders.

Deficiencies characterizing Groups (1), (2), and (3)

In most of the cults except the neo-fundamentalist ones:

Supreme authority rests in the visions or mystical intuitions of the founder of the movement. Father Divine is God. "No tongue or pen" taught Mrs. Eddy the science for her textbook. Emanuel Swedenborg was appointed of Jehovah to formulate the true concept of Christianity. God the Father and Jesus Christ personally appeared to Joseph Smith. To be sure, historic Christianity has always held to the validity of mystical experience. Such phenomena are authoritative, however, only for the experiencer, and only if they meet specific tests of their origin and cogency. Christianity has never held that the mystical intuitions of one individual are binding upon another individual, and therein lies its sharpest distinction from most of these movements.

The world of history and nature loses significance and may even be *denied to exist.* At best, the temporal order is but a "manifestation" of the divine, at worst an expression of the unreal human mind.

Man is placed nearly or actually on the level with God. This follows naturally from the second point since, if history and nature are unreal or without genuine significance, then man himself exists only in the supratemporal and divine sphere.

There is therefore no room for a real Incarnation or a real sacrament. Yet these are at the very heart of historic Christianity.

Deficiencies characterizing Groups (1) and (2) only

Certain shortcomings of the non-Christian and the mentalist bodies are peculiar to these, and yet grow naturally out of deficiencies shared with the other groups. That they are found only in Groups (1) and (2) indicates that these movements more frequently push their teachings to extremes, or else do not balance them with other, modifying doctrines.

Cults of these types usually *depreciate personality*. This is regarded as a false concept of man's nature, whose true reality stems from an impersonal or superpersonal Power. Religious life is simply the application of impersonal cosmic law. The Deity Himself (or rather, Itself) is thought of as either unknowable (Astrology, Spiritualism usually) or as a cosmic Principle, Mind or Over-Soul. In all this there is frequently a strong tendency toward pantheism.

Though personality is not highly regarded, yet these movements generally *cater to the individual's preoccupation with himself*. Sometimes he seems disposed to *use* his God to gain his own ends. Now the availability of religion to meet personal need is, as we have recognized, a prime desideratum. Nevertheless, the almost exclusive emphasis on what religion *gets* for *oneself* must be condemned on many grounds. It increases introversion. It rarely or never produces genuine stability. It makes for selfishness and social blindness. It ignores the basic psychological fact that the surest cure for maladjustment is often the complete abandonment of self to an interest in one's fellow.

The significance of sin is minimized. Attention is drawn chiefly to the removal of pain rather than of moral obliquity. The individual is blinded to his own selfishness. He may even feel himself to live in a supratemporal order that is exempt from mundane moral obligations.

The evil of occult and irrational religious movements consists, thus, not simply in the fact that they seem foolish to us. It lies far deeper. Such practices provide easy escape from personal and public moral responsibility. They depreciate hard and straight thinking. They encourage the desire to fly from reality, into magic and mystification. They weaken moral fiber. These are a high price to pay, even for real release from deep misery.

8. THE ANSWER OF THE CHURCH

The challenge of the cults, whether for good or for ill, confronts the Church at nearly every point of its historic faith. When they deny or transmute that faith, they must be vigorously contradicted. Therefore we shall affirm, against them, the supreme worth of personality, the reality and significance of time and history, the centrality of sacramental religion, and mankind's personal and social moral responsibility before God.

We have also to *learn* from the cults:

First, to reconstitute the Church's mission to the underprivileged. It is a damning charge against the history of many denominations that they have begun among the humble, only to continue as societies of the comfortable. Yet Christianity has been strong always and only to the extent that it has foregone privilege, and reached out to the weary, the unschooled and the needy.

Second, to study and apply the truth that bodily health and spiritual health go hand in hand. Steps in this direction already have been taken by several denominations. They ought to be extended, until psychosomatic medicine receives fullest aid from the techniques of religious counseling and from the religious life of the layman.

Third, to bring home to people the immediacy and avail of God in every department of life. The college girl who said, "God is nice, but not much use in an emergency," put in words a frustration that too many have felt in standard religious pursuits. Yet *God is really true.* It ought to be possible, and the cults have shown that it is possible, to make religion not only clear, but absorbingly interesting, and practically effective in the daily round.

Every cult exists because someone has needed what it claims to give. This proffered gift, coming under many guises, is in fact quite simple. It is spiritual religion. The bent of the human spirit to the Divine Spirit is innate, and testifies to a Reality of the universe. Therefore, while we oppose the cults when they are wrong, and learn from them when they are right, a greater, a supreme task lies before us. It is to recover and make available to our time Christianity's ancient doctrine of the Holy Spirit.

FURTHER READING

ATKINS, GAIUS GLENN. *Modern Religious Cults and Movements.* New York: Fleming H. Revell Company, 1923.

CHESTERTON, G. K., *et al. Twelve Modern Apostles and Their Creeds.* New York: Duffield, 1926.

JONES, RUFUS M. *The Church's Debt to Heretics.* London: James Clarke & Co., Ltd.

WEBER, JULIUS A., compiler. *Religions and Philosophies in the United States of America.* Los Angeles: Wetzel, 1931.

PART III

The Church: Basic Response

CHAPTER 9

Christianity and the Non-Christian Religions

HUGH VERNON WHITE

CHAPTER 10

Resources in a Genuinely Christian Church

EDWARD L. PARSONS

9

CHRISTIANITY AND THE NON-CHRISTIAN RELIGIONS

Hugh Vernon White

Introduction.   1.   The nature of religion: its determinative character.   2. Christianity a missionary religion.   3. The nature of the Christian faith: truth and reality.   4. Relations with non-Christian religions: the realm of religiousness, the realm of truth, the realm of works.   5. The Christian mission as an asset.

Other chapters of this volume have dealt with the forces and influences that favor or oppose the purposes of Christianity *within* Christendom. The book begins with the recognition that there are secular rivals to the Christian faith that presume to supplant it as a basic conception of reality and of the nature and destiny of man. All the other chapters seek to distinguish in the organized activities of human society the elements of non-Christian and anti-Christian conceptions of life. In facing all these influences that are antagonistic to Christianity, the truth of Christian faith and the validity of the Christian way of life are not argued but assumed.

We must, however, face the fact that there are other religions in the world that call in question the unqualified truth and validity of Christianity, and that the majority of mankind are followers of those religions. These are not like the secular substitutes for religion which constitute the problem within Christendom. They are themselves historic faiths which furnish to men an ultimate orientation to reality and a sense of meaning and destiny. They provide the fundamental norms for man's thought and conduct; they claim to be the true spiritual and moral basis of human life.

1. THE NATURE OF RELIGION

If the world were neatly divided among the religions and if societies could develop in intimate and undisturbed dependence upon their several spiritual faiths, the world situation itself would not present to Christianity the problem of its relation to other faiths. But, of course, this never has been the case and, in our time, is not even thinkable. Today the world is one community and the different religions of mankind are in the presence of one another. It is demanded of Christianity, therefore, that it shall discover the true basis of its relations with other religions. What that basis is will depend upon our conception of religion in general and of the proper function of religion in the totality of human life. Even more determinative will be our understanding of the character of the Christian religion.

These questions are answered by many educated men by the relegation of religion to the role of an inward and individual form of belief, the only legitimate outward expression of which is in the act of social worship. From this point of view even organized religion is characteristically occupied with transcendental and supernatural or otherworldly interests and has no relation in principle to the social, cultural or even the moral life of men. Accordingly, even though the religions are in the presence of one another in a world or national community, all that is required of them is the practice of tolerance. So far as the practical business of life is concerned it can and will go on in response to needs and by virtue of forces and interests that have nothing to do with religion but are self-explanatory and self-sufficient. The popular expression of this point of view is that "it doesn't matter much what your religion is if you are sincere in your belief."

A determinative force

This position is consistent with the presuppositions of a secular society, but it belies the place of religion in the history of man and it is allied to an inadequate and faulty knowledge of the human spirit. The basis of our present inquiry is the conviction that religion is a formative and determinative force in every aspect of man's life, individual and social, and that the good ends Christianity seeks in the practical or, more correctly, secular affairs of human life are directly and inwardly related to the religious faith and commitment of the Christian Church. Christian faith is the source of Christian works; the Christian religion is the dynamic of a Christian civilization.

When, therefore, the Christian Church assumes responsibility for civilization it can only be on the assumption that it can undertake its task with confidence in the spiritual potencies of the Christian faith. At this point Christianity faces the necessity of determining its relation to other religions, each of which, in its own way, assumes a similar responsibility for the character of the common life. This necessity exists also because Christianity is, in principle, a universal religion. There are in the world tribal religions that do not claim validity beyond the human group to which they belong. Among advanced peoples the tribal becomes the ethnic faith, but still the idea holds that religion is the spiritual heritage and possession of a section of mankind and that the counterpart of cultural pluralism is religious pluralism. Let each man follow the faith of his fathers and of his environing society and respect others in doing the same. Such religions in our day are Hinduism and Judaism and, one might add, Shinto which has been, also, a national religion.

But there are also in the world universal religions, notably Buddhism, Mohammedanism and Christianity. Each one of these religions represents a historic rejection of tribal, ethnic and national ideas in the sphere of religion and claims to be equally true and valid for all men. The universal religion deals radically with man as man and holds that its truth about man and his destiny, whether received through revelation, as in Islam, or discovered by the exercise of human thought, as in Buddhism, is a truth that has no national boundaries and is limited to no one form of human culture.

2. CHRISTIANITY A MISSIONARY RELIGION

Christianity, being such a universal faith, must deny the religious pluralism of the ethnic faiths and must come into inevitable rivalry with those religions which make the same claim to the assent and acceptance of all men. For what Christianity seeks is both the fullest and most complete communication to each individual of the truth and grace of God, and the regeneration and redemption of the common life, that is, the creation of a Christian civilization.[1] This means that Christianity, in the broadest sense of the word, is a missionary religion. No one except the religious isolationist is troubled by the positive aspect of the missionary character of our Christian faith. Rather we find in it a source of inspiration; it gives us confidence in our profession of Christianity to feel that there is nothing narrow or provincial about it and that in its vision and essential adequacy it includes all men and all sorts and conditions of men. We do not feel that, by being Christians, we are accepting any permanent and necessary spiritual separation from any man or any part of the race. We value our religion precisely because it is not peculiarly "ours" but is a faith true enough and fundamental enough and hospitable enough to embrace men of every race and culture, without doing violence to any of the legitimate variations of custom and cultural form.

But many Christians of liberal and tolerant spirit are offended by the fact that such a program, though consistent with and even demanded by the essential character of the faith, does set

[1] The term "Christian civilization" is used here not as applying to the cultural aspects of the common life, still less to the technological, but to the moral basis and spiritual assumptions of a human society.

the Christian in opposition to, and in rivalry with, the religions of those to whom he presents his universal gospel. We shrink from religious controversy. Looking back over the theological wrangling within Christendom and the sectarian rivalries that have been a scandal in Christian history, we are prone to assume a "peace at any price" attitude in the realm of religion. It seems unfitting that the spirit of competition and conflict which as Christians we seek to purge from the secular life should be admitted into the realm of worship and the service of God. Above all do we deplore any affront to the religious feelings and beliefs of other men and any effort to force our own views upon them.

There is much that is right and Christian in these feelings. But alongside such worthy sentiments, in this connection, must be put the fact that too many are cool to the missionary effort of the Church from sheer lack of imagination, from parochialism and from a temper of "sweet reasonableness" in religion that derives in part from lack of clear and strong Christian conviction and in part from the tendency to exalt an urbane spirit above the weightiest considerations in man's service to God.

Beset by the tension between these positive and negative considerations as we confront the missionary imperative of our faith we are called upon to do clear and discriminating thinking. We should act not upon the basis of threadbare parodies of the missionary and such slogans as "thrusting our religion down other people's throats," and "one religion is as good as another," but according to sound knowledge of the world situation in religion, and acquaintance with the actual practice of Christian missions and with their characteristic results in the lives of men. The missionaries themselves, by and large, are at least as sensitive to the negative considerations regarding their task as are the rest of us. They are respectful and considerate toward the beliefs and practices of those they seek to win to Christ. Their approach is on a basis of friendship and frankness. There is no coercion; in fact, there is seldom a situation in which

coercion could be exercised. Nor does the missionary who represents the great body of Protestant Christendom seek to impose
his dogmatic beliefs upon his converts. Like the preacher in a
pulpit here at home he preaches "not himself but Christ Jesus as
Lord" and witnesses to a truth and grace that are not of himself
but of God. Departures from this, when they occur, are bad and
unchristian missionary practice, just as they are wrong when
the Church at home is guilty of them.

As to the feeling that rivalry in religion is disgraceful we
ought rather to say that in no other area of human life is a
faithful and persistent search for truth and rejection of error so
necessary. What the truth about God is, what His will for man
is, these are of supreme importance. No false delicacy of feeling, no dilettantism should be allowed to protect us from the
element of difference or even of conflict in so far as it is involved
in making our testimony to the Christian revelation. We must
contend earnestly, even though lovingly, for the faith entrusted
to us. We expect those of other religions also to defend and to
propagate their faith.

One might well hesitate to urge a private preference or a
personal theory of the spiritual life upon others, but the missionary witness of the Christian is no such subjective thing. The
faith of the Church in its Lord is God's saving message to all
men. Christians are not pushing their preferences on other men
when they proclaim that faith. On the other hand, they fail in
a fundamental obligation to God and man when they do not
participate in its proclamation. Here the shoe is squarely on
the other foot: the Christian has received a trust, a divine gift
in which is bound up his and all men's salvation, and he has
no right to withhold that gift from any man. The Church lies
under absolute and permanent necessity to make Christ known
and to teach his ways to all peoples. It cannot determine the
response of men nor the ultimate outcome of its testimony;
these are in the hands of God. But it betrays its Lord and
renounces its primary function if it fails to preach his gospel.

3. THE NATURE OF THE
CHRISTIAN FAITH

One other point needs to be clarified regarding the general situation confronted by the Church in its missionary task. This has to do with the question of truth in religion and with the authenticity of the revelation of God in Jesus Christ. We can easily fall into complete relativism if we are not perfectly clear as to our meaning of "truth" and as to the reality of the Christian revelation in Christ. We are here involved in the whole problem of religious knowledge and of faith and its object. Manifestly such a theme cannot be treated adequately in a subsection of one chapter which itself is only part of one volume in a series. But some recognition of the problem must be made and some attempt at an outline of the way it must be approached if the missionary claim of Christianity is to be rationally validated. Accordingly I make the following comments:

(1). Our grasp or apprehension of truth is always limited and imperfect. This is largely due to the fact that we think in terms of concepts which, just in the degree that they are precise and clearly defined, lose something of the reality to which they refer. This is a limitation of all human knowledge but more so of thought about spiritual reality than in knowledge of the physical order. The conception and expression of truth in religion often issues in myth and paradox, but these myths and paradoxes are themselves true or false, that is, they either point on to the fuller meaning that rational thought cannot clearly grasp, or they point away from that meaning. Indeed, poetry, drama and works of creative imagination often represent more vividly the full meaning of our ideas than do clearly defined concepts. They clothe the bare structure of intellectual forms with something of the warmth and color and energy of reality. But the structure of our thought is still rational and we must deal responsibly with truth in rational terms despite their limitations. The qualitative supplements the conceptual and the conceptual disciplines the qualitative imagery of religious truth.

(2). The Christian faith, in so far as it is a system of beliefs held in terms of human thought, is thus not Truth absolute for there is no absolute Truth in such terms. Viewed objectively, it is one among many more or less completely articulated and successfully expressed systems of religious ideas. The Christian and his theology suffer from the native imperfection and inadequacy of all human thought. There is every reason, therefore, why the Christian should be modest and humble in his discussion of religious truth with those who hold to other beliefs.

(3). The Christian cannot but hold, however, that, so far as the mind can go in its grasp of truth, the basic convictions of his faith are true and that the affirmations that are made in the face of paradox or even in the form of myth are substantially right and to be trusted, and that the outcome of any other system of human thought in religion that contradicts those affirmations is misleading and not to be received. Whatever areas of belief and affirmation of truth the Christian may have in common with the non-Christian, and these areas are larger than we are likely to think, the body of faith as a whole is in contradiction with Christianity when it issues in ultimate affirmations and demands that deny the ultimate meaning of Christian faith. Such a denial is found in each of the other universal religions. Therefore, while the Church holds with due humility its Christian *doctrine,* it must assume responsibility for patient teaching of the *truth* that its doctrine tries to express. This means that there is a challenge to the non-Christian system as a totality even while there is much common understanding and agreement in specific matters and in particular areas of belief. Were there not such common ground it would be difficult if not impossible ever to win a convert, or for one who has become a Christian to understand the change of belief that has taken place in him.

(4). We must go further and observe that the object of the Christian's faith is not primarily truth conceived as a system of ideas however well articulated and expressed. His confidence does not rest upon the greater competence of this theological thinking but upon the manifestation of God in the historic tradition of the Hebrew people and his definitive embodiment in the person of Jesus of Nazareth. The Christian shares with religious men in all traditions the revelation of God in nature and in the inner consciousness. He has the same rational faculties with which to construct concepts and to develop ideas about God. But he has something that neither Buddhism nor Mohammedanism even claims to present to its adherents, namely, the historic manifestation of God in a human person. To say this does not carry endorsement of the Chalcedonian or any other christology but it does constitute one of the ultimate affirmations of the Christian faith. It affirms that God, who is infinitely above and greater than man, is, also, completely one with man, and that Jesus of Nazareth is the factual evidence of this oneness. Christian belief and thought thus rest back upon the historic reality of God as He has come to man rather than upon the most profound speculative insight of religious genius derived from the universal experience of God in creation and in human consciousness. The belief of the Christian is not primarily in a Truth but in a Reality.

Truth and reality

While human thought in theology as well as in other realms may issue in paradox and the myth that point beyond rational concepts, the Christ in whom the Christian believes and the God whom he reveals are neither paradox nor myth but substantial Reality. The difference between these two forms or stages of the object of faith, *truth* and *reality*, comes to light in the discussion of the Christian world mission in *Re-Thinking Missions*, where Professor Hocking writes, regarding the universal quest for truth in religion: ". . . a part of the life of any living religion is its groping for a better grasp of truth. The truth which rectifies the faults of any religious system is already foreshadowed in its search. Hence all fences and private properties in truth are futile; the final truth, whatever it may be, is the New Testament of every existing faith."[2] In so far as the Christian has the impulse to a better understanding of the truth, and in so far as with human limitations he is engaged in that quest, he shares a common experience of mankind, just as he does when he seeks a better solution of political or economic problems, or progress in scientific knowledge.

On the other hand, Hocking arrives at the definitely Christian basis of faith in his later book, *Living Religions and a World Faith*, where, following an appreciative treatment of the universal search for truth in religion, he declares, that "the moral tetanus due to the rooted suspicion of human nature (which is our most radical sin) that the ideal is a *mere ideal*, an eternal Platonism, has to be broken. To break that palsy would be to release for action the torrent of the pent-up idealism of mankind, and this would be the saving of the world." He finds in the person of Christ the illustration or symbol of the reality, ". . . the veridical traits of actuality are there; and the full idea is embodied. Christianity is the only religion which inclines to substitute its founder for its entire doctrine, and knows that it has gained rather than lost by so doing."[3]

But if we are not still to remain within the bonds of a Platonic idealism we must go on to the full Christian affirmation that Christ is not merely the embodiment of an Idea but the incarnation of the living God. For God is not *mere idea* but Reality. Philosophy seeks an adequate Idea as the goal of thought. Hocking, as a Christian philosopher, finds the most adequate expression of that Idea not in a rational concept but in the personal symbol. Religious faith boldly says "God" instead of "Idea," and looks beyond the terms of its own discursive reason to that God whose eternal being determines the form of the Idea. And it sees in Christ not alone the symbol but also the reality of God. Christian faith can thus be analyzed into these

[2] W. E. Hocking, *Re-Thinking Missions* (New York: Harper & Brothers, 1932), p. 44.

[3] W. E. Hocking, *Living Religions and a World Faith* (New York: Harper & Brothers, 1940), pp. 235-236.

elements or stages: (1) the mind itself; (2) our formulated beliefs or doctrines about God; (3) the perfect Idea which is the unattained goal of thought and which the limited truth of Christian doctrine approximated; and, finally, (4) the Living God, present in Christ, Who is the object of knowledge and faith, of belief and trust, and whose being determines the Idea just as the Idea determines the degree of truth or error to be found in any doctrine or system of doctrine.

Great confusion arises here through the failure, from which Professor Hocking is not entirely free, to distinguish between truth as the Idea in terms of thought, and Reality as the self-subsistent Object, the living God of Christian faith. The Idea is the hypothetically perfect mental form, but a form that refers beyond itself to God. Men worship not the Idea but God both before they try to conceive the Idea and while they are engaged in the attempt. The absolute idealist, of course, identifies the Idea with God and under the influence of Hegel a good deal of modern thought about God has made that identification. But it leads to confusion to do that and then to say that a historic person is the real object of faith or that he can, with profit, be substituted for the entire doctrine of Christianity. But if we say that the historic person is the embodiment or incarnation of the true and living God who is something more than even the most perfect idea of God, then Christianity has clarified its meaning.

It has also established the basis for its universal appeal and for its claim to the acceptance of all men. For the object of its faith is not a more highly developed truth about God, beyond which it hopes to go, nor merely a more expressive symbol, but God Himself as He appears in Christ, beyond whom there is none to seek. With complete humility, therefore, and with no pretensions to moral or intellectual or cultural superiority the Christian can and must preach the gospel to men and invite them to participation in a faith not only more adequate in content but different in this essential point from that which they have followed. The Hebrew-Christian idea of God as creator and of His self-revelation in historic events gives to the time process profound reality and moral significance. The Christian affirmation of His incarnation in Jesus Christ denies all doctrines of the evil or unreality of matter. This incarnation is not a mere theophany but a revelation of God in terms of the moral personality of an actual man in a specific historical nexus, making the reality of God a part of the life of man. The divine imperative for human righteousness derives from the character of God thus revealed. It calls men to individual God-likeness and to a fellowship that Jesus called the kingdom of God. This is a personal matter throughout; God is revealed in a human person, the redemption of man is reconciliation to God through repentance and forgiveness, the coming of the kingdom in history and beyond history is the creation of a fellowship by the love of God communicated to man and made the law of his social existence.

The Christian enjoys an advantage both doctrinally and morally that other religious men do not have because of the historic basis and character of his faith. But this is an advantage that he must share; it is not given for any limited section of humanity but is for all. The missionary character of Christianity is determined by the absolute obligation to continue the act of revelation that is in principle complete in Christ but that requires the faithful testimony and life of the Church to make it complete in historic and spiritual fact.

4. RELATIONS WITH NON-CHRISTIAN RELIGIONS

So far we have been dealing with the radical, missionary character of the Christian faith. This is a necessary preliminary to any discussion of the relation of Christianity to other religions from the standpoints both of resistance and resource. It must first be made clear that the Christian Church understands and assumes its missionary task without misgivings before we consider the relations of co-operation or conflict that arise through the presence together of the different religions in the same human scene.

Although Christianity is a universal and missionary religion, indeed, just because it is such a faith, it must look for those elements in the other religious systems that contribute to Christian ends. It must also identify clearly those things that are essentially opposed. Some illustrations may be presented to indicate what sort of thing may be found in either case, but no survey of the total world situation can even be attempted here. However, there are three areas in which the principles involved can be stated. They are (1) the forms of religiousness, (2) the truths and (3) the works of the non-Christian religions.

Much has been said in recent years about "sharing" as a missionary method. It has been urged that sharing is a two-way process; the Christian shares his faith and he also shares in the values of the other religions. He both gives and receives. This principle is involved in the intercourse with other religions in which we discover things that help and detect those that hinder realization of the Christian purpose. (We ought to note clearly that it is the *Christian* purpose that is normative.) This sharing process or, for our present purposes, this process of discrimination does not deal with the God who is revealed in Christ, but with the elements of the human response to that revelation in the forms of devotion, thought and moral effort. There is one God; He is not ours to share or for others to share with us. There is one Christ; we do not exchange something of him for a portion from some other personal embodiment of God. This is the absolute of religion. Christ is to be shared in that we are to give all men the knowledge of him, but not in the sense in which we engage with the followers of other faiths in marshaling the resources of the human spirit to achieve ends already determined by the word and spirit of Christ. It is, therefore, in the realms of worship, of theology and of ethics, all activities of the human spirit, that we can properly explore the non-Christian systems to discover resources for our task and to be warned of points of resistance to it.

The realm of religiousness

This is the area of the psychology of religion, of the cultivation of attitudes, sentiments and spiritual habits, of the "spiritual exercises" found in religious orders as well as the general practice of religion as a cult. It is not the realm of absolute values for there are both values and dangers in religiousness. Jesus directed his sharpest criticisms to the perverted religiousness of his contemporaries and Christianity has continued to be beset by similar perversions. On the other hand the practice of religion both inwardly and outwardly, that is, both individually and socially, is necessary to the full release of the Spirit of God in human life. It is a technique, a technique of the spiritual life. It is not unconnected with either thought or morality and, therefore, cannot be discussed in complete isolation from either. When religiousness becomes an end in itself it causes men to forget God and to develop a false confidence in themselves. It must always be made subject to the reality of God and to His demands upon men; here both the knowledge and the service of God are involved. Worship, theology and morality are of a piece, and all are subject to God, Who is worshipped, Who is believed in and Who is obeyed.

But in the important even though relative matter of religious practice men can learn from one another across the lines that most critically divide those of Christian and of non-Christian faith. Protestant Christians especially have need to learn in this way; not merely to copy superficially the methods and habits of those who seem to be spiritually mature, but to discover and appropriate the motions of the spirit in which religious living really consists. The accumulated wisdom and experience of the Roman Catholic tradition in this realm were so completely rejected by the Reformation that much of sound worth was lost to Protestantism. A certain cheapness, crudeness and superficiality have often filled the void, or religion has just been deficient in spiritual practices.

Now with the multiplied contacts and freer intercourse with the ancient religious traditions of the Orient and with a more sympathetic and informed acquaintance with the world of Islam we have a maximum opportunity to observe and appropriate those ways of the spirit which are of universal application.

What they are can only be suggested. Professor Hocking has pointed to some of them in *Living Religions and a World Faith*:[4] the sense of the majesty of God and the dignity of man to be found in Islam, the meditative element in Hinduism and Buddhism, the impersonal aspect of truth in Buddhism, the intense humanity of Confucianism. It is quite generally assumed that the Orient and especially India is much more conscious of the reality of the spiritual than are we of the West. Without sacrificing any of our sense of the historical and the practical we may well learn from the authentic saints of the East how to keep alive the consciousness of the presence of God. Of course, much of this spiritual methodology is to be found in the Christian heritage and literature of devotion. We have our Augustine, our Francis of Assisi, our *Theologica Germanica*, our Bunyan, our Groot and many others. Thus we can meet on a ground of common understanding as we share in the life of meditation and devotion and remembrance of God with men of other faiths. We have both something to receive and something to give. And in such giving and receiving both parties are enriched. We also recognize therein the common religious need and nature of all men.

The realm of truth

We are dealing here not with the Reality, the God of Christian faith and worship, nor even with the Idea which is the unattained thought form that truly corresponds to the Living God, but with the relative and growing body of interpretations and meanings of religious doctrine. It is this level of thought, the conceptual, in which no finality can be claimed, that every stimulus and contribution can be welcomed. The insights, the spiritual discoveries of Buddhist and Hindu, the reflections of religious thinkers upon the nature of the spiritual life, when brought into the stream of Christian thinking, help in various ways toward the clarification of truth. Sometimes, by contrast, the teaching of another religion will draw out more clearly the meaning of

[4] *Ibid.*, pp. 254-262.

Christian truth; sometimes, more positively, it will show a development not yet taken.

One illustration of the emphasis by contrast, is the fact that the meaning of love as *agape* in Christianity is made more apparent when compared with the meaning of love in other religious traditions. Through the work of the Lundensian theologians we have become aware of the great significance of this distinctive Christian conception. But the contrast between *agape* and *eros* is to be found not only in the interplay of Christian and Hellenistic elements in Christian history. Dr. J. E. Graefe, in a little book entitled *Christ and the Hindu Heart*, has revealed the same contrast between the Christian and the Hindu ideas of love. Accordingly, in translating the first epistle of John for Hindus, he could not find any word or idea in Indian religious thought that corresponds to *agape* but had to write "self-giving love" to make the meaning clear.[5] Thus apart from the theologian's historic research, a Christian missionary was called upon to define and express more fully the value of a Christian truth. This is but one of a number of similar instances where fuller exposition of truth was required in translation.

The most constant stimulus to the further development and expression of truth in Christianity has come always from the necessity to communicate it to those whose ideas, beliefs and general mental patterns were different from those of the existing Christian thought world. It is generally true that we learn by teaching, that we discover the fuller significance of our beliefs by communicating them to others. It is a commonplace of Christian history that the first Christian theology was developed in the process of expressing the faith in terms of the Greek mind. In this process much of the "intellectual apparatus" of Greek philosophy was employed. Not even this rich and flexible instrument was sufficient for the task, and in some cases Christian doctrine was prematurely set in dogmatic forms. But the essential undertaking was inevitable and the gain was great.

[5] J. E. Graefe, *Christ and the Hindu Heart* (New York: Fleming H. Revell Company, 1938), p. 76.

We are now engaged in reinterpreting Christian faith in terms of modern scientific and philosophical thought. It would not be strange if a similar reinterpretation should come from the inter-action of Christian thought with the thought systems of the great non-Christian religions. In this way those religions will supply a positive resource toward developing the meanings and implications of Christian truth. Such creative interaction in the realm of religious truth is not likely to take place quickly or by design. Much less will it be the work of Christian missionaries who broadmindedly try to understand, appreciate and appropriate the "truths" of other religions. It will come in due course as the growing Christian community in any traditionally non-Christian society grapples seriously with its own tradition and environment, and in terms of that heritage undertakes to express as well as can be done the essential and eternal truth of the Christian faith. This is a task of continuous interpretation and reinterpretation.

There are two recent attempts to deal with the nature of this process that are quite opposite in theory and yet are closer together in the outcome than might be expected: Professor Hocking's doctrine of reconception and Hendrick Kraemer's principle of discontinuity. According to the former the Christian recognizes the essential soundness of the quest of the non-Christian and assumes that what his present formulation of belief "means" or aims at is the truth. Since it is truth that the Christian also wants and has defined for himself in his doctrine there is no irreconcilable conflict but a call for more funda-mental reconception of the points at issue. In the course of this further exploration there emerges a higher integration of thought in which the non-Christian finds that his essential meaning is not only preserved but expressed better than he had understood it before. The Christian, on his part, finds that instead of com-promising or losing his truth he has simply carried it on to fuller development where he discovers that it includes the real meaning of the other belief which had heretofore been expressed in dim and perhaps objectionable terms.

This is a positive and even optimistic way of viewing the co-operation of Christianity with other religions in the realm of truth. It needs, however, to be taken critically. To begin with, this friendly interaction is strictly limited to the conceptual or symbolic forms of the development of truth and does not extend to the essential truth of Christianity even as conceived in terms of the ultimate Idea. It must also be noted that there is a negative side to the matter that Professor Hocking does not bring out and that is, that this reconceiving of the doctrine of the non-Christian is not only a matter of showing him what he was really looking for and expressing better what he really "means," but also involves the exposing of error in his original belief, and, if he is to progress toward the truth, his rejection of that error. All of us have had the experience of being compelled to renounce and reject ideas that we have held in good conscience. Honest intent in the quest for truth does not mean that what one actually believes is at the worst only a poorly developed or badly formulated truth. Reconception has both negative and positive functions; there is rejection of error as well as confirmation and development of truth. When Professor Hocking shifts the ground to the personal embodiment of the Idea, or, as the Christian says, of God in Jesus Christ he goes beyond this "conceiving" process and affirms the object of Christian faith which is not an idea to be thought and re-thought in endless interaction with other similar but less perfect presentations of truth, but the primary reality and point of reference of all thought for the Christian.

The other systematic treatment of this problem is that by Hendrick Kraemer. In *The Christian Message in a Non-Christian World*,[6] Kraemer deals with the "point of contact" between Christianity and other religious systems. He emphasizes the distinctive "apprehension of the totality of existence" of each religious system and the radical difference and contradiction between any non-Christian religion and Christianity when both

[6] Hendrick Kraemer, *The Christian Message in a Non-Christian World* (New York: Harper & Brothers, 1938), pp. 130-141 and 299-307.

are viewed in their totality. All other religions represent the attainment of a basic conception of reality and of human destiny that are contradicted at certain vital points by the self-revelation of God in Christ. In terms of doctrinal thought there is no concrete point of contact or of continuous development between the pagan faith, even at its best, and Christianity. This is due to the fact that Christianity is not merely a structure of religious thought and insight built up by doctrinal development but the revelation of the true and saving relation between God the creator and redeemer, and man the sinful and needy child of God. Man cannot by searching find out God, the appetite does not create the food to satisfy itself, man's felt need of God and all his efforts to satisfy that need do not give true knowledge or possession of God. This is the same distinction we have been making above between Idea and Reality, between thought and God.

But with all this stress upon the absolute difference between Christianity and the other religions Kraemer admits, in the realm of method and understanding, the possibility and necessity of interaction of thought. He observes that the language and meanings and, by implication, the concepts of the other religions must be understood and employed with complete sympathy and appreciation in order to convey the truth of Christianity. Hocking deals too exclusively with the positive side of this process and sees in it an outcome of mutual benefit even though it issues in showing the non-Christian that what he really meant was the truth that Christianity is trying to give him. On the other hand, Kraemer puts undue emphasis upon the radically contradictory character of the Christian revelation as it confronts the human apprehension of the divine within the other faiths. Even though there is crucial reconstruction of thought and rejection of the essential position of the other religion involved when a non-Christian accepts the Christian faith, there is still a wide area in the discussion between Christian and non-Christian in which terms held wholly or partly in common constitute the language and the forms of thought and expression through which the

Christian gospel is intelligibly and in the end successfully im-
parted and received.

The realm of works

Christians are sometimes surprised to discover among non-
Christians works of unselfishness and men of high integrity and
character. But morality is not a peculiarly Christian thing. All
men, at every stage of cultural development, must work out in
some way the problem of living together and must accept some
system of obligations and duties to one another. Individuals,
whatever the system, will vary from the most virtuous who seek
to fulfill the spirit as well as the letter of the law to those who
perform the minimum of outward acts of righteousness with no
inner understanding or acceptance of its meaning.

Back of every system of morality lies the basic principle,
either implicitly or consciously held, of man's moral obligation.
That principle may be obedience to a divine lawgiver in the
hope of gaining reward and escaping punishment in this world
or another. Or it may be the endless endeavor to reduce bad
karma and to increase good karma with the hope of ultimate
release from the burden of individual existence. Or it may be
response to the law of love and the quest for a fellowship of
men of good will in this present world and in the world to come.

In every religious system the implied or expressed system of
obligation, or the moral impulse, is related to the religious
belief as regards the nature of the divine, whether personal or
impersonal, and the nature and destiny of man. The religious
background of good works may not be apparent on the surface,
but it cannot be ignored by the Christian who seeks co-operation
with those of other faiths. He must understand the religious
basis of conduct in order to discern both the points of legitimate
co-operation and those at which the moral intent of Christianity
is denied and subverted. Two men may do the same act from
different motives and with divergent and conflicting expectations.
One man may give alms in order to build up merit for himself;
another may give alms for the benefit of the needy. On the

surface the two are the same, but they are quite different acts when viewed in their wholeness and intent.

The possibility of co-operation to be found in other religions lies primarily in the moral integrity and intention of individuals and in their higher ideals. Men and women of moral sensitiveness in other religious traditions often respond to the Christian ethic of love with an enthusiasm and appreciation that put to shame the average Christian. The moral ideals of these non-Christians find in the Christian ethic a more adequate base and a more expansive scope for the expression of their moral impulses than they had known before. Filial love, humility, the capacity for self-denial, and similar moral attitudes find in the Christian way of love their true fulfillment.

The Christian world stands to be enriched by these discoveries of its own moral values both by those who become Christians through conversion and by the many who, though retaining their original faith, claim the Christian vision and impulse for their own. We may be convinced that in the end the religious source of Christian morality must and will be recognized. But in the fruitful period of discovery and communication the matter of conversion need not be pressed. After all, that is a matter between a man and God and any true conversion is the free response of the spirit to the God who speaks to man in Christ. The influence of Christian moral ideals is being widely recognized today among those of non-Christian cultures. Illustrations of this in India, China and Japan are numerous and convincing. A cultured Brahmin once declared in my presence, "Christianity has been like a searchlight thrown on the complex mass of Hinduism to reveal what is true and noble and what is weak and base."

On the other hand, it is sentimental and fallacious to idealize the virtues of non-Christians. There are moral evils in non-Christian systems that are the direct result of religious misconceptions and of defects in the moral principles underlying conduct. A Buddhist archbishop from Japan once said to a group of Christians in Hawaii, "We Buddhists do not object to the Christian Church sending missionaries to Japan if they do not interfere with the social customs of the country." Buddhist noninterference in the social morality of the people is one of the religious and moral defects of the system. Moral regeneration and social reform are natural results of authentic Christian faith. The whole non-Christian world must be brought under the criticism and moral motivation of Christianity. As this goes on we may expect a powerful reaction upon Christendom itself through the ever renewed awareness of the moral demand of its own faith.

We may sum up the results of this brief survey of the nature of Christianity as a missionary religion in the light of the elements of resource and resistance in the other religions somewhat as follows:

(1) Christianity approaches other religions as itself a missionary faith seeking to win all men to itself.

(2) The ultimate object of Christian faith is not a body of doctrine nor a mere Idea, but the living God who reveals Himself in Christ.

(3) There are areas of the activities of the human spirit in which Christianity discriminates between the helpful and the opposed elements in other religions, namely, in matters of religiousness, of truth and of practical goodness.

Social co-operation in efforts for community betterment or for the advancement of world objectives of justice, humanity and peace are supported and also limited by these fundamental factors in the religious situation. Wherever co-operation with non-Christians either as individuals or organized bodies is possible it should be welcomed. There are occasional instances of such co-operation. It must be recognized, however, that thus far they consist mainly in joint expressions of agreement in very general objectives. Much more is required if any co-operative program is to be significant. And no one acquainted with the general world situation can be blind to the fact that the moral power and organized effort for the realization of a better world community come from Christianity and from a small part of the Christian community at that. Whatever occasional and tentative response of co-operation may be found and however such responses may increase in the future, the Christian Church must assume the initiative and responsibility under God for the realization in the world of its own hopes and objectives.

5. THE CHRISTIAN MISSION AS AN ASSET

The conscious and organized effort of the Church to extend the faith and to create Christian communities in all parts of the world is itself one of the great resources of the Church. Much of the preaching of the Gospel, and of the teaching of Christian truth has been theoretical and unproductive because it has been unrelated to missionary action. The world mission of the Church is Christianity at work exhibiting its love for man, the universality of its doctrine and the acceptance of its God-given task. To cherish a high and universal truth and witness to it only in words is stultifying; the spiritual impotence of the Church has often been due to this kind of witness. The Church has both an intensive and an extensive mission; it must try to make Christian the life of the immediate neighborhood and it must sow the seeds of Christian community in all the earth.

The fruits of the missionary movement in modern times have been rich, varied and, in some respects, unexpected. There has been, for example, the reaction of the geographic outreach upon tasks near at hand. The Church has been awakened and sensitized to the human needs of the homeland by its very zeal for the welfare of men overseas. It has come to see as a glaring defect of its concern for men as men that missionaries devote themselves to the service of black and brown and yellow men in other parts of the world while color prejudice and race discrimination flourish in our home communities and even in our churches. As the Christian mission has broadened into educational, health and social services and as Christianity has defined itself as respect and concern for human persons, it has strength-

232   *Hugh Vernon White*

ened the Christian purpose and sharpened its conscience regarding social injustices in our own society. The Christian mission is the protagonist of man. It indicts forms of religion that debase him and it also opposes political, social and economic practices that exploit him and deny him the opportunity of full personal development. It sets up a standard by which the society of the home country is judged as well as those in "mission" lands.

The Christian mission has been the chief contributor to the world mindedness of the Church. Its missionaries move back and forth between the countries of Europe and North America on the one hand and those of Africa, Latin America and Asia on the other. They are at home in two worlds and interpreters of each to the other. They know the languages, the mentalities and the aspirations of two sections of the human race. They represent the best of their homelands to others and they bring home a real knowledge of those with whom they work. They are ambassadors of good will busily weaving among the peoples of the earth friendship, understanding and the sense of our oneness under God. The peace movement of recent times has been mightily undergirded by this substantial work of human service and interpretation. As Horace Greeley said long ago, "The missionary movement has put a map of the world in the vestibule of every village church of the land."

The Christian mission has been a major support for the ecumenical movement. It was out of the missionary conference at Edinburgh in 1910 that the world councils on Faith and Order and on Life and Work grew. The International Missionary Council represents the greatest united enterprise of non-Roman Catholic Christianity. It furnishes the ecumenical movement with a going concern, a network of activities all over the world engaging tens of thousands of missionaries and hundreds of thousands of national workers. It has made the word "ecumenical" geographically realistic because it has literally carried the Church into the whole inhabited earth. It has brought into the ecumenical gatherings men and women from most of the countries of the world so that the world Church is not any longer a Church of the Western Hemisphere, much less a Church of

Western Europe and North America. It has made Christianity in fact a global faith.

The missionary movement has contributed greatly to the purification and clearer definition of the faith. Beginning with the New Testament much of the literature that has set forth and developed the meaning of the Christian faith has been produced in the endeavor to present the faith to the non-Christian. It is in this expository kind of interpretation rather than in the definition of dogma for controversial purposes that the finest expressions of Christianity have been achieved. The best way to become conscious of one's faith and its values is to engage in communicating them to someone else. It is in this that the missionary work of the Church consists.

The Church itself has been constantly renewed in its spiritual vitality and zeal by the stimulus of the world mission. It is almost a truism that a high degree of missionary intelligence and activity deepens the spiritual life of a congregation and that a lack of such interest tends to stagnation. Missions are as much a cause as they are a result of missionary vigor. Every aspect of the task of the Church is illuminated and vitalized by a strong missionary interest; concern for realization of the social ideals of Christianity, awareness of the need of world peace and unity, the transcendence of sectarianism within the Church and, finally, growth into fulness of life in Christ.

FURTHER READING

HOCKING, W. E. *Living Religions and a World Faith.* New York: Harper & Brothers, 1940.

KRAEMER, H. *The Christian Message in a Non-Christian World.* New York: Harper & Brothers, 1938.

GRAEFE, J. E. *Christ and the Hindu Heart.* New York: Fleming H. Revell Company, 1938.

VAN KIRK, W. W. *A Christian Global Strategy.* Chicago: Willett, Clark & Company, 1945.

LATOURETTE, KENNETH SCOTT. *Anno Domini.* New York: Harper & Brothers, 1940.

10

RESOURCES IN A
GENUINELY CHRISTIAN CHURCH
Edward L. Parsons

*Introduction. 1. Opportunity, the accessibility of the world.
2. Fundamental moral integrity and stability. 3. A faith which
integrates total experience. 4. A spiritual power, compelling
and conquering.*

~~~~~~

This is not a sermon, but if it were it would have at least two
texts. One is that great charter of the Christian faith which
seems to burst from St. Paul's heart as he writes to his beloved
Philippians. This new faith of theirs is no one-track road. It is
no confining fanatic-breeding creed. It reaches out to all life.
"Whatsoever things are true, whatsoever things are honorable,
whatsoever things are just, whatsoever things are pure, whatsoever things are lovely, whatsoever things are of good report;
if there be any virtue, and if there be any praise think on these
things."

It touches all life; but, not as the dilettante, not, to use Dr.
Mackay's phrase, as the observer on the balcony. It touches it
with power. "I can do all things through him who strengtheneth
me," says St. Paul speaking to those same Philippians. And yet
again he tells the Corinthians how when the sense of his weakness overwhelmed him he heard God's voice: "My grace is
sufficient for thee for my power is made perfect in weakness."

It is a troubled, chaotic and sinful world we face today. The
demonic powers which contested in the war for its dominance

have been defeated in battle. They have not been destroyed, for they were only the embodiment focused at one point of the evil, the selfishness and pride which live in the hearts of men. The task of the Christian faith is to conquer that evil. It is always the same old enemy. He merely puts on different armor and uses different weapons. He merely substitutes atomic bombs for lances and sabers, radio for grapevine, secular radicalism for antinomian heresies, weird new cults for ancient pagan superstitions. But the evil is the same: the pride, the lust, the greed of men.

But because the weapons change, the Church has at each new era in human history to consider anew the nature of the attack and its own resources, not, let it be clear at the start, for defense, but for that instant counteroffensive which moves on to victory under the banner of the cross.

The work of the Church ought never to be defensive. To talk of saving the Church is a kind of defeatism, unworthy of those who believe that God is King. The business of the Church is to save the world; not to save itself.

Today the vast new discoveries which have changed the outward aspect of life have put an unprecedented demand upon the Church for this study of strategy and tactics. This book is one illustration. The previous chapters have surveyed one by one the various competing interests which contest with the Church for control of men's hearts and minds. Its particular burden has not been with obvious evil. Many of the chapters have discussed interests which in themselves are desirable or even necessary in the workaday life of the world. The difficulty lies in the fact that they claim men's time or men's loyalties in such fashion as to block the way of the Gospel to men's hearts. Some are bad. Some only substitute a good for the best. Each has been studied in its various manifestations; its strength and weakness portrayed, its evil and its good appraised. That has been a kind of Christian intelligence service.

There remains to sum up the resources of the Church, their character and striking power. They are often latent. They are obscured when faith is weak. They are revealed when faith is strong. The account of them, which at best is a summary, may be made in terms of four classes which build up into a picture of the vast resources of power which the Church possesses. They are:

(1) Opportunity; the accessibility of the world.
(2) Fundamental moral integrity and stability.
(3) A faith which interprets total experience.
(4) A spiritual power, compelling and conquering.

1. OPPORTUNITY

Once in awhile a parson feels isolated. He does not go down to business day by day. He does not put on overalls and work in a steel mill. He is never invited to the inner political circles of the town. He seems to be out of touch with the realities of life and it is possible that brooding over his position, he takes comfort in what has been the refuge of many troubled Christian souls since the beginning. He flees to the desert. It may be the literal desert of an Anthony. It may be the spiritual desert of his own heart. It is likely to be the social desert of his own small congregation. There he broods. There he basks in its light. Thence he looks out upon a world still in darkness. It is true that we do not find in American Christianity today many people taking refuge in the *Vita Monastica.* But we do find many ministers of Christ who are perpetually on the edge of a social and spiritual desert. They conduct services and preach sermons. They visit sick people and attend gatherings within their own congregation. But the scope of their work, as of their thought, is limited. They have actually come to living and working as if their very faith had separated them from the common life of the community.

No greater fallacy could get a foothold in a man's mind. There is literally no other profession which gives such wide opportunities for reaching people; no other calling to which the world of men and women is more accessible. The businessman's life is cramped. The lawyer's life moves in a groove. The journalist for all his wealth of opportunity meets people on the surface. The minister, if he is alert, indeed if he merely does the things which his profession asks him to do, is set in the midst of the life of the world.

I have put this in the singular and made it personal. But that is only one way of approach to the big task of surveying the opportunity of the Church in carrying out its mission of reaching men with the gospel of Christ. All the people who give themselves to these competing interests, who drift out of the Church or are hostile to it—are these people accessible? we ask.

They are. Pastoral opportunities are capable of almost unlimited expansion. Homes are open; sick people are touched and cheered and helped to healing; chance acquaintances become friends; troubled souls are advised and divided families are reunited. The friendship of the congregation reaches out with succor to the unfortunate. All true pastoral work constantly expands. It constantly reaches new people and it constantly enlarges the number of those within the congregation who would strengthen the fellowship. Ward politicians, fraternal orders, service clubs, have done this thing. The Church often does not do it very well, but it has done it and it can do it. It can make evident to the world that there is a deeper fellowship which can underlie and enrich all these others.

Neither the Church in a local congregation or such groups as men's clubs or women's missionary societies within that congregation exist to draw men and women away from Rotary or the Masons or the League of Women Voters. Their function is to reveal and develop the deeper loyalties out of which the lesser loyalties grow. Christianity is in essence never a negation. It is a fulfillment. "In Him is Yea," says St. Paul. But that touches another area of our resources. Here we are concerned with reaching people.

We have the same opportunity in civic interests and welfare work. Endless avenues open and as he moves along any one of them the minister of Christ or the Christian layman is bringing to those with whom he works the never-failing witness to the faith in which his service is grounded. The small town, and the big city alike are responsive to the Church's help in matters of the common good. Occasionally welfare workers suspect the competence of clergy. Now and then civic groups grow "political" and are not eager for too much church influence. But, taking American society as a whole, the co-operation of the Church is everywhere welcomed. Many a parson becomes the most influential citizen of his community. He does not rate high in getting publicity, but he is the person to whom those who are seriously concerned with civic welfare turn first. Of course he may get into trouble. He is likely to be more "radical" or progressive or liberal than many of the "best people." Sometimes he wins, sometimes he loses. But as St. Paul said of another situation, that does not really matter for "in every way Christ is proclaimed." People become aware that here is a man whose life is built on a foundation deeper and more solid than the social fellowships which engross the interests of so many people. Who can measure the impact upon the community of the courage of that young Congregationalist missionary David Burgess of whose fight to save the homes of a community of farmers in Missouri we read recently. There are hundreds of unrecorded stories of such courage, such clear-headed leadership. The "interests" don't like it; but the Lord Christ is exalted.

Here too must be included the teaching opportunity of the Church. There is no field lying beyond that of worship and pastoral care in which the minister of Christ can make his service count more effectively, nor any field in which the Church, through ministers and laity alike, can touch more effectively the springs of national life. In the church school on Sunday, in release time classes, on weekday afternoons and evenings, children and adults alike may be reached. The opportunity is great. There is no area in which the Protestant churches of America have failed more completely; no area to which, regarded as a resource, the word "latent" applies more appropriately.

But the matter does not need to be labored. Looking over the vast field of American life and tabulating the varied interests which block the way of the Gospel, the Church can never fall back upon the excuse that this and that area of life is inaccessible. Many hearts are as yet inaccessible. There is blindness and there is a burden of sin to be swept away. But the first resource of the Church in fighting successfully the battle of Christ is that the whole terrain lies open before it. In St. Paul's great charter the Church lays claim to all life. Week by week and day by day in worship, it cries, "Christ is Lord of Life." There are plenty of fights to be won before men accept that Lordship. But none of the competing interests has a greater, indeed none has so great, an opportunity to carry the struggle into every field of human endeavor.

But granted that the Church has reached people, has made contact with their lives and, to keep the military language, that the fight is on, what resources are at its command? What, for example, are the deeper loyalties which can illumine the meaning of the lodges and the clubs, make secular radicalism seem superficial, reveal the ends of social work, and accomplish the fulfillment of all religion in Christ?

2. MORAL INTEGRITY AND STABILITY

Christianity's first obvious resource in this struggle is its moral integrity and stability. We shall see (as indeed everyone who has kept abreast of Christian thinking knows) that Christianity is not a code of morals. It is an ethical religion, the ethics of which grow from its faith. But the first and simplest contact of Christianity with the life of men today lies within the range of the broad and simple principles which guide or should guide conduct.

In a world none too sure of itself, or, perhaps it would be

more accurate to say, a world which has been badly shaken out of its certainties and become entirely unsure of itself, the Church can speak with moral authority. It does know the difference between right and wrong. It does know what brings and alone can bring to any society or to any individual integrity and stability.

But before we note the bearing of this upon contemporary life we must recognize that the inconsistencies and limitations of actual everyday conduct are nowhere more apparent than in the Church. Just because these fundamental moral principles are factors in all life all the time, men's inconsistencies are more obvious there than elsewhere. We need not concern ourselves with manifest hypocrisy. Within the Church the chief source of trouble, again passing over the obvious dominance of sin, lies in failure of perspective. The Church's witness is obscured on the one hand by those who fail to realize that their faith reaches to all areas of life. "Business is business" is a maxim which has broken down many a man's witness to Christ. On the other hand, it is obscured by the exaltation of one particular virtue or the condemnation of one particular sin. It has been often pointed out that our Anglo-Saxon puritanism has led us to lay such emphasis upon sex morality that the very term "immoral" needs no adjective to relate it to sex misconduct. To some Christians few or no sins seem to equal that of traffic with the liquor trade! Not only Savonarola but the founder of the Jesuits himself exhorted good Christians to throw their "vanities" in the fire. Dancing, theater-going, cards, Sunday games are all anathema to many devout people while the equally devout count them innocent recreation.

All that makes for confusion. It leads some Christians to appeasing the world and some to living in a state of perpetual irritation with the world, a very different thing be it remarked from the moral indignation of the Lord Christ and of great Christian saints like Paul or Augustine. It leads many of the best kind of people who are not Christians to look with condescending contempt upon the Church. It does hamper us in the effort to reach men with the Gospel.

But it is largely a difficulty which lies on the surface. It often obscures the profound moral contribution of the Church to human life, but it never destroys it. Over the centuries the Church has proclaimed the supremacy of righteousness and justice in the affairs of men. It has differed in details of application. It has been woefully lax. It has compromised. But always in the worship and wherever its prophetic message has been heard the Psalmist's cry has echoed: "Righteousness and justice are the habitation of his seat." "Who shall ascend into the hill of the Lord? even he that hath clean hands and a pure heart." Wherever the Scriptures have been open to men Paul's words have rung in their ears. They have heard Jesus—"By their fruits ye shall know them." "Blessed are they that hunger and thirst after righteousness." The Church has proclaimed these things for the individual and for society; and it can point to the history of mankind as confirmation of its message. The house founded on sand is swept away in the flood. The house built on rock stands.

This has direct bearing on today's task. Morals in America are not on a very high level; but that has been true of any society at any time. Our trouble today lies in the fact that the standards of reference which a few generations back were questioned by few seem now uncertain to many. "Decalogue-morality" is not fashionable. Furthermore large numbers of young people under the influence of what appears to be up-to-date psychology, sociology, philosophy, what you will, and under the terrible impact of a chaotic world are very uncertain, genuinely doubtful as to fundamental moral standards. Are there any? If so what are they? Is duty an essential principle of life or not? Is chastity really worth while? All that has become fairly apparent, if we have any doubt about it, in the preceding chapters of this book. Look, for example, at social work, humanism, secular radicalism and the cults. All along the line there is moral uncertainty, wavering. In such a world the

Church may not speak authoritatively; but it can. It is no latent
resource in the sense of something hidden which needs to be
forced up to the surface, discovered as a surprise. It is there.
Integrity, honesty, chastity, self-control, courage, all the things
which, whether in the Decalogue or not, may be called Decalogue-morality are a constant part of the Church's message.

Now it is not within the scope of this paper to discuss fundamental ethical questions. Whatever we may conclude about universal natural law or whatever ethical theory we may hold, the
Christian Church has never doubted that these basic ethical
concepts belong to man everywhere, that men do know the
distinction between right and wrong, that the moral consciousness is part of the normal man. The Christian Church has,
therefore, never doubted that the moral law has authority. It
may not be obeyed, but it is there. Into the uncertainties of today
the Church carries its message. Men may ignore it. They cannot
refute it. Upon these fundamental virtues civilization, the stability of personality and the stability of nations depend. With
them, expressed in crude fashion, primitive society holds together. Without them, the desperate moments of the present
have come upon us.

But Decalogue-morality (like patriotism) is not enough. It
never has been enough. These moral standards, however high
they may be and however noble the life they nourish, always
need the sanctions of Sinai. On the tables of stone the hand of
God must write. The hand of man has no strength for the task.
Which is to say, in a figure, that wherever elementary moral
law has had power over men's lives it has rested upon sanctions
which bound it up with their fundamental faiths concerning the
world. Religion is not morality and morality is not religion; but
a moral code finds power over men because very vaguely perhaps men believe it is more than a mere creation of the social
order. A few intellectuals may be satisfied with such a theory,
but if they are any more than mere observers of the human
scene, if they take a real part in it, there is always the consciousness of a hidden universal sanction. It is found in men

like Dewey. It is found in humanists. And when one turns to the great and dominating movements of today, those which have caught and carried with them ordinary average people, there is no doubt of it. Marxian morality is based upon a philosophy as universal as that of Christianity. The fanatical devotion of the Hitler youth was certainly religious in the deep sense of contact with what was believed to be eternal. The morality (or immorality) of Nihilism was conceived to have a universal basis.

We need not labor the familiar story. It brings us at once to the third category of the Church's resources:

3. A FAITH WHICH INTEGRATES TOTAL EXPERIENCE

The faith of the Church has suffered more from the divisions among Christians than any other aspect of its life. In its basic teachings it has been constantly, week by week, day by day, proclaimed to the world. But it has been obscured. It has been distorted. It has been presented in such diversity of expression that men have failed to see its profound meaning and the essential unity of all faithful people. But it has always been there and its possession has always marked off the Christian from the non-Christian. That which in a so-called Christian land is often forgotten is very clear when a few Christians find themselves along in a pagan world. The mission field today is a constant and living witness to that fact. If the problems of unity could be left to the "younger churches" the life of the "older churches" would have already been revolutionized.

But this central and universal faith is after all a very simple thing. In the language and thought forms of another day it is enshrined in the great creeds of Christendom, and what these creeds say is that this vast universe in which we live is no fortuitous product of impersonal forces. It depends for its very being upon a living righteous God who is at once Ruler and Father.

Men are God's children; sin is men's hopeless alienation from

God; history is the theater in which God acts to reconcile men to Himself. The story of His activity, everywhere to be read by those who have eyes to see, is all of it the story of God giving Himself. It culminates when in Jesus Christ the Word becomes flesh and dwells among us. In Him the meaning of human life is revealed and through union with Him (a thousand theories about it but always the same principle) men's broken lives find reconciliation with God. This is the message of which the Church is not only witness but embodiment. Upon the Church falls the task of bringing to men this life which, as the very Body of Christ, it possesses. Under the guidance of the Eternal Spirit it brings its message of love and reconciliation to the souls of men and to the society of men. It foreshadows in its fellowship the kingdom of God which is the commonwealth of love.

Now no such attempt as the above to put this Christian faith in a few words is ever adequate. The only really adequate statement of the faith is that it is Christ Himself. He is the Truth, the test of all our theories, the standard of all our values, the searching judge of all our interpretations. That from a somewhat different approach was the burden of William Adams Brown's last book. That is the core of our acceptance of the Scriptures as the ultimate standard of faith.

But if we are to think of this faith in relation to the world of today, we must, it would seem, have some framework of interpretation and some phrasing in familiar language. For what we are doing is bringing to men a world view. We put it alongside other views. We challenge men's reason, will and emotions. We ask what they can offer that can promise, as does this faith, the fullest interpretation of life, the fullest development of personality, the clue to history and the goal of the social order.

This is no apologetic, no defense, that we have to offer. All too often we Christians fall into a kind of Bishop Butler attitude. "There are difficulties in our position; but look at those in yours," we say. Good, true, quite right, but there is nothing conquering about that attitude. There is nothing stirring, moving, inspiring. There is nothing of evangelical fervor. We need evangelical fervor in our thinking. We need the tone of Athanasius, not of Anselm, when we tell men of the Incarnation of the Son of God. For this world view of ours is our one nearly ultimate resource. It is our great task to make it live among men.

Look at the way in which it touches life. It sets us at the very beginning in a world which is governed by purpose. "In these days of anxiety and fear and impending tribulation," says Dr. Hebert, "Christians have their witness to bear of the reality of God as the owner of his world and the Master in his own house." In history men and nations do not escape Him. His righteous judgment is upon them but His judgment is only an instrument of love and as judgment falls, so equally is revealed the goal towards which history is moving. That is foreshadowed and in a sense consummated in Christ. In Him men discover what fullness of life means, the way to God and the joy of God. Direction comes to the life of men when they discover direction in the life of the world. God is master.

This is clear cut. It challenges every world view which falls back on impersonal force, whether it be good, orthodox, dialectic materialism or the new naturalism or any kind of pragmatic optimism about men's future. It comes with withering power upon the momentary pessimism wrought by the revelation of atomic force. Man may blow his world to pieces; but it is still God's world and somewhere and somehow his purposes will be achieved.

Then there is implicit in it all, the dignity of man and the essential unity of mankind. As we have already noted, beneath the humanitarianism of organized social work it puts the divine heritage of men. It gives depth to humanism, meaning to the fellowship of clubs and lodges, and lifts secular radicalism out of the mire of power politics. In the same breath it destroys fascism (imposition of rule from above) and gives the only solid foundation for the uniting of the peoples of the world in one organic community. Democracy, that much used and much abused word, is its child; for wherever men have sought freedom they have been led by the light that lighteth every man. And finally, it exalts all Decalogue-morality as it sets it back upon the love of God. The common virtues achieve their meaning only as they are transcended in a love which is the fulfilling of the law.

It is in love likewise that men learn to read something of the meaning of the vast load of sorrow and suffering which humanity has borne. A new cult offers men health and prosperity. It has no message when the magic formulas fail and suffering and misfortune come. But this Christian world view has a message. It is in suffering and through suffering that love works. On the cross the Lord of life gathers into himself the suffering of the world and conquers it. We often point out in our contacts with these cults, of which Christian Science is the chief, that the Church too can bring the healing power of religion to bear upon disease. That is true. What we often forget is that the essential message of the Church sanctifies suffering. There is no word anywhere except in Christ which makes tolerable the vast sufferings of the world today, the pitiful hunger and misery of body and the worse agonies of soul. The Old Testament moves toward it. There are glimpses of many times and places where men have gone groping after God, for God has always been there first; but the interlocking of God with love and suffering waited for Calvary.

Or turn from these more tragic aspects of men's life and note that great charter of St. Paul's with which we began these reflections. Since this is God's world all that is true and beautiful and good is open to the Christian. We are leaving behind us in these days the fear that beauty may turn us away from God and the serious moral purposes of life. In Church architecture as well as in Church ceremonial we are beginning to recognize the place of beauty in life. The results are a little weird at times, but the direction is right. Beauty, truth and goodness are all of God, are all part of God's world, are all therefore open to the wide searching joy of men. The great charter of Chris-

tianity claims the scientist, the artist and the poet, as it does
the mechanic and the farmer and the doctor and the lawyer.

The final area in which the Christian world view challenges
all other views is in religion itself. Two points may suffice in
this matter to reveal the resources which the Church has at command. The first touches human personality. Nowhere is there
on any wide scale such power to interpret personality, balance
it, release its best powers as is constantly revealed in men's
relation to God through Christ. The perfect balance and un-
wavering direction of Jesus himself is transmitted to those who
seek God in him.

And the second is the way in which this Christian world
view fulfills the meaning of other religions. In Christ is the
"Yea" of them all. It would carry this paper to too great length
to enter on so great a field of discussion. The essential fact may
be put like this: Whether he approaches other religions from
the point of view of Kraemer or of Hocking, shares the attitude
of the preceding chapter of this book or some other philosophy
of missions, the Christian minister or the Christian layman
turning to his own faith knows that it possesses this fulfilling
quality. Whatever men have sought in God, groping blindly
but honestly and humbly, has been given them in and through
Christ. In Him God has spoken and through Him the world is
both judged and saved.

But this certainty of faith is far more than a certainty of
knowledge. It carries with it a compelling power, a persuasive
conviction. All these resources which are at hand and which we
can so easily tabulate, all of them together are of little value
unless we can use them with wisdom and with power.

Of the need of wisdom Jesus speaks frequently. "Be ye wise
as serpents" was no mere proverbial phrase. Throughout his
ministry we catch glimpses of the way in which he balanced
the choices that lay before him and took no step without reckon-
ing its bearing upon his mission. The wise householder, the
men who used their talents, the king who was planning war, all

suggest the importance to him and to us of wisdom, of a divine canniness in dealing with people. He knows when to be persuasive and simple, when to be stern, when to lift the scourge and overturn the tables of the money-changers. In a brief ministry of two or three years the mission which God laid upon him is accomplished so completely that the course of history is changed. Men in their moments of adoring prayer say of it "full perfect and sufficient."

Now we cannot attain that degree of wisdom. We shall make in the future as we have in the past countless mistakes, but at least here in America we need no special exhortation to plan wisely. We are deluged with plans. To make them is one of our major sports. They are as plentiful in our church headquarters as they are in any secular agency. Indeed for the average congregation and the parson of ordinary ability they are likely to be too plentiful. Too much is planned. The plans themselves are probably good. Where they lack wisdom is in holding the right balance and in emphasis upon the essential things. We constantly smother the Gospel by the plans we make for proclaiming it.

But to repeat, the Gospel is in itself a simple thing and the highest wisdom in proclaiming it seems to point to one fact. We have a fairly good understanding of our opportunity to reach the world. We have a profoundly convincing declaration of essential moral standards. We have a world view, a faith, which touches all life and integrates all experience. But over and over again, we lack, the Church lacks power from on high. It speaks as the scribes and not with authority. There is no compelling force. There is no burning inward fire, that kind of fire which lies behind and makes utterly convincing the simple words of the Sermon on the Mount; and which gives his greatness to every great figure in Christian history: Paul, Augustine, Aquinas, the turbulent Luther, the logical Calvin. Into whosoever's heart we look there the fire burns. It is in that power that our deepest resource lies.

4. A SPIRITUAL POWER,
COMPELLING AND CONQUERING

There is no doubt about the lack of it. We look at the fanatical devotion of the Nazi youth and wonder why our Christian youth seem to show nothing to equal it. The steady persistence of the Communist seems to us sometimes to find no match in Christian congregations. It is possible that we are partly wrong on that point. We pick out and admire in the other faiths those who are most thoroughly committed, but we judge ourselves by our own average groups. For the fire from on high has never been lost since it fell upon those gathered in the upper room at Pentecost. The early church was a Spirit-guided and Spirit-empowered body. The church which sent out its missionaries as the great nineteenth century opened was Spirit-guided and Spirit-empowered. What but the Spirit of Power has made strong the Niemöllers and Berggravs, the Confessional pastors and the Roman priests of Germany during the days of Nazi dominance, or kept the missions living centers of courage and unselfish devotion in Japanese-occupied China?

No, when we look at our ordinary congregations and wonder at their slow response to appeals and their contentment with their own small ways and search in vain for a trace of the burning fire of the Holy Spirit, we must never forget that the fire is there. It is hidden, banked under ashes of conventionality, but it is there. It is our ultimate resource.

How then are we to stir these latent fires into flame and give the power of the Spirit to our proclamation of the Gospel?

It is again very simple. The first and primary need is to lead the Church (or the churches) back to a life in which worship stands first. The primary function of the Church is worship. Its primary concern is God; not human souls or human society, but God. Its missionary work, its saving of souls and its social responsibilities, all grow out of its relation to God. Worship can be formal and conventional and that is true in nonliturgical as well as in liturgical churches. It can be chiefly emotional. It can be a mere gathering to hear a preacher. In other words, there can be many a service of worship which generates no power. Those who participated go out from it as cold as when they went in.

And yet this common worship is the powerhouse of the Church. It was so back in Jerusalem of old. It is so today. The Holy Spirit falls upon the fellowship of believers. He is given first to the corporate life of the Body of Christ. But it is when the congregation of the faithful, gathered in the Word of God service, at the Holy Communion or in the prayer meeting, waits breathlessly for the heavens to open that Pentecost can come again. When Christians worship because they want God, God comes to them in power.

Implicit in this waiting for the Spirit, this wanting God, is the call to complete self-surrender. The exaltation dies, the power fades, unless the high moment of worship has carried with it the gift of self-giving. When this congregation of the faithful, each several and separate member conscious of its meaning can pray, "We offer and present unto thee O Lord ourselves our souls and bodies," then, though the exaltation fades, the power lasts. In self-surrender the channel of power is widened and secured.

There are many specific channels of this power which are part of or supplement the corporate worship of the Church. The Bible is one of them. Indeed in all Christian experience there are few things stranger or more miraculous than the power of the Bible to bring God to men and so to light the flame within them. It is a book stemming from the life of only one small people. There is much in it hard to understand, much which raises questions in the mind of modern men; and yet men want it. Millions of new copies flood the world each year. Men seize on it. They read it. They find strength, courage, joy in it. God comes to them and with God comes power.

Another source of power is the prayer of the individual Christian. A praying Church means not only a Church which prays corporately but a Church which is warmed and strengthened by the prayers of countless Christian souls. What prayer does can never be measured. It has no statistical value. But the corporate life of the Church grows weak without it.

But the corporate Church is more than the single worshiping congregation. Every small Christian fellowship; the Church in Jerusalem or Corinth or Rome; the Church in St. John's Cathedral, New York, or in the First Baptist Church of Tulsa; every congregation receives power through the prayers of the world-wide Church and the world-wide Church is the stronger for the multitude of praying groups. Indeed we must often pray better than we know. Our prayers overflow. They bring power not only to the churches which perhaps we call our own, but help to open channels for God's power to enter groups of fellow Christians whom we know not, to whom it may be we have sometimes denied the very name of Christ. This is true when we are divided. The access of power is again immeasurable when we are united. Dr. Van Kirk's recent book on global strategy is a telling illustration of that fact. Church unity, not just friendly relations, but an organically united life of the divided Christian Church is a divine necessity if the full resources of power are to be released. That must be so because a religion which proclaims that God is love repudiates its own profession by its divisions. That must be so because if the Church is the Body of Christ divisions are its bleeding wounds. They must be healed if the Body is to reveal the full power of the Spirit.

All these various aspects of the power from on high cluster about the one great central fact of Christian experience: the Person of the Lord Christ. If the power of the Bible (the Word which speaks) is a strange and miraculous kind of thing, the power of the Christ (the Word made flesh) is more so. The great Christian fellowship, the Church throughout the world, is His Church, His Body. The Word which speaks tells of Him. The prayers which open channels for the grace of God are in His name. The Holy Spirit which guides and gives strength, which falls upon men like a flame from heaven, is His Spirit. It is He who in the imagery of the Apocalypse comes riding the white horse and, making war in righteousness, leads the Christian hosts to victory. He is the Victor, He is the King who conquered the great Empire of the West and gave law to a continent. He is the "Young Hero" who a thousand years ago tamed the rude warriors from the North. He is the Leader who has taken His armies to the uttermost parts of the earth. His is the Name before which every knee shall bow! Christ the Victor. The whole consideration of the Church's resources in this troubled and evil world comes back in the end to the one fact that the Christian religion is Christ; and the Church's power is measured by its loyalty to Him.

It is in that supreme faith that we make our proclamation to the world. As we have passed in review the resources of the Church we have been acutely and constantly aware of its failure to use them as they can be used. Our certainty, our sense of power and our joy in the greatness of our faith have been shot through with the knowledge of the sinful selfishness which lies behind these failures and of our need of penitence. But still the certainty, the power, the joy remain. They are not ours. They are God's. They are Christ's. From our hearts we make our own the words of the Madras Conference report: "No one so fully knows the failings, the pettiness, the faithlessness which infect the Church's life as we who are its members. Yet, in all humility and penitence, we are constrained to declare to a baffled and needy world that the Church, under God, is its greatest hope."

FURTHER READING

ATHANASIUS. *The Incarnation of the Word.*

AUGUSTINE. *The City of God.*

BENNETT, JOHN C. *Social Salvation.* New York: Charles Scribner's Sons, 1935.

LATOURETTE, KENNETH SCOTT. *The Great Century,* 3 vols. New York: Harper & Brothers, 1941-44.

———. *Advance Through Storm.* New York: Harper & Brothers, 1945.

LUTHER. *A Treatise on Christian Liberty.*

TEMPLE, WILLIAM. *Nature, Man and God.* London: The Macmillan Company, Ltd., 1935.

THOMAS, GEORGE, ed. *The Vitality of the Christian Tradition.* New York: Harper & Brothers, 1944.

SUBJECTS AND MEMBERSHIP OF THE COMMISSIONS

COMMISSION I-A

VOLUME I. *The Challenge of Our Culture*

CLARENCE T. CRAIG: *Chairman*
JAMES LUTHER ADAMS
ELMER J. F. ARNDT
JOHN K. BENTON
CONRAD BERGENDOFF
BUELL G. GALLAGHER
H. C. GOERNER
GEORGIA HARKNESS
JOSEPH HAROUTUNIAN

WALTER M. HORTON
JAMES H. NICHOLS
VICTOR OBENHAUS
WILHELM PAUCK
ROLLAND W. SCHLOERB
EDMUND D. SOPER
ERNEST F. TITTLE
AMOS N. WILDER
DANIEL D. WILLIAMS

COMMISSION I-B

VOLUME II. *The Church and Organized Movements*

The Pacific Coast Theological Group:

RANDOLPH CRUMP MILLER: *Chairman*
JAMES C. BAKER
EUGENE BLAKE
KARL MORGAN BLOCK
JOHN WICK BOWMAN
ELLIOTT VAN N. DILLER

GALEN FISHER
ROBERT M. FITCH
BUELL G. GALLAGHER
CYRIL GLOYN
GEORGE HEDLEY

John Krumm
Morgan Odell
Pierson Parker
Clarence Reidenbach
John Skoglund
Dwight Smith
Frederic Spiegelberg

Everett Thomson
Elton Trueblood
Aaron Ungersma
Hugh Vernon White
Lynn T. White
George Williams

Guests of the Theological Group:

John H. Ballard
Theodore H. Greene
Edward Ohrenstein
Edward L. Parsons

Howard Thurman
Stacy Warburton
Frederick West

COMMISSION II

Volume III. *The Gospel, The Church and The World*

Kenneth Scott Latourette: *Chairman*

Earl Ballou
John C. Bennett
Nels F. S. Ferré
Joseph Fletcher
Herbert Gezork
Edward R. Hardy, Jr.
Elmer Homrighausen
Stanley Hopper
John Knox
Benjamin Mays

William Stuart Nelson
Richard Niebuhr
Justin Nixon
Norman Pittenger
James McD. Richards
Luman J. Shafer
Paul Scherer
Wyatt A. Smart
George F. Thomas
Frank Wilson

COMMISSION III

Volume IV. *Toward World-Wide Christianity*

O. Frederick Nolde: *Chairman*
Edwin R. Aubrey

Roswell P. Barnes
John C. Bennett

ARLO A. BROWN

E. FAY CAMPBELL

J. W. DECKER

H. PAUL DOUGLASS

CHARLES IGLEHART

F. ERNEST JOHNSON

CHARLES T. LEBER

HENRY SMITH LEIPER

JOHN A. MACKAY

ELMORE N. McKEE

LAWRENCE ROSE

STANLEY RYCROFT

MATTHEW SPINKA

A. L. WARNSHUIS

A. R. WENTZ

ALEXANDER C. ZABRISKIE

VOLUME V. *What Must the Church Do?*

HENRY P. VAN DUSEN